THE STATES AND THE NATION SERIES, of which this volume is a part, is designed to assist the American people in a serious look at the ideals they have espoused and the experiences they have undergone in the history of the nation. The content of every volume represents the scholarship, experience, and opinions of its author. The costs of writing and editing were met mainly by grants from the National Endowment for the Humanities, a federal agency. The project was administered by the American Association for State and Local History, a nonprofit learned society, working with an Editorial Board of distinguished editors, authors, and historians, whose names are listed below.

Wisconsin

A Bicentennial History

Richard Nelson Current

W. W. Norton & Company, Inc.
New York

American Association for State and Local History
Nashville

Author and publishers make grateful acknowledgment to The Viking Press, Inc. for permission to quote from *Two Lives, A Poem* by William Ellery Leonard (Copyright, 1923 by V. W. Huebsch, Inc.; copyright renewed 1951 by Charlotte Charlton Leonard).

Library of Congress Cataloging in Publication Data

Current, Richard Nelson.
   Wisconsin: a Bicentennial history.

   (The States and the Nation series)
   Bibliography: p.
   Includes index.
   1. Wisconsin—History.   I. Title.   II. Series.
F581.C87   977.5   77-2176
ISBN 0-393-05624-4

Published and distributed by
W. W. Norton & Company, Inc.
500 Fifth Avenue
New York, New York 10036
Printed in the United States of America

2 3 4 5 6 7 8 9 0

To Jeremy and Barnaby

Contents

Illustrations

Invitation to the Reader

IN 1807, former President John Adams argued that a complete history of the American Revolution could not be written until the history of change in each state was known, because the principles of the Revolution were as various as the states that went through it. Two hundred years after the Declaration of Independence, the American nation has spread over a continent and beyond. The states have grown in number from thirteen to fifty. And democratic principles have been interpreted differently in every one of them.

We therefore invite you to consider that the history of your state may have more to do with the bicentennial review of the American Revolution than does the story of Bunker Hill or Valley Forge. The Revolution has continued as Americans extended liberty and democracy over a vast territory. John Adams was right: the states are part of that story, and the story is incomplete without an account of their diversity.

The Declaration of Independence stressed life, liberty, and the pursuit of happiness; accordingly, it shattered the notion of holding new territories in the subordinate status of colonies. The Northwest Ordinance of 1787 set forth a procedure for new states to enter the Union on an equal footing with the old. The Federal Constitution shortly confirmed this novel means of building a nation out of equal states. The step-by-step process through which territories have achieved self-government and national representation is among the most important of the Founding Fathers' legacies.

The method of state-making reconciled the ancient conflict between liberty and empire, resulting in what Thomas Jefferson called an empire for liberty. The system has worked and remains unaltered, despite enormous changes that have taken place in the nation. The country's extent and variety now surpass anything the patriots of '76 could likely have imagined. The United States has changed from an agrarian republic into a highly industrial and urban democracy, from a fledgling nation into a major world power. As Oliver Wendell Holmes remarked in 1920, the creators of the nation could not have seen completely how it and its constitution and its states would develop. Any meaningful review in the bicentennial era must consider what the country has become, as well as what it was.

The new nation of equal states took as its motto *E Pluribus Unum*—"out of many, one." But just as many peoples have become Americans without complete loss of ethnic and cultural identities, so have the states retained differences of character. Some have been superficial, expressed in stereotyped images— big, boastful Texas, "sophisticated" New York, "hillbilly" Arkansas. Other differences have been more real, sometimes instructively, sometimes amusingly; democracy has embraced Huey Long's Louisiana, bilingual New Mexico, unicameral Nebraska, and a Texas that once taxed fortunetellers and spawned politicians called "Woodpecker Republicans" and "Skunk Democrats." Some differences have been profound, as when South Carolina secessionists led other states out of the Union in opposition to abolitionists in Massachusetts and Ohio. The result was a bitter Civil War.

The Revolution's first shots may have sounded in Lexington and Concord; but fights over what democracy should mean and who should have independence have erupted from Pennsylvania's Gettysburg to the "Bleeding Kansas" of John Brown, from the Alamo in Texas to the Indian battles at Montana's Little Bighorn. Utah Mormons have known the strain of isolation; Hawaiians at Pearl Harbor, the terror of attack; Georgians during Sherman's march, the sadness of defeat and devastation. Each state's experience differs instructively; each adds understanding to the whole.

The purpose of this series of books is to make that kind of understanding accessible, in a way that will last in value far beyond the bicentennial fireworks. The series offers a volume on every state, plus the District of Columbia—fifty-one, in all.

Each book contains, besides the text, a view of the state through eyes other than the author's—a "photographer's essay," in which a skilled photographer presents his own personal perceptions of the state's contemporary flavor.

We have asked authors not for comprehensive chronicles, nor for research monographs or new data for scholars. Bibliographies and footnotes are minimal. We have asked each author for a summing up—interpretive, sensitive, thoughtful, individual, even personal—of what seems significant about his or her state's history. What distinguishes it? What has mattered about it, to its own people and to the rest of the nation? What has it come to now?

To interpret the states in all their variety, we have sought a variety of backgrounds in authors themselves and have encouraged variety in the approaches they take. They have in common only these things: historical knowledge, writing skill, and strong personal feelings about a particular state. Each has wide latitude for the use of the short space. And if each succeeds, it will be by offering you, in your capacity as a *citizen* of a state *and* of a nation, stimulating insights to test against your own.

James Morton Smith
General Editor

Preface

$\mathcal{T}$HIS volume attempts to show how American life has specially manifested itself in one of the fifty states, Wisconsin, and how events in this particular state have influenced the nation's development. That is to say, the book is concerned with an aspect of the American character—the aspect that may be termed the Wisconsin character. So it concentrates on those persons and happenings that are distinctive of the state.

If the book seems to refer too frequently to Wisconsin firsts, bests, and greatests, it does so in no spirit of braggadocio. Such a spirit would misrepresent Wisconsinites, for they are not characteristically braggarts, not at all. The superlatives are used only to help delineate the uniqueness of Wisconsin and its history. Really, they are too few, but no matter how numerous, they would probably not be enough. The more one looks into Wisconsin's past, the more one is inclined to feel that no number of superlatives could quite do justice to the superlativeness of the state.

By its very nature this brief account is selective and interpretive, not comprehensive or encyclopedic. It leaves out a great deal that, in some other context, would be indispensable. Indeed, it includes no name simply because the person had a distinguished career in Wisconsin, and it mentions no event simply because of the event's importance to large numbers of people in the state. The test for inclusion has been Wisconsinianness.

Readers who understand this will not wonder why, for example, the Green Bay Packers rate several pages and the Milwaukee Braves, Brewers, and Bucks, not a single word.

A historian, not a press agent, the author has proceeded on the principle that the names of living persons are to be omitted from the text. Exceptions to this principle are few.

R. N. C.

August, 15, 1976

Wisconsin

1

Wonderful Wisconsin

AT the bicentennial of the United States, Wisconsin was 128 years old, having become the thirtieth state in 1848. As a place known to Europeans, however, it was much older than that. Frenchmen had begun to penetrate its wilds at about the same time as Englishmen were founding their first colonies on the Massachusetts coast. But the remote region between Lake Michigan and the Mississippi River remained essentially a wilderness for more than two centuries. Only after 1848 did the process we call "civilization" get well under way there. In the process the landscape was transformed and much of its natural beauty destroyed. Still, a great deal of scenic wonder was retained or recovered, though more or less altered. The changing face of Wisconsin had a unique and enduring charm.

1

We can get some idea of the charm of the primeval scene from men and women who were privileged to view it, were bewitched by it, and wrote down their impressions for us to read.

Nobody knows for sure who was the first European to set eyes on this particular piece of the North American continent. Most likely it was Jean Nicolet, one of the bright young men in the service of Samuel de Champlain, the founder of Quebec and the leader of New France. Champlain was interested in extending the fur trade, finding a water route to the Orient, and getting on good terms with the "People of the Sea," a distant tribe who, he had heard, occupied a strategic position along that route. In 1634, together with seven Huron braves, Nicolet journeyed westward by canoe, probably paddling through the Straits of Mackinac into Lake Michigan and finally stepping ashore near the head of Green Bay. Awaiting him were the Winnebago. "They meet him; they escort him, and carry all his baggage," a friend, who doubtless had the story from Nicolet himself, wrote several years later, after Nicolet's untimely death by drowning. "He wore a grand robe of China damask, all strewn with flowers and birds of many colors. No sooner did they perceive him than the women and children fled, at the sight of a man who carried thunder in both hands—for thus they called the two pistols that he held." [1] Nicolet's encounter with Wisconsin was brief, and he left no written account of it.

Twenty-five years later Médard Chouart Des Groseilliers and his brother-in-law, Pierre Esprit Radisson, both of them fur traders, arrived by way of Lake Superior and landed on the shore of Chequamegon Bay. Three years they wintered in the forest of northern Wisconsin. "The countrey is beautifull, with very few mountaines, the woods cleare," Radisson wrote after the two men had made a trip inland from the lake. [2] On another occasion he was ecstatic. "The country was so pleasant, so beautifull & fruitfull that it grieved me to see yt ye world could not discover such enticing countrys to live in," he declared. "What conquest would that bee at litle or no cost; what laborinth of pleasure should millions of people have, instead that millions complaine of misery & poverty!" [3]

1. Louise Phelps Kellogg, ed., *Early Narratives of the Northwest, 1634–1699* (New York: Charles Scribner's Sons, 1917), p. 16.

2. Alice E. Smith, *From Exploration to Statehood,* State Historical Society of Wisconsin, *History of Wisconsin,* 6 vols. (Madison: State Historical Society of Wisconsin, 1973), 1:17.

3. Grace Lee Nute, *Caesars of the Wilderness: Médard Chouart, Sieur des Groseilliers, and Pierre Esprit Radisson, 1618–1710* (New York: D. Appleton-Century Company, 1943), pp. 37–38.

The first Europeans to cross what was to become the state of Wisconsin were Jacques Marquette and Louis Jolliet. Father Marquette was one of the many Jesuit priests who devoted their lives to the Christianizing of the Indians and who, if they failed to make so many lasting converts as they hoped to, at least succeeded in revealing the land and its inhabitants in accurate maps and descriptions. (*The Jesuit Relations and Allied Documents: Travels and Explorations of the Jesuit Missionaries in New France, 1610–1791,* as edited by Reuben Gold Thwaites and published in Cleveland, 1896–1901, were to fill 73 volumes.) Jolliet had studied for the priesthood but chose a career in the fur business instead. In 1672 he received instructions from the government of New France to go in search of the rumored "great river," the Mississippi, and to take Marquette along. The next year Jolliet and Marquette, with five other men and two canoes, entered Green Bay, ascended the Fox River to Lake Winnebago, and then followed the winding uppper Fox to a point where it was only a mile and a half from a larger river flowing in the opposite direction, a river that the Indians called, according to Jolliet's spelling, the "Miskonsing." Carrying their canoes across the portage, the explorers floated and paddled downstream. Finally, as Marquette recorded, "we safely entered Missisipi on the 17th of June, with a joy that I cannot express." [4]

The Fox-Wisconsin waterway became an important route for fur traders and continued to be the main passage through the area during the nearly a century that the region still remained under the sovereignty of the French, and for many years beyond that. After the British, with the aid of their American colonists, had won the French and Indian War (1758–1763) and taken over the territory, a Massachusetts surveyor and veteran of the war, Jonathan Carver, undertook to explore it.

In September 1766 Carver, traveling with a group of traders and Indians, headed upriver from Green Bay. He was hospitably entertained at the "great town of the Winnebagoes" on the small island in the river where it flows out of Lake Winnebago.

---

4. Smith, *Exploration to Statehood,* 1:30.

He was impressed by the bountiful yield of the lake and its surroundings—the fish, geese, ducks, and teal; the wild rice; the
grapes, plums, and other wild fruits; and the corn, beans, pump-
kins, squash, tobacco, and watermelons that the Winnebago cul-
tivated. "About twelve miles before I reached the Carrying
Place," he wrote with regard to his approach to the portage, "I
observed several small mountains which extended quite to it.
These indeed would only be esteemed as molehills when compared with those on the back of the colonies, but as they were
the first I had seen since my leaving Niagara, a track of nearly
eleven hundred miles, I could not leave them unnoticed." They
were worth noticing, and some of them were, geologically, true
mountains. The Baraboo Range, which Carver saw, had been
far higher in the remote past than the Appalachians were in his
time. Canoeing down the "Ouisconsin," Carver was amazed at
seeing the "Great Town of the Saukies" on the site of the later
villages of Sauk City and Prairie du Sac. "This is the largest
and best built Indian town I ever saw," he wrote. It looked
"more like a civilized town than the abode of savages." As
Carver proceeded downriver, the land nearby "seemed to be, in
general, excellent; but that at a distance is very full of mountains, where it is said there are many lead mines." Going up the
Mississippi from the Wisconsin's mouth, he beheld on both
sides rocky heights "resembling old ruinous towers," some of
which he climbed. "From thence the most beautiful and extensive prospect that imagination can form opens to your view." It
was a sight to "attract your imagination and excite your wonder." [5]

The Wisconsin scene changed little when the Americans
gained their independence and, along with it, the title to the
land stretching westward from the Appalachians to the Mississippi. French voyageurs continued to roam the woods to gather
furs, and British agents continued to control the trade as well as

5. Jonathan Carver, *Travels Through the Interior Parts of North America, in the
Years 1766, 1767, and 1768* (London, 1781; facsimile edition, Minneapolis: Ross &
Haines, Inc., 1956), pp. 32, 37–38, 41, 46–47, 54–56.

to command the loyalty of the Indian tribes. Only after the War of 1812 did the United States make its authority complete. The army erected Fort Crawford at the mouth of the Wisconsin, Fort Howard at the mouth of the Fox, and later Fort Winnebago in between, at the portage. Then the army laid out a military road to connect the three forts. Meanwhile, from 1818 to 1836, the area was governed as a part of Michigan Territory.

When Lieutenant Jefferson Davis, then a young graduate of West Point, was transferred from Fort Crawford to Fort Winnebago in 1829, Prairie du Chien and Green Bay were long-established communities, but the land away from the well-traveled Fox-Wisconsin route was still not only unsettled but, so far as the army was concerned, largely unknown. That summer Davis camped in the locality where, in seven years, the city of Madison was to be platted. "Nothing, I think, was known to the garrison of Fort Winnebago, about the Four Lakes, before I saw them," he recalled as ex-president of the Confederate States of America nearly sixty years later. "Indeed, sir, it may astonish you to learn, in view of the (now) densely populated condition of that country, that I and the file of soldiers who accompanied me were the first white men who ever passed over the country between the Portage of the Wisconsin and Fox Rivers and the then village of Chicago." [6] Possibly they were the first Americans to do so.

Lieutenant Davis's friends Juliette Kinzie and her husband, the federal Indian agent at Fort Winnebago, made a similar trip, on horseback, about two years after Davis, in March of 1831. Mrs. Kinzie, a sharp-eyed and well-educated New Englander, twenty-four years old at the time, recorded the sights along the way in both words and pictures. The Kinzies and their party camped beside "a beautiful stream, a tributary of one of the Four Lakes, that chain whose banks are unrivalled for romantic loveliness." The next day they went past the northernmost of the four (now Lake Mendota), along the shore of which was a

6. Varina Howell Davis, *Jefferson Davis, Ex-President of the Confederate States of America: A Memoir by His Wife,* 2 vols. (New York: Belford Company, 1890), 1:75.

Winnebago encampment. "How beautiful the encampment looked in the morning sun! The matted lodges, with the blue smoke curling from their tops—the trees and bushes powdered with a light snow which had fallen through the night—the lake, shining and sparkling, almost at our feet—even the Indians, in their peculiar costume, added to the picturesque!" On the return trip, three days out from Chicago, the travelers found themselves in a "much more diversified country" than they had been passing through in Illinois. "Gently swelling hills, lovely valleys, and bright sparkling streams were the features of the landscape." When on a balmy spring day they came upon Big-foot Lake (now Lake Geneva), a "shout of delight burst involuntarily from the whole party . . . 'What could be imagined more charming? Oh! if our friends at the East could but enjoy it with us!' " [7]

Another and more famous artist touring Wisconsin in the 1830s was George Catlin, a Pennsylvanian who for several years traveled up and down the Mississippi Valley to paint Indian portraits and frontier landscapes. In the "rude untouched scenes of nature"—the Wisconsin and Minnesota bluffs of the Mississippi—Catlin found "scenes of grandeur worthy the whole soul's devotion and admiration." Along the Fox-Wisconsin route he delighted in the "inimitable scenes of beauty and romance." He said, "The Ouisconsin, which the French most appropriately denominate 'La belle riviere,' may certainly vie with any other on the Continent or in the world, for its beautifully skirted banks and prairie bluffs." [8]

The river gave its name to the territory, which was separated from Michigan in 1836, and to the state, which was admitted twelve years later. The spelling had varied—Meskousing, Miskonsing, Ouisconsin, Wiskonsan. But it became Wisconsin Ter-

7. Mrs. John H. Kinzie, *Wau-Bun: The Early Day in the Northwest* (1856; Chicago and New York: Rand, McNally and Company, 1901), pp. 107–110, 246–249.

8. George Catlin, *North American Indians: Being Letters and Notes on Their Manners, Customs, and Conditions, Written During Eight Years' Travel Amongst the Wildest Tribes of Indians in North America, 1832–1839*, 2 vols. (1841; London: published by the author, 1880), 2:160–162, 185.

ritory, and in 1845 the territorial legislature made that spelling official. That the word comes from one of the Indian languages there can be no doubt, but uncertainty persists as to which one and also as to the original meaning. The Indians themselves gave various definitions. Two of the favorites are ''a gathering of the waters'' and ''the stream of the thousand isles.'' One may take one's choice.

When the separate territory was set off, Milwaukee was already a boom town, and settlers were beginning to take up farms in the southeast, near the Lake Michigan shore. But the area most heavily populated with Americans was in the southwest, where men from Missouri, Illinois, and other states had been digging and smelting lead for a decade or more. The surface mines with their piles of dug earth looked like gigantic badger holes, and, much as the badgers did, the miners burrowed into the ground to make shelters against the winter cold. Hence Wisconsinites came to be known as Badgers.

''I consider the Wisconsin territory as the finest portion of North America, not only from its soil, but its climate.'' So declared the English novelist Frederick Marryat after a visit in 1838. Marryat greatly admired the rocky ridges, the thick forests, the rolling prairies of tall grass, and the ''oak openings''—''imagine an inland country covered with splendid trees, about as thickly planted as in our English parks; in fact, it is English park scenery.'' Wisconsin was wonderful. Indeed, Marryat concluded, ''the whole of this beautiful and fertile region appears as if nature had so arranged it that man should have all troubles cleared from before him, and have but little to do but to take possession and enjoy.'' [9]

After Wisconsin became a state, more and more enthusiasts gave testimony to its natural attractions. The chancellor of the new state university, for one, rhapsodized: ''Among the ten thousand undulations, there is scarcely one which lifts its

9. Frederick Marryat, *A Diary in America, with Remarks on Its Institutions,* edited by Sydney Jackman (1839; New York: Alfred A. Knopf, Inc., 1962), pp. 174–176, 179, 181, 188.

crown above its fellows, which does not disclose to the prophetic eye of taste a possible Eden, a vision of loveliness, which time and the hand of cultivation will not fail to realize and to verify." [10] By this time, settlers were arriving by the tens of thousands. They were to make great changes in the appearance of the land, changes almost as great in a century as man and nature had made in all the millennia since the region had recovered from the last ice age.

2

A few million years ago the air began to turn colder. More and more snow fell, and less and less of it melted. Gradually the snow was compacted into ice. Great ice caps in or near the Arctic Zone spread slowly southward, glaciers hundreds and even thousands of feet thick inching along until they covered much of northern Europe, Asia, and North America. Then the world warmed up again and a gigantic thaw occurred. Several times the process was repeated. Finally, quite recently by geologic time, ten to twenty-five thousand years ago, the last of the continental ice sheets melted away.

In all the vast sea of ice only one large island had remained, only one uncovered piece of land of significant size. Glaciers moving down from caps near Hudson Bay spread over most of Wisconsin and extended as far south as the Ohio and Missouri rivers. But a large part of Wisconsin was spared—more than a fourth of the state (along with a small adjoining strip in Minnesota, Iowa, and Illinois). This area was protected by the highland to the north of it and, beyond that, the deep trough of Lake Superior, both of which slowed down the movement of the ice. Glacial lobes came together below the protected area, and others were pushing in toward it from the east and the west when the final thaw began.

The unique Driftless Area of southwestern Wisconsin ("drift-

<hr>

10. J. H. Lathrop, "Wisconsin and the Growth of the Northwest," *De Bow's Review,* 14 (March 1853):230.

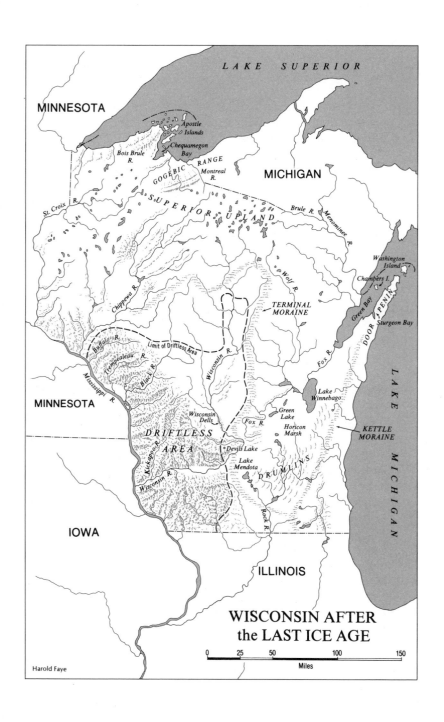

WISCONSIN AFTER
the LAST ICE AGE

Harold Faye

less'' because lacking in glacial drift or deposit) shows today what much of the rest of Wisconsin and the northeastern United States must have been like before the glaciers arrived. The topography here is the result of much older geologic activity, activity that had been going on for hundreds of millions of years. At successive periods, Wisconsin had been folded into mountains, worn down by weathering to a low plain with a few hills, submerged beneath an ocean to receive its sediment, and lifted up again, to be further eroded and sculptured by wind, rain, and frost.

The results are seen in spectacular landscapes of a kind not to be found anywhere else in the United States east of the Mississippi River. There are mesas, buttes, and other rock formations comparable to those of Colorado. Near Camp Douglas, for example, a broad and very flat plain is interrupted by castellated hills, sandstone towers, and steep bluffs with rock outcroppings. In the Kickapoo Valley, in the Dells of the Wisconsin, in the vicinity of Viroqua, and in other places, columns and crags of limestone or sandstone or some combination of the two appear in a variety of fantastic shapes.

Outside the Driftless Area the glaciers obliterated such features as those. The grinding, crunching ice smoothed off the rough terrain as it advanced. Though it gouged out new hollows in some stretches, it filled in existing depressions elsewhere. As the ice melted away, it left deposits of boulders, gravel, and soil that it had scraped up and carried along, polishing and pulverizing as it went. Thus it created new hills and ridges, gentler and more rounded than the old ones. Terminal moraines, such as the Wisconsin bluffs opposite Prairie du Sac, appeared at the glacier's edges. Drumlins, oval mounds of dropped materials, were widely scattered over southeastern Wisconsin. Kettle moraines, knolls with a kettlelike depression on top, occurred where huge blocks of ice were deposited with piles of glacial drift, to melt and leave a void. A string of such kettles stretches through Sheboygan, Fond du Lac, and Waukesha counties, in the eastern part of the state.

The advancing ice, by damming streams, and the retreating ice, by yielding up its water, caused floods that produced some remarkable scenery. Rivers changed their directions. The Wisconsin, having been turned aside from its previous course, wore a channel through several miles of red sandstone, thus forming the Wisconsin Dells. The St. Croix, along the Minnesota border, cut a long, deep gorge through gray and black lava. When the glacier melted there, it loosed not only granite boulders but also a mighty torrent that swirled them about in the softer rock of the gorge to form dozens of potholes, some of them more than ten feet wide and equally deep.

Thanks to the glaciers, which carved out the Great Lakes, Wisconsin has five hundred miles of Lake Michigan and Lake Superior shoreline, much of it picturesque. Wisconsin also has thousands of other natural bodies of water, ranging from mere ponds to Lake Winnebago, which is more than ten miles wide and almost thirty miles long. Nearly four thousand lakes have been mapped—seemingly a large enough number to justify Wisconsin's claim to more lakes than any other state. In the entire world there are few areas of comparable size where so large a proportion of the earth's surface is covered with lakes (in this case quite small ones) as a wide expanse of northern Wisconsin near the Michigan border.

Practically all the natural lakes have resulted from glaciation (some ponds are the work of beavers). There are none within the Driftless Area. Some of the inland bodies of water, as well as the Great Lakes, occupy basins that the glacier scooped out, Green Lake being the deepest of them at 237 feet. Most of the lakes lie behind dams of glacial detritus. One of the most interesting, both scenically and geologically, is Devil's Lake. It was left in a gap the preglacial Wisconsin River had cut through the Baraboo Range. Tongues of ice, moving from east to west on both sides of the range, blocked the river and forced it to detour. For a time the lake lay between two ice cliffs, which were replaced by two terminal moraines when the thaw came. Elsewhere, in places where the glacially dammed water was too shallow to constitute lakes, it formed marshes, bogs, and swamps, some of them quite extensive, though the largest in the state, the Great Swamp of central Wisconsin, which lies in a flat and poorly drained part of the Driftless Area, was not a result of glacial action.

In consequence of its geologic history, Wisconsin has a more varied topography than other midwestern states. It has not only plains and rolling hills but also horizons that appear to be truly mountainous, even though the highest elevation is slightly less than two thousand feet and the lowest nearly six hundred. The soils on some bottoms and plains were rich, but on the whole the land the first white settlers found was less fertile than in some of the neighboring states, particularly Illinois. Still, in the northern two thirds of Wisconsin, the soil supported a vast and valuable forest of solid white pine in some tracts and mixed evergreens and hardwoods in others. In the southern third it bore a cover of tall prairie grass interspersed with groves of oak (the oak openings), hickory, and other trees.

The climate of Wisconsin is probably much the same as it has always been since the land first rose from the primordial ooze—except during the abnormal cold of the successive ice ages. Rainfall and snowfall vary from one part of the state to another, but the annual precipitation for the state as a whole averages about 35 inches (as compared with about 10 inches for Nevada and 60 for Florida) and is fairly evenly distributed throughout the year. Temperatures range from a record high of 111 degrees to a record low of about 50 degrees below zero Fahrenheit. Summers are short and cool, especially in the north, where, along the Michigan border, the growing season is limited to 75 days; near the lakeshore below Milwaukee it extends to 175. Even in the central south, there are seldom more than a half-dozen summer days on which the thermometer goes above 90. Winters, though quite sunny, are long and cold, colder on the average than in any other state except North Dakota and Minnesota. Some geologists think that we are living in an interglacial period and that the ice eventually will come back. This is easy to believe on a subzero January day in Wisconsin.

3

One autumn day in 1836 a newcomer to Wisconsin Territory stood gazing at the golden foliage of oak openings and the golden expanse of unplowed prairie. In front of him, where the land sloped down to the Crawfish riverbank, he noticed something unnatural about the terrain—three hillocks that were not irregular and rounded but quite geometrical in shape. On closer inspection he saw that they were, indeed, flat-topped earthen pyramids. These must have been made by human beings! Among the curious whom the news quickly attracted was a Milwaukee judge who had been reading about the Aztecs. In Mexico the Aztecs had constructed pyramids, much larger ones of stone, and possessed a tradition that their ancestors had come from Aztalan, a place in the distant north. The judge jumped to the conclusion that this was the place, and he named it Aztalan.

As settlers looked over the land in southern Wisconsin, they discovered a great many other artificial mounds. These were not pyramidal but conical or domelike, linear, or pictorial, that is, representing animal and even human forms. The pictorial or effigy mounds, viewed from above, revealed the outlines of bears, panthers, wolves, foxes, deer, buffalo, turtles, eagles, swallows, and wild geese. The man-mound near Baraboo outlined a human figure 214 feet long. Such animal and human effigies were characteristic of Wisconsin; comparatively few of them have been found in other states. The tumuli of all kinds in Wisconsin numbered between ten and fifteen thousand, probably more than in any other area of comparable size in the mound regions of the country. The settlers assumed that such remarkable work could not have been performed by "savages" like those they were familiar with. It must have been the doing of some ancient people lost to history, a race of exceptional ability and amazing civilization, the mysterious Mound Builders.

At first the archaeologists endorsed and, indeed, developed that belief, the Mound Builder myth. An exception was Increase A. Lapham, Wisconsin's own pioneer scientist and one of the nation's leaders in prehistoric research from the 1830s to the

1870s. Lapham believed that the builders of the mounds, except possibly those at Aztalan, were ancestors of existing Wisconsin tribes. In his *Antiquities of Wisconsin* (1855) he described the state's mounds and mapped and diagrammed many of them, including those at Aztalan. It is a good thing he did so, for furrows steadily leveled the pyramids and erased thousands of other mounds, while a county road amputated the Baraboo man-mound at the knees. After its organization in 1901, the Wisconsin Archaeological Society encouraged both preservation and research. "Investigations conducted by the Society," the state archaeologist of Ohio declared in 1931, "have made the archaeology of Wisconsin well known and have served as an inspiration to more backward states." [11] The society acquired the Aztalan site as a gift from the citizens of Jefferson County and transferred it to the state as soon as the latter was ready to convert it into a state park. In 1950 the restoration of the pyramids, palisaded walls, and other prehistoric structures was begun, largely on the basis of Lapham's drawings and descriptions.

Agreeing with Lapham, later archaeological and ethnological experts arrived at the following consensus: The people who made the mounds were essentially similar to, and in some cases closely related to, the Indians of historic time. Wisconsin's earliest inhabitants moved in from the south after the last ice sheet had disappeared and had been replaced by vegetation. A second folk movement occurred a few thousand years before the birth of Christ; it included the ancestors of the Menominee. A third, about A.D. 1000, consisted of the people who were to be known as the Winnebago. Some of the early arrivals covered their graves with rounded or elongated heaps of earth. Later arrivals built the effigy mounds, between about A.D. 700 and about 1300, to serve both as totems and as tombs. A fourth migration

11. Henry Clyde Shetrone, *The Mound Builders: A Reconstruction of the Life of a Prehistoric American Race, Through Exploration and Interpretation of Their Earth Mounds, Their Burials, and Their Cultural Remains* (New York and London: D. Appleton and Co., 1931), pp. 307–308.

began around A.D. 1200 or 1300 and brought the builders of Aztalan up from the region around what is now Cahokia, Illinois, where (and farther south in the Mississippi Valley) their relatives constructed even more impressive earthen works. The Aztalanians were careful farmers as well as skilled engineers. They were also cannibals. They stayed on in Wisconsin until approximately the year 1600, when they inexplicably disappeared.

At that time, just before the first Frenchmen arrived, there were perhaps 20,000 Indians within the confines of the future state. Among them were the Menominee, who had been present for thousands of years and were occupying the Menominee Valley in the northeast, and the Winnebago, who had been present for several hundred years and were scattered from the Door peninsula to Lake Winnebago and around it. Other tribes destined to figure in Wisconsin history were beginning to force their way into the area from the northeast and the southeast, fleeing from the terrible scourge of the rampaging Iroquois. Along the southern shore of Lake Superior the Chippewa took up hunting grounds. In the valleys of the Fox River and the lower Wisconsin the Fox Indians and the related Sauk made their settlements. Elsewhere the Potawatomi, Kickapoo, and others found at least temporary living space. Continual wars resulted from the intrusions, wars that proved disastrous for some tribes, especially the once powerful Winnebago. The identity and distribution of Wisconsin's Indians changed considerably, whether or not the total numbers did.

During the seventeenth and eighteenth centuries the tribal cultures deteriorated through exposure directly or indirectly to European influences. Previously the Menominee and the Winnebago had been more or less settled people with a somewhat diversified economy. For a living they hunted and fished; gathered wild rice, fruit, and berries; and raised garden crops. The fur trade changed that way of life. It converted the Indians into trappers who worked for the white man and depended on him for their necessities. The beaver, one Indian remarked, ''makes kettles, hatchets, swords, knives, bread; and, in short, it makes everything." [12] Adapting most readily to the demands of the fur business were the Chippewa, who already had a comparatively simple hunting-and-fishing economy. Other tribes, in Wisconsin and throughout the northeast, used the Chippewa language as a second tongue, a lingua franca. They began to approximate the Chippewa culture in other respects also.

In the early nineteenth century some of the Wisconsin tribes faced desperation as the fur trade declined, as white settlers pressed in to work the lead mines or take up farms, and as the United States government began its program of Indian removal. The Indians now had to choose between adopting the white man's ways and accepting confinement on reservations somewhere west of the Mississippi River. When, in 1827, some of the Winnebago resisted by killing several whites, federal troops and territorial militia converged on the tribe. To save his people from hostilities, Chief Red Bird surrendered, hoping to be put immediately to death. Instead, a tragic figure, he lingered and died in jail.

More serious trouble broke out five years later, in the spring of 1832, when about a thousand Sauk and Fox men, women, and children under the leadership of Black Hawk crossed into Illinois from the west bank of the Mississippi, to which the two tribes had been consigned by treaty. The followers of Black Hawk were known as the "British band" of the Sauk and Fox; he had sided with the British during the War of 1812, and he still entertained vague hopes of British aid. He also expected help from the disgruntled Winnebago. But he got no such assistance, and he ran into the opposition of Menominee, Potawatomi, and Sioux warriors as well as white soldiers. Recently the Menominee had lost a war party of twenty-six in a Sauk and Fox attack; now they were seeking revenge. A hundred years

---

12. Felix M. Keesing, *The Menomini Indians of Wisconsin: A Study of Three Centuries of Cultural Contact and Change* (Philadelphia: American Philosophical Society, 1939), p. 79, quoting the *Jesuit Relations,* 73 vols. (Cleveland: Arthur H. Clark Co., 1896–1901), 6:297.

later, descendants of the Menominee were to speak of the American forces as allies in what was, according to tribal tradition, essentially a Menominee campaign.

Black Hawk soon realized the futility of trying to recover his people's lost corn-planting ground, but he was rebuffed when he proposed to talk peace. Compelled to give battle, he put to flight a militia force much larger than his truce party. To escape the federal troops, he took his people up the valley of the Rock River and into Wisconsin, then past the Four Lakes and toward the Wisconsin River, whence he intended to make his way back across the Mississippi to safety. On the bluffs of the Wisconsin, near the site of the old Sauk town that had so much impressed Jonathan Carver, he delayed his pursuers in a short, sharp engagement, the Battle of Wisconsin Heights. He and some of his followers finally managed to cross the Mississippi on rafts and get away (to be captured later), but others, including women and children, were slaughtered on the riverbank. Such was the Black Hawk War, in which Jefferson Davis served as a lieutenant of the regular army and Abraham Lincoln as a captain of Illinois militia.

That was the last of the Indian wars in Wisconsin. The relocation of the tribes proceeded. The Winnebago were assigned to reservations west of the Mississippi, but many of these people could not suppress their longing for their ancestral homeland. Four times they were rounded up and shipped out, yet they kept straggling back, to lead a wandering existence in western Wisconsin. Some exiled Potawatomi also returned. The Chippewa and Menominee managed to get reservations inside the state, including parts of the very area in which they had been living. Others, recent arrivals from the east, the Stockbridge and the Oneida, also received reservations in the state. Both were English-speaking groups of settled farmers. The Oneida were descendants of a member-tribe of the famous Iroquois League. The Stockbridge were close relatives of the Mohicans, whom the Iroquois once had defeated and practically wiped out. Thus the "last of the Mohicans" ended up in Wisconsin.

Reservation life further demoralized many of the Indians, as the federal government fluctuated from one policy to another, now trying to break down the tribes and "civilize" the individual members, now proposing to restore tribal culture, organization, and responsibility. After more than a century of this, the reservation Indians of whatever tribe were dismally poor and practically resourceless. The Menominee seemed to be worse rather than better off after the government, in 1961, terminated their reservation, which then became Menominee County.

As of the 1970s, Wisconsin had the largest Indian population of any state east of the Mississippi except for North Carolina and New York. The Wisconsin total probably came to more than 15,000, though it was hard to estimate since it depended on the definition and identification of "Indians," including a majority with varying degrees of Caucasian blood. The number was smaller than in many western states, but the variety was greater than in any of them except Oklahoma, Arizona, New Mexico, and California. Most of the Wisconsin Indians were living off the reservations, a half or more of them in cities, but this did not necessarily mean that they had lost their Indian character and had been assimilated into the larger society of the state. "From treaty to termination," an able student observed, "the boundaries of the state of Wisconsin encompass an astonishingly representative illustration of the total development of federal Indian policy and Indian adaptation and resistance to it." [13]

4

The Indians left their mark on the landscape not only in the mounds but also in traces of garden plots and, more striking and more extensive than either, in much of the ground cover as it was when the Caucasians arrived. To drive game, the Indians used to set fires, which, together with those the lightning started, kept down the growth of timber and accounted for the

13. Nancy Oestreich Lurie, "Wisconsin: A Natural Laboratory for North American Indian Studies," *Wisconsin Magazine of History,* 53 (Autumn 1969):3.

existence of the prairies and the oak openings. The Caucasians could be expected to make a much more noticeable impress if only because they became far more numerous. Wisconsin's population reached nearly four and a half million by 1970 (making this the sixteenth most populous of the fifty states). By then the population density was more than two hundred times as great as it had ever been when the Indians alone occupied the area. But the whites had a deeper effect on the land not so much because of their sheer numbers as because of their peculiar activities—their clearing, plowing, ditching, draining, damming, lumbering, road making, railway construction, industrialization, and urbanization.

From the viewpoint of the typical pioneer, the wilderness itself along with its aboriginal inhabitants was an adversary to be eliminated or tamed. The frontiersman might have moods in which he romanticized its beauty, yet he knew he must demand its sacrifice, since he was at heart a bringer of civilization, a man of progress. He rejoiced to see the passing of the "dark and silent forest" and the "green rolling prairie" along with the "roving tribes of native Indians that claimed the wild but beautiful region as their inheritance." He welcomed the "ocean of waving crops," the "bustle of the busy reaper," and the "hum, clatter, and other sounds of industry," which were "daily and hourly banishing silence from the wilderness." [14] To him, civilization apparently meant, among other things, noise.

As the settler cleared trees off his land, he burned most of the wood just to get rid of it. As he plowed his fields, however, he unintentionally created fire-stops that checked the formerly periodic prairie fires. "Seedling oaks forthwith romped over the grasslands in legions, and what had been the prairie region became a region of woodlot farms." [15] Much of southern Wisconsin acquired more trees than ever before in recorded history.

14. John Gregory, *Industrial Resources of Wisconsin* (Milwaukee: Starr's Book and Job Printing Office, 1855), pp. 6–7, 22–25, 28.

15. Aldo Leopold, *A Sand County Almanac, with Essays on Conservation from Round River* (New York: Oxford University Press, 1953), p. 31.

Back in 1766 Jonathan Carver had climbed one of the Blue Mounds to get a look at the countryside. ''For many miles nothing was to be seen but lesser mountains, which appeared at a distance like haycocks, they being free from trees.'' [16] Today those hills are quite heavily wooded.

It was a different story with the great pine forests of the north. There the white man cut the timber for its own sake, not for the purpose of making farms, and by 1900 the best of the pine was practically gone. The lumber industry operated with enormous waste, less than half of the usable timber ever reaching the sawmill, the rest being left to rot or burn, or sinking irretrievably in sloughs and backwaters as logs were floated downstream. Rare was the summer without a serious forest fire.

The most terrible holocaust struck northeastern Wisconsin, on both sides of the Green Bay, in 1871. In that part of the state there had been little or no rain all summer long. Even the marshes dried up, and small fires here and there began to smolder along the ground, occasionally flaring up in the tree tops. On Sunday evening, October 8, a sudden wind stirred up thick clouds of smoke, showers of sparks, and long, leaping tongues of flame. These turned into veritable tornadoes of fire. Only seventeen of about eighty inhabitants survived the blaze in the shingle-manufacturing settlement of Williamsonville, near Sturgeon Bay. In the village of Peshtigo hundreds died, and others saved themselves only by standing neck-deep in the Peshtigo River and dousing themselves to avoid the flames that billowed out over the water. By the next day a sixty-mile swath above the Green Bay and a fifty-mile strip on the Door peninsula lay in ashes and charred ruins, and a total of 1,200 to 1,300 people were dead. On the very same night the great Chicago fire had occurred, causing more property damage but far fewer deaths (about 250). It drew the world's attention away from the much deadlier Wisconsin conflagration.

Plundering the forest and plowing the grassland let rains wash off the once protected topsoil. Wheat growing exhausted the soil

16. Carver, *Travels,* pp. 47–48.

of its nitrogen. Careless disposal of human wastes fouled the waters above ground and below; as early as 1877 the state board of health found most of the state's water supplies contaminated. Papermaking and pea canning added industrial wastes to the rivers, and munitions making polluted the air. When, in 1941, the federal government announced plans for a powder plant— the largest in the world, according to anticipations—Sauk County farmers objected not so much on ecological as on personal and economic grounds. The project would take *their* land, some of the most fertile in the entire state. Once built, the Badger Ordnance Works spewed its noxious fumes over its beautiful surroundings all during the Second World War and again during the Vietnam adventure.

Among the early settlers were some who, standing apart from the rest, pleaded for mercy for things natural and wild. John Muir, for one, arriving from Scotland as a boy of eleven in 1849, immediately fell in love with the spot in Marquette County—"the sunny woods, overlooking a flowery glacier meadow and a lake rimmed with white water-lilies"—that his father had chosen for starting a farm. "Oh, that glorious Wisconsin Wilderness!" [17] In 1865, after leaving the University of Wisconsin, Muir wanted to convert the farm, which his brother now owned, into a sanctuary for the wild flowers that had gladdened his youth. His brother declined to sell the farm but took up the idea and put it into effect—the first such experiment in wildlife preservation in Wisconsin. Muir himself went on to roam through California and much of the rest of North America and through South America and Africa, studying nature as he went. Before his death in 1914 he was recognized as one of the foremost of American naturalists and conservationists.

By 1867 so many citizens were concerned about the depletion of the forests that the legislature set up a commission to look into it. As chairman of the commission the self-made scientist Increase A. Lapham put together a hundred-page *Report of the*

17. John Muir, *The Story of My Boyhood and Youth* (Boston: Houghton Mifflin Co., 1913), pp. 51, 53.

Disastrous Effects of the Destruction of Forest Trees Now Going on So Rapidly in the State of Wisconsin (Madison, 1867). The report clearly showed that stripping the land of forest cover not only threatened the wood supply but also harmed the natural environment, diminishing the flow of springs while increasing the destructiveness of floods. In response to the report, the legislature did nothing to regulate the cutting of timber and passed only an ineffectual measure to encourage the planting of trees.

Charles R. Van Hise, a geologist and president of the University of Wisconsin, contributed to the national conservationist cause one of its most useful books, *The Conservation of Natural Resources in the United States* (New York, 1910). Aldo Leopold, who became professor of game management at the university, the first such professor in the country, left a classic work on that subject (1930). He also wrote (1949, 1953) essays on nature in a spirit reminiscent of Henry David Thoreau and John Muir. Leopold emphasized the complex relationships among all forms of life, both animal and vegetable, both macroscopic and microscopic. "For the biotic community to survive, its internal processes must balance, else its member-species would disappear," he pointed out. "Our grandfathers did not, could not, know the origin of their prairie empire. They killed off the prairie fauna and drove the flora to a last refuge on railroad embankments and roadsides." [18]

From the early years of statehood Wisconsin had game laws, but these were neither comprehensive nor well enforced. They did not prevent the destruction of the passenger pigeons, which once had darkened the sky each spring, nor the decimation of the prairie chickens. Buffalo, bear, moose, and elk sooner or later disappeared. Deer recovered and thrived, though they were indiscriminately slaughtered despite the tightening of the laws. "The hunters promise to outnumber the deer," one of the hunters remarked as early as the season of 1878. After a century of statehood, game expert Leopold observed that "Wisconsin

18. Leopold, *Sand County Almanac*, pp. 191, 193.

deer-hunters, in their pursuit of a legal buck, kill and abandon in the woods at least one doe, fawn, or spike buck for every two legal bucks taken out. In other words, approximately half the hunters shoot any deer until a legal deer is killed." [19]

In 1897 the state began a serious effort to conserve and restore the forests. A state forestry warden was named and given power to appoint and supervise town wardens who, in turn, were authorized to call out citizens as firefighters. Gradually the state expanded its system of fire detection and suppression, with a regular force of wardens and with watchtowers, two-way radios, and observation planes. By the 1970s the extent of forest annually burned had been reduced from more than 500,000 to less than 9,000 acres. The state commenced reforestation with the establishment of a nursery in 1911. A forest crop law of 1927 encouraged tree farming by deferring taxes on privately owned land until the timber harvest. More and more of the land, nearly half of northern Wisconsin, was converted into publicly owned forest preserves. By the time of the Second World War the state held 187,000 acres of forest and 13,000 acres of wooded parks; the counties held 1,886,000 acres and the federal government 1,300,000, including two national forests, Chequamegon and Nicolet.

Wisconsin led the nation in developing methods of checking soil erosion. Before the First World War the state university began to experiment with planting rows of trees to shelter the land from the ravages of wind. During the Great Depression there were nearly three thousand miles of growing "shelter belt" in six counties of the sandy central plain of Wisconsin. This device was widely copied, especially in the dust bowl of the Great Plains. In 1933 the United States Department of Agriculture in co-operation with the University of Wisconsin set up, in Coon Valley, the first soil-conservation demonstration project. In 1940 this was succeeded by a federally assisted program in which local farmers agreed to set up a soil-conservation district and adapt to practical farm management such means of

19. Leopold, *Sand County Almanac,* pp. 15, 213.

erosion control as reforestation, dam construction, terracing, and contour plowing. Tours brought farmers from other parts of the state to learn from the demonstrations.

Dead fish in the Flambeau River, poisonous with industrial wastes, set off a campaign, starting in 1927, to clean up the waters of the state. Industry co-operated with government. Pulp and paper mills, the worst polluters, made the most spectacular clean-up effort, spending more than $50,000,000 on it during the next five decades. After fifteen years of research Marathon Paper Mills of Rothschild discovered ways of transforming wastes into a variety of useful products, among them vanillin, tanning chemicals, a synthetic rubber ingredient, and plastics for laminated sheets. The canning industry found means of treating and utilizing cannery wastes. The city of Milwaukee converted sewage into a saleable fertilizer, Milorganite. By the Resource Management Act of 1966 the legislature provided for a comprehensive antipollution program. Though Wisconsin had been a leader in this field, increasing population and industrialization continued to threaten its water resources. Slime, scum, and sludge floated on too many of the lakes and streams, and people ate fish from the Wisconsin River only at the risk of mercury poisoning.

A spectacular success for Wisconsin conservationists was the restoration of Horicon Marsh, a victory that came only after a long and bitter struggle. At one time the marsh, on the Rock River near its headwaters, had been a bounteous source of wild rice, fish, beaver, and muskrat for the Winnebago. In the 1840s businessmen interested in water power built a dam that produced a lake fourteen miles long and six miles wide, the largest artificial body of water in the world, some said. Lawsuits by farmers with flooded lands led the owners of the dam to break it down in 1869. After the marsh recovered and again attracted seasonal flocks of waterfowl, wealthy eastern sportsmen leased parts of the area and used them as private hunting preserves. In the early 1900s a land company bought 18,000 acres, drained the marsh, and sold the land to farmers. Drainage left a desolate, hideous, stinking morass of no value for industry or recreation and, as experience proved, of little value even for agriculture. The Wisconsin chapter of the Izaak Walton League persuaded the legislature, in 1927, to restore the marsh as a wildlife refuge, but landowners, complaining that the reflooding damaged their crops, sued the state and compelled it to let the water out again. Finally the state and federal governments acquired the affected land, and Horicon Marsh became once more a paradise for hunters, fishers, and nature lovers.

On the whole, the Wisconsin of the late twentieth century presented a prospect that, if different from what it once had been, was still pleasing. If some parts of the north country were bleak, cutover lands, covered with scrubby aspen instead of the once majestic pine, other parts had a luxuriant new growth of evergreen. If pollution and industrial blight marred portions of the south, most of the area had a special kind of latter-day beauty. This was the result of dairying, in itself a conservationist activity, one that the landscape closely reflected. Woodlots topped the ridges, pastures covered the slopes, and fields of hay or grain lay in the valleys. Long, high barns dotted the rolling countryside, and tall cylindrical silos stood beside them, more silos than in any other state. It was, indeed, a vision of pastoral loveliness.

5

Wisconsin remained less urban than the United States as a whole. Though it was one of the highly industrialized states, comparatively few of its people were concentrated in large cities. The majority lived in small or medium-sized ones (under 50,000), in villages, or in the country, but only about a fifth of the total population on farms. Most of the farmers were close to town; most of the businessmen and factory workers were close to pleasant lakes and game-filled woods. There was a remarkable intimacy between town and country. Taking advantage of the opportunity, an unusually high proportion of the people devoted themselves to outdoor recreation, not just on annual vacations but on weekends and even weekdays throughout the

year. The same attractions also brought in yearly millions of
outsiders, mainly from the neighboring states and especially
from Chicago. Tourism was one of Wisconsin's biggest businesses.

The state's attractions had begun to draw vacationists soon
after the Civil War. More and more people were acquiring the
leisure for travel, and more and more of them were learning
about the advantages of Wisconsin as a destination.

The scenery of Wisconsin Dells and Devil's Lake first gained
widespread publicity through the work of Henry H. Bennett,
one of America's great landscape photographers. After serving
in the Union army, Bennett opened a photographic studio in
Kilbourn City (now Wisconsin Dells). Soon he was clambering
about the rocky ledges and making his way along the gulches to
take pictures for the stereoscope, a then popular device for
viewing photographs, one that gave them a three-dimensional
effect. Besides his primitive, homemade camera, he had to
carry with him a load of cumbersome equipment, including a
light-tight tent as a portable darkroom for developing the wet
glass plates, which had to be processed in a hurry. By the
1870s, families throughout the country were gazing, in their
parlors, at Bennett's marvelous stereoscopic views. Sightseers
who went to Kilbourn City could buy the pictures at his shop,
and they found local enterprisers more than willing, for a consideration, to take them on boat tours to behold nature's originals.

For the time being, however, not the Dells area but Waukesha was Wisconsin's leading summer resort. Waukesha had
been a quite ordinary village before Colonel Richard Dunbar
happened to stop there in August 1868. The colonel, from New
York, was wealthy but he was also diabetic. Thirstily he drank
from a mineral spring in a pasture near the edge of town. Over-
night he was cured of his diabetes, or so he believed. The next
year he bought the spring, named it Bethesda, erected a pavilion
over it, and began to advertise its water as God's own elixir.
Other promoters developed neighboring springs and built hotels
and boarding houses. Soon Waukesha aspired to be the Saratoga

of the West. In its heyday during the 1880s and 1890s it was indeed a fashionable and a busy place, offering not only therapy but also amusement—dancing, bicycling, bathing, boating, hayrides, croquet, lawn tennis, billiards, bowling, concerts, theater. After 1900, with the multiplication of the automobile, such resorts as Waukesha lost popularity, and its springs even began to dry up. One company, White Rock, continued to bottle and sell Waukesha water under a trademark that became nationally familiar: Psyche, seminude, with butterfly wings and a shapely figure, kneeling on a rock and peering into a pool. She is still kneeling there, as she has been since about 1893.

Besides the Dells and Waukesha, a number of other Wisconsin places gained renown as summer resorts from the 1870s on. Among those most often recommended were Madison, Oconomowoc, Pewaukee, Palmyra, Sheboygan, Neenah, Menasha, Lake Geneva, Devil's Lake, and Green Lake. Tourists' and sportsmen's guides listed the places and proclaimed their delights—the bracing air, the sparkling waters, the fishing, hunting, and other sports. Railroads, advertising their "palace cars," joined in boosting the travel to Wisconsin. In the early 1900s the Milwaukee Road promoted Delavan Lake, only three hours from Chicago, as a versatile resort offering, among other features, yacht races, Chautauqua meetings, and a large golf course. That railroad's *Guide to Summer Homes* in 1915 mentioned sixty-three Wisconsin locations, among which Kilbourn City had the most hotel facilities.

By the turn of the century, sportsmen were already venturing into the north woods, which tempted the angler with a variety of catch, the top prize being the musky, or muskellunge, the toughest and fightingest of freshwater fish (a monster weighing nearly seventy pounds, a world's record, was one day to be taken from Chippewa Lake, near Hayward, after a forty-five-minute contest). The early commercial resorts of the north offered primitive cabins and a central dining hall, where on chill evenings the guests could gather before the crackling flames of the fireplace. Quite different was the private estate of Henry Clay Pierce, a New York and St. Louis financier and oilman, on the Bois Brule River. The ultimate in rustic luxury, it cost $1,200,000, not counting the price of the four thousand acres. Its master bungalow, Cedar Island Lodge, was the summer White House in 1928, when President Calvin Coolidge spent three months there as Pierce's guest, while secret-service agents tramped over the grounds. The president's stay gave tremendous publicity to the region, making it a much greater tourist attraction than it had ever been before.

The area attracted bootleggers and gangsters, among others. Hurley, once a rowdy lumber camp, became a rowdy vacation spot. During the days of Prohibition it had dozens of speakeasies in addition to a much larger number of available whores. It was a haven for criminals on the lam, as was the neighboring resort of Little Bohemia. At Little Bohemia the FBI's most wanted man, John Dillinger, hid out with his mob and their molls in 1934. When G-men surrounded the place, Dillinger and his men emerged shooting and made good their escape.

During the 1930s Wisconsin's recreation industry suffered from the effects of the general business depression. Resort proprietors, no longer the beneficiaries of the railroads' boosting, reached only a limited market with the individual advertising they could afford. So, in 1936, the state stepped in. It added a recreational publicity department to the existing conservation commission, the assumption being that conservation and recreation were closely allied. The publicity department, with public funds, began a systematic advertising campaign. Directed mainly at the neighboring states and particularly at Chicago, the advertisements of "Wonderful Wisconsin" kept reminding prospective vacationists that within an easy day's drive there was an inviting countryside quite different from the corn belt. To make the drive still easier, the state closed its highways to truck traffic on summer weekends. By midnight on Sundays trucks would be lined up at the borders, waiting to get into Wisconsin.

All along, Wisconsin had been touted as a summer vacation land. When the long winter came, the strangers departed, the hotels were closed and the cottages boarded up, to be left in stillness and isolation amid the drifting snow. The winter scene began to change shortly before the Second World War. Enterprisers installed ski-tows on the long slopes of some of the northern hills, and "snow trains" ran from Chicago and Milwaukee to Rhinelander, Eagle River, Ashland, and other northern points. Resort owners on many of the lakes made arrangements for skating, hockey, iceboating, and ice fishing. Visitors learned to enjoy sports that the local people previously had had all to themselves. Wisconsinites redesigned the iceboat and made it more maneuverable by putting the rudder in front of a set of fixed runners; going much faster than the wind, an Oshkosh boater claimed a record speed of 150 miles an hour on Lake Winnebago in 1953. Through holes cut in the ice of various lakes and especially Winnebago, which was reputed to have more sturgeon than any other lake in the world, patient fishermen managed to spear specimens of this "living fossil" weighing from 30 to 40 to a record 168 pounds.

More than anything else, the snowmobile transformed Wisconsin into a winter playground. Predecessors of this vehicle had appeared in the state as early as the 1920s, when Wisconsinites converted Model-T Fords into "snowbuggies" by substituting skis for the front wheels and half-track treads for the rear wheels. Carl Eliason, of Lost Lake Resort in far-northern Vilas County, invented an "autoboggan"—a toboggan powered by a motorcycle engine, propelled by an endless track in the rear and steered by two skis in front—which he patented in 1927. A number of Eliason's motor toboggans were manufactured in Clintonville and used by the United States Army in the Second World War. The snowmobile of the present type, however, came out of Quebec in 1958. Its use quickly spread, especially in Wisconsin. At the end of the following decade, Wisconsin was the home of six of the twenty-three major manufacturers, 56,000 of the country's 500,000 machines, and more snowmobile trails and cruising areas than any other state. Wisconsin laid claim to the title of snowmobile capital of the United States, as snowmobile cruising, camping, racing, and skijoring (ski-towing) brought an end to what remained of the winter solitude in the north.

In the age of affluence following the Second World War, Wisconsin's recreation industry boomed as never before. By 1960, vacation-recreation visits (counting each stay of one day or part of a day) had reached an annual total of 56 million for out-of-staters and 114 million for Wisconsin residents. The totals increased with the completion of interstate highways 90 and 94 across the state during the 1960s. A quarter-billion-dollar industry in 1940, Wisconsin tourism became a three-billion-dollar-a-year industry by 1975.

While tourists multiplied, so did owners of vacation property, both inside and outside of developers' tracts. According to an informed estimate, the number of vacation homes in the state grew from 55,000 in 1959 to 92,000 in 1965 and would reach 120,000 by 1970. Some Wisconsinites suspected that Chicagoans, buying up marginal but scenic farmland, were engrossing the vacation sites. Such was not the case according to a 1970 survey, which indicated that only about 15 percent of the buyers of such properties in Wisconsin were residents of other states.

Though yielding profits and tax revenues, the tourist business and the recreational real estate developments caused difficulties for Wisconsin. Highways, lakes, state parks, and much of the countryside itself were overcrowded. Resorts, notably Wisconsin Dells, were blighted by the crassness of their commercialism. Automobiles and snowmobiles left litter, stench, and nerve-wracking noise in their wake. Wastes seeped into the earth and the water in rural areas where neither the developers nor the purchasers of lots were willing to pay for sewerage systems and where soil conditions were unsuitable for the proper functioning of septic tanks. Of Wisconsin's scenic beauty, one could aptly say that to enjoy it was to destroy it.

To preserve the landscape, and at the same time to promote its enjoyment, the legislature in 1961 passed an outdoor recreation act that provided for an advanced and comprehensive program of environmental planning. Environmentalists maintained, however, that there was an inherent conflict between promoting and preserving, between recreation and conservation. Recognizing the truth of this, the legislature in its 1975–1977 state budget took the promotion of tourism from the department of natural resources (successor to the conservation commission) and put it in the department of business development. "Unless we are to adopt a xenophobic attitude toward outsiders," a Madison newspaper commented in approving the change, "we are going to continue to play hosts to the millions of vacationers who seek respite in our vistas, in our resorts. Heaven knows, there is beauty enough and vistas enough and resorts enough to share with our neighbors." [20]

20. *Madison Capital Times,* August 9, 1975.

2

A German State?

$\mathcal{W}$ISCONSIN'S population was composed of "heteroge-neous masses collected together from every quarter of the globe," an Irish-born promoter of immigration and real estate wrote in 1855, exaggerating a bit. He conceded that the "ad-mixture of different habits, customs, passions and feelings" would generate a certain amount of "gaseous" discord. "But though these elements may jar for a moment, like different met-als in the furnace, yet the amalgamation of the races, by inter-marriage, must produce the most perfect race of men that has ever appeared upon earth." [1] Here, by a Wisconsinite, was an early statement of the theory of the melting pot.

Not all authorities agreed, however, that the Wisconsin pot ever would or even should melt down the various peoples and cultures into a new, unique amalgam. An English-born Wiscon-sin physician predicted in 1880 that the "general intermingling" of the state's nationalities would "tend to preserve the good old Anglo-Saxon character, rather than to create any new character for our people." [2] A Wisconsin newpaperman and historian, a native of Maine, took a somewhat different view in 1899. "It

---

1. Gregory, *Industrial Resources of Wisconsin,* pp. 12–13, 22–25.
2. Joseph Hobbins, "Health of Wisconsin," *History of Sauk County, Wisconsin* (Chicago: Western Publishing Company, 1880), p. 237.

has sometimes been a matter of wonder that Wisconsin, so over-whelmingly foreign in its population, should be so distinctively American in all its institutions and government, in its educational impulse and its progress,'' this son of the Puritans declared. ''Wisconsin institutions have been dominated by Americans of the Puritan seed from the beginning.'' [3] Looking at the same situation as of about the same time, a scholar of German background concluded: ''In Wisconsin, whose population is three-fourths of foreign origin, the German element has always predominated.'' [4]

A distinctive, blended society emerging? A re-creation of England, or of New England? An essentially German state?

1

At the time Wisconsin became a state, in 1848, Americans and Europeans were swarming westward in search of cheap land and an opportunity to start life anew. During the 1850s one American in every four moved from one state to another, and from some of the older states of the northeast the departure rate was as high as one in three. During the same decade a larger number of Europeans migrated to America than had done so in all the preceding decades since Independence.

Wisconsin welcomed the home-seekers, both native and foreign-born. Those who had already arrived might prefer newcomers of their own kind, but few doubted that rapid population growth would lead to rapid economic development or that this would be a good thing for the new state and hence for themselves. Wisconsinites with relatives in the east or abroad, land promoters, emigration societies of particular nationalities, representatives of churches, all tried to attract migrants. The state government added its efforts, thus setting an example for other

3. Ellis B. Usher, ''The Influence of New England on Wisconsin,'' *Proceedings of the State Historical Society of Wisconsin . . . 1899* (Madison: 1900), p. 27.

4. Albert B. Faust, *The German Element in the United States,* 2 vols. (Boston: Houghton Mifflin Company, 1909), 1:481.

states of the northwest. Laws of 1852 and 1853 provided for a commissioner of emigration with an office in New York and for a traveling agent who was to advertise Wisconsin's resources, prospects, and presumed advantages for the settler. Though dropping the program after a few years, the state resumed it in 1867 and continued it into the twentieth century.

Those who heeded the appeal and headed for Wisconsin looked, as a rule, for some place in the state where people of their own kind or kindred were already settled. They preferred neighbors with the same language, religion, and ways of life. Thus, from the beginning, Wisconsin became largely a patchwork of separate ethnic communities. These were more widely scattered, less heavily concentrated in the metropolis, than they were in other states. Wisconsin's immigrants did not crowd into Milwaukee in such disproportionate numbers as others did into New York, New Orleans, Chicago, Cincinnati, Baltimore, and Boston—even though Milwaukee, as early as 1860, had a population with a higher percentage of the foreign-born than did any other American city except St. Louis.

The 1860 census showed that Wisconsin, in proportion to its population, contained more immigrants than any other state except California. Yet the figures for Wisconsin gave the impression that it was still very much a Yankee state. Only a little more than a third of the inhabitants had been born abroad. The statistics, however, failed to show the real ethnic composition of the people, since a sizeable number of the American-born were the children of immigrants. If this number were subtracted from the native total and added to the foreign-born, the state's 1860 population would consist of two approximately equal parts. Already there were in Wisconsin about as many immigrant families (the foreign-born together with their American-born children) as families of older American stock.

Of Wisconsin's American-born at that time, nearly half were natives of the state, and the next largest numbers were natives of New York, Ohio, Pennsylvania, and Vermont, in that order. Of the foreign-born, the most numerous were the Germans, who made up a larger part of Wisconsin's population (nearly 16 percent) than of any other state's. Next in order were the Irish, the British (English, Scottish, Welsh), and the Norwegians, of whom there were about as many in Wisconsin as in all the rest of the country. There was a considerable number from British America, but the census did not tell how many of that number were English-speaking and how many were French Canadians. There were much smaller numbers of Dutch, Swiss, and Belgians, and a still smaller number of people of African descent. Indeed, the blacks totaled only 1,171, or less than two-tenths of one percent of the state's 1860 population.

In whole counties near Lake Michigan and in entire townships elsewhere, as in Sauk County, the German settlers outnumbered all others. The English-speaking immigrants, along with the people of native American stock, were fairly well scattered throughout the settled portions of the state. Still, the Irish, as construction workers, were especially numerous in places where canals or railroads were being built, and in one township of St. Croix County nearly all the family heads were natives of Ireland. The English had colonies of their own in Racine, Columbia, and Dane counties, and some (the Cornish) were clustered in the lead-mining region of the southwest, as were the Welsh. A number of settlements in the southeast and in an extensive strip along the Mississippi, north and south of La Crosse, were solidly Norwegian. Hollanders kept to themselves in communities in the lower Fox Valley and along the Lake Michigan shore near Sheboygan. Belgians on the Door peninsula formed the largest rural settlement of their nationality in the United States. In the Green County township of New Glarus practically every adult was of Swiss birth.

Immigration into the United States fell off during the Civil War, but it rose again in the 1870s and reached new heights in the 1880s. Wisconsin continued to receive a large share of the immigrants, particularly Germans and Scandinavians. According to the 1890 census, only a little more than a fourth of all Wisconsinites (434,650 of 1,686,880) were strictly "American" in the sense of having parents both of whom were born in the United States. A considerably larger number (519,200) were of foreign birth, and a still larger number (726,835) were the American-born children of parents one or both of whom were immigrants. Half of the foreign-born had come from Germany, and so it could be presumed that close to half of the American-born of foreign parentage had German ancestors. By the outbreak of the First World War in 1914, a clear majority of Wisconsinites were of German origin or background. In this respect, at least, Wisconsin had become a German state.

Meanwhile, increasing numbers of eastern and southern Europeans had joined the immigrant tide. After rising to an unprecedented volume, the flood was stemmed by the First World War and then by the restrictive laws of the 1920s. "Wisconsin is probably the only state in the Union," an outsider commented in 1925, ". . . in which an American of the 'old stock'—meaning, thereby, of British ancestry and of long family residence in this country—is perfectly naively called a 'Yankee' to distinguish him from the majority of his neighbors." [5] Wisconsin's ethnic makeup was changing, however, in response to the newer immigration trends. As of 1930, the foreign-born constituted only 13.2 percent of the population, a percentage lower than in fifteen other states. Comprising 50.2 percent of Wisconsin's people were the foreign-born plus the American-born of mixed parentage. Of that number, the people of German birth or background composed less than half, or 41.2 percent. Another 13.1 percent were Scandinavian (Norwegian and Swedish, not counting the Danish), 9.4 percent Polish, and 4 percent Czechoslovakian. Smaller percentages were distributed among a variety of nationalities, including such comparatively recent Wisconsin arrivals as the Finns, Icelanders, Russians, Yugoslavs, Italians, and Greeks. No longer were the German-Americans a majority among Wisconsinites.

As late as the 1930s, and for some time thereafter, separate and clearly identifiable ethnic communities continued to exist. This was especially true in regard to the newer groups—the

5. French Strother, "The Death of the 'Wisconsin Idea,'" World's Work, 50 (October, 1925):624.

Finns and the Russians in the far north, the Icelanders on Washington Island, most of the Czechs, Yugoslavs, Italians, and Greeks and about half of the Poles in and around Milwaukee. The city, once primarily German and secondarily Irish, had become ethnically much more diverse. In the state as a whole, people of German and other older immigrant backgrounds were more widely dispersed than they once had been. Yet among these groups, too, concentrations were still to be found. There were, for example, the Swiss in Monroe and New Glarus, the Norwegians in Westby, Stoughton, and Mount Horeb, and the Danes in Racine, the "most Danish city in America." [6]

During the first three decades following the Second World War the most noticeable changes in Wisconsin's ethnic character were the advent of Spanish-speaking Americans, Chicanos who stayed on after arriving as migrant farm workers, and—much more striking—the rapid increase in the number of blacks, who were concentrated in the cities, especially Milwaukee. As late as 1910 there had been fewer than a thousand blacks in Milwaukee County and only about three times that many in all of Wisconsin. By 1930 the number in Milwaukee had risen to 7,500 and by 1970 to 105,000, nearly 15 percent of the city's population. For the entire state, however, the black percentage remained less than three, which was much lower than it was for the nation as a whole.

2

"The religious institutions of Wisconsin bear, in good degree, the impress of New England." [7] So declared a Congregational minister when the state was only a few years old. The descendants of the Puritans hoped to keep it a sanctuary of evangelistic Protestantism of the American type, as did the

6. Fred L. Holmes, *Old World Wisconsin: Around Europe in the Badger State* (Eau Claire: E. M. Hale and Company, 1944), p. 301.

7. Stephen Peet, *History of the Presbyterian and Congregational Churches and Ministers in Wisconsin* (Milwaukee: Silas Chapman, 1851), p. 187.

Methodists, Presbyterians, Baptists, and members of other long
domesticated sects. But in time the waves of immigration over-
whelmed them. About half of the arriving Germans were
Roman Catholics, and so were about half of the Dutch, the great
majority of the Irish (a minority were Protestants from northern
Ireland), and practically all the Belgians and the French Canadians, not to mention such later arrivals as the Poles, Czechs,
and Italians. A large proportion of the Germans and practically
all the Scandinavians were of the Lutheran faith. As early as
1870 the Catholics, with almost a fourth of all the church members, could claim to be the largest of the state's religious
groups, and the Lutherans were one of the largest. By 1940 the
Catholic Church included only a little less than half of the total
membership, and the Lutheran Church about a third. The rest
was divided among some fifty other denominations, and those
of Puritan origin had only a tiny share.

From the beginning, however, the Catholic Church in Wisconsin was subject to internal strains on account of its ethnic
diversity. Its first bishop of Milwaukee, later its first archbishop
of Wisconsin, John Martin Henni, was a German-speaking
Swiss. Most of the state's hierarchy consisted of Germans.
Henni aimed to give each parish a priest of the same nationality
as the majority of the parishioners, but he could not always
manage to do so, and when he did, he ran the risk of displeasing
the minority. The Irish in particular resented the ecclesiastical
power of the Germans. Often the Irish withdrew from mixed
parishes, to form separate congregations of their own, and so
did Catholics of other nationalities. When, in 1857, Henni visited the French and German churches in Green Bay—to speak
on the "necessity of union in faith"—the Irish were about to
leave the French and form an Irish church, and the Hollanders
were already separating from the Germans and beginning to
worship in a newly built Dutch church.

Having no single organization such as the Catholics had, the
Lutherans suffered far more from differences among them-
selves. They came from separate state churches in the various
German and Scandinavian countries, each of the churches hav-

ing its distinctive forms of governance, ritual, and belief. Once arrived, the Lutherans founded independent congregations, and these sooner or later affiliated with one or another of several American synods. Lutherans disagreed not only on points of doctrine but also on the basis of ethnic loyalties. Germans remained distinct from Scandinavians, and Germans from Pomerania found it difficult to co-operate with Germans from Mecklenburg. Norwegians had their own dissensions, especially as between the orthodox Lutherans and the Haugeans, pietists who wished to reform the Church of Norway much as the Puritans had once aspired to reform the Church of England. Only in the twentieth century did the Lutherans in Wisconsin, along with those in the rest of the United States, manage to achieve something approaching ecclesiastical unity.

Also divided were the native American Protestants. Their rivalries and jealousies often grew bitter as missionaries and ministers of the various denominations competed for converts. Yet these denominations—the Methodists, Congregationalists, Presbyterians, Baptists, and even the Episcopalians—recognized a certain spiritual kinship among themselves, and they co-operated as well as competed with one another. They drew a sharp distinction between their kind of Protestantism and both Catholicism and Lutheranism. They did not view the Lutherans as "evangelical" in the same sense as they themselves were. But they accepted, as true Protestants, the Dutch Reformed and many of the German and other foreign Calvinistic or pietistic sects. The American denominations welcomed these groups, joined forces with them, and gained proselytes from them. As early as 1851 there were, in the village of Cambridge, enough Norwegian converts to Methodism to build their own handsome stone church, which was said to be the first Norwegian Methodist house of worship in the world.

Neither of Wisconsin's largest immigrant groups—neither the Scandinavians nor the much more numerous Germans—formed a complete unity in a social or cultural sense. Not only were the Scandinavians divided as among Norwegians, Swedes, and Danes, but the Norwegians differed among themselves in religious views and also in dialect and identity, which varied according to the native valley of the mountainous homeland. Germans were not simply Germans before the unification of Germany in 1871, nor necessarily even after that; they were Prussians, Bavarians, Hessians, Pomeranians, Mecklenburgers, Lippe-Detmolders—natives of one or another of the various German states. In religion they were Catholic, Lutheran, Reformed, Evangelical, Methodist, or nothing at all. Some thought of themselves as humanists or freethinkers.

The freethinkers included most of the Forty-Eighters, those German revolutionaries who fled the fatherland after their failure to liberalize and unify it in the uprisings of 1848. Once in America, the Forty-Eighters kept on with their radical ways, joining *Turnvereine* or turner societies to preach socialism while practicing physical culture. Antireligious in general and anti-Catholic in particular, the Forty-Eighters and other freethinkers denounced the Church of Rome as a fount of superstition and a bulwark of political reaction. Among them were some of the most intellectual and artistic of all the Germans in America. In Wisconsin the most conspicuous of the Forty-Eighters was Carl Schurz, bony, bespectacled, and brilliant, who quickly learned to speak English almost as well as German, and spoke both languages with surpassing eloquence. Schurz met native politicians on their own ground and made them take him into account. He has often been described as typifying, in his liberty-loving spirit, the great mass of his fellow countrymen in early Wisconsin. Nothing could be further from the truth. The revolutionary exiles were a minute minority among the nineteenth-century German immigrants. Schurz himself neither led nor represented the great majority of devout Catholic and Lutheran Germans. To them he was anathema, a godless fanatic.

Whether Catholics, Lutherans, or freethinkers, most of the Germans agreed upon at least one thing: Sunday was a time for enjoyment. They spent the day—the churchgoers after church—in beer drinking, dancing, target shooting, bowling, and other games. Similar to the German Sunday was that of the Dutch (the Catholics, not the Protestants) and the Belgians.After a week of hard work, rural Dutch families took their ease on Sunday afternoon, gathering at a neighbor's home where the men played cards and drank from a liquor jug, the women chatted and sipped tea or coffee, and the children engaged in pastimes of their own. Belgians went from the celebration of mass to the conviviality of round after round of weak beer, a feast, patriotic French and Belgian songs, athletic contests, and finally a dance lasting until late at night.

Sunday was intended for no such activity in the opinion of evangelistic Americans and like-minded immigrants, such as the German, Norwegian, British, and Dutch pietists or Calvinists. To all these people, Sunday was a day of rest, of worship, prayer, and contemplation, of complete abstention from pleasure as well as work. According to the sermons of Methodist, Presbyterian, Baptist, and other such Protestant pastors, it was a sin to drink, dance, or play cards at any time, and it was doubly wicked to do so on Sunday. Some members of the flock might steal away on a sunny Sunday to go boating, fishing, or hunting, and they might even take a bottle or two along, but they ran the risk of suffering the community's disapproval if not also their own pangs of guilt. From the viewpoint of the puritanical, the Germans and others with their heathenish carryings-on were not remembering the Seventh Day to keep it holy but were profaning the Sabbath.

Other customs of the foreigners, especially the Catholics, seemed outlandish to many of the Americans of old stock. An early Methodist missionary remarked, regarding an Irishman who had drowned in Lake Superior, that "his friends had an Irish drunken revel over his corpse." [8] The behavior of some of the American sects was equally absurd in the eyes of foreign-born Catholics and also Lutherans. After attending a Methodist revival a German settler said he had "never been in an insane

8. Diary of James Peet, August 2, 1856, manuscript in the State Historical Society of Wisconsin.

asylum, but truly it could not be worse there." [9] Yet the Lutherans themselves were in varying degrees anti-Catholic. In the mid-nineteenth century the Missouri Synod, to which many of Wisconsin's German Lutherans belonged, still endorsed the old doctrine that the pope was Antichrist. Lutheran along with other Protestant ministers criticized Catholic beliefs and practices, one Norwegian Lutheran informing his congregation (in 1874) that Catholics were taught an erroneous view of marriage, since they were led to believe that monkish celibacy was a "holy and perfect state." [10] Zealots of whatever faith, of domestic Protestantism as well as Roman Catholicism and German or Norwegian Lutheranism, were unrelenting in their hostility to atheism and agnosticism.

Antagonism between Catholics and Protestants was not due merely to bigotry on either side. It resulted from fundamental differences in belief, differences in outlook upon this world as well as the next. Catholics, like Protestants, considered the earth a sinful place, but the Catholics believed that, on the whole, it had to be accepted as it was. The evangelistic Protestants felt a duty to save the world from what they considered sin—to create ultimately a heaven on earth. On this question the Lutherans stood somewhere in between. Though anti-Catholic in some respects, they shared much of the Catholic aversion to the evangelistic, millenarian view.

Both sides were equally convinced of the other's error, and each was alike determined to make its own conception of the truth prevail. If, in the early years, some Protestants wished to keep Wisconsin as a religious outpost of New England, some Catholics hoped and expected to make it eventually a religious province of Rome. In 1850 the leading Catholic spokesman in America, Archbishop John Hughes of New York, declared: "Everybody should know that we have for our mission to con-

9. Joseph Schafer, ed. and transl., "Documents: Christian Traugott Ficker's Advice to Emigrants," *Wisconsin Magazine of History,* 25 (June 1942):463–466.

10. Herman A. Preus, "Second Sunday After Holy Three Kings Day, Muskego, 1874," manuscript sermon in Luther College Library, Decorah, Iowa.

vert the world—including the inhabitants of the United States
. . . ." There was, he said, no secret about "the intention of
the Pope with regard to the Valley of the Mississippi," which,
of course, included Wisconsin.[11] Two decades later the *Star of
Bethlehem,* a Catholic family magazine appearing under the auspices of Bishop Henni of Milwaukee, contended that the freedom and prosperity of the United States were "not due to the
principles of Protestantism, but to Catholicity," and the magazine also proclaimed: "The Republic is becoming Catholic." [12]
If Wisconsin Catholics at one time felt like an oppressed minority, Wisconsin Protestants of native stock found themselves
more and more on the defensive as the Catholics, not through
conversion but through immigration, steadily gained in numeri-
cal strength. And when conflicts arose, neither group, any more
than the other, could properly be called the aggressor.

In the cultural conflicts the antagonists were not simply Protestants as against Catholics, nor native Americans as against the
foreign-born. At times the foreign-born Protestants divided, the
German Lutherans taking a stand alongside the German Catholics and even the German freethinkers in opposition to the Methodists, while the German pietists and many of the Norwegian
Lutherans joined the Methodists and their American-bred allies.
At other times the foreign-born Catholics divided, the Irish and
the Germans drifting apart. The alignment at a given moment
depended on the particular issues that were then at stake.

3

Throughout its first century the state of Wisconsin was trou-
bled by ethnic and religious tensions that brought on periodic
crises. Recurring issues had to do with the privileges and ob-
ligations of citizenship, with sabbatarian and temperance laws,
and with the control and support of schools, both public and pa-

11. Quoted in Ray A. Billington, *The Protestant Crusade, 1800–1860: A Study in the Origins of American Nativism* (New York: Rinehart and Company, 1938), pp. 289–291.

12. *Star of Bethlehem,* Milwaukee, October 1869, June 1870.

rochial. These issues involved the powers of local, state, and federal government. Hence the questions got into politics, and cultural conflicts took the form of political clashes.

At the outset the men of New York and New England ancestry had the government pretty much to themselves. Yet, when they drew up the state constitution, they shared political rights with the immigrants from Europe, allowing them to vote as soon as they had declared their intention of becoming citizens and had resided in the state for a single year. Wisconsin was thus more generous with the suffrage—to foreigners but not to American Negroes, whom the constitution did not enfranchise— than any other state at the time. Reflecting their Yankee backgrounds, the members of the 1849 legislature revised and retained the existing common-school system, which had been modeled on that of New York. The legislature also kept a territorial act regarding the observance of Sunday, a statute that was to remain on the books into the twentieth century. This "Sunday law" prohibited, on the Lord's day, all kinds of business or work (except in cases of necessity or charity), attendance at dancing or any sort of public diversion, and participation in any game or sport. But the law was seldom enforced in those communities that opposed it. The Germans disregarded it in enjoying their Sunday *Gemuetlichkeit*.

Puritanical Wisconsinites desired legislation not only to put down revelry on the Sabbath but also to discourage drunkenness throughout the week. A state law of 1849 dealt with the problem by making saloon keepers personally responsible for any harm their intoxicated patrons might do. Germans demanded repeal, but in 1850 temperance legislators, under the lead of John B. Smith, strengthened the law instead. A mob of infuriated Germans then marched upon Smith's house in Milwaukee and smashed the windows. The next year, the legislature gave in and replaced the liability law with an ordinary licensing act.

On the temperance issue the Democratic party sided with the Germans and other foreigners who opposed legislation against drink. That party, in the state constitutional convention, had also been responsible for the generous grant of suffrage to immigrants. Most of them understandably became loyal Democrats. This confirmed the opposition party, the Whig, in its doubts about the wisdom of welcoming the immigrants, particularly the Catholics, and giving them a share in political life. Not all the Wisconsin Whigs were so extreme as to approve the new antiforeigner, anti-Catholic secret organization that arose in the northeast in the 1850s—the Native American party, as it termed itself, or the Know Nothing party as outsiders called it because its members professed to know nothing about its secrets. Yet the movement gained some following in the state and an official organ in Milwaukee, the *Daily American.*

"You cannot have failed to observe the significant transition of the foreigner and Romanist from a character quiet, retiring, and even abject, to one bold, threatening, turbulent, and *despotic* in its appearance and assumptions," the *Daily American* told its native Protestant readers. Still, those "peculiar traits of *foreignism,* coming under the heads of Socialism and Red Republicanism," were "ten thousand times more to be feared" than even the "worst features of Catholicism." Protestants must meet the danger by preventing the foreigner or the Catholic from holding office, and by other means. "Let us keep *down* the newly arrived flood of emigration until they understand our language and our laws . . . while their *children* are educated and become Americanized—then we are safe." [13]

As native Protestants saw it, the public school was the hope of the future. Not only would it teach English and patriotism; it would also instill Protestant values. True, the state constitution prohibited "sectarian instruction" in the public schools, as well as state aid to any religious organization. But the state superintendent of public instruction could interpret and apply those constitutional clauses, and in the early years one superintendent after another was a Protestant leader, either an actual clergyman or an influential layman. Generally he ruled that the Bible was not a sectarian book and that prayer was not necessarily a sec-

13. *Milwaukee Daily American,* October 19, 1855.

tarian exercise. Many of the public schools required Bible reading and praying in the classroom. Catholics objected to the use of the King James version and to Protestant forms of prayer; freethinkers refused to accept any version or any forms. The controversy raged in the 1850s and revived from time to time after that. Finally, in 1890, the state supreme court declared such classroom exercises unconstitutional.

The Know Nothings made little headway in Wisconsin, managing only to polarize in resistance to them a large mass of people of heterogeneous nationalities. Germans in West Bend lynched one of the Know Nothings, a not-very-bright youth named George De Bar, a New York native who had worked as a farmhand, quarreled with his German employer, wounded him and his wife, and killed their hired boy. The Know Nothings went into the Republican party after it had established itself as the successor to the Whig party in the state. Thus the Republicans acquired an odor of nativism that repelled most of the foreign-born. Nevertheless, they succeeded in attracting some of the immigrants, not only the British but also most of the Norwegians and many of the non-Catholic Germans, especially Carl Schurz and his freethinking followers among the revolutionaries of 1848. The Republicans did so by playing down the nativist causes, including sabbatarianism and temperance, and by playing up the more broadly appealing program of antislavery and free soil.

In the election of 1860 the Irish and German Catholics and most of the German Lutherans voted against Abraham Lincoln. Understandably they had little enthusiasm for Mr. Lincoln's war when it began the next year. They tended to lose what little they had when President Lincoln put the draft into effect and issued his Emancipation Proclamation. Many of the immigrants had come to America, free country that it was reputed to be, partly to get away or to get their sons away from the hated military conscription of the Old World. Now the German-language newspaper *Seebote* of Milwaukee, the voice of Wisconsin's Catholic hierarchy, expressed its horror that men from Europe should be "used as fodder for cannons" in an abolitionist war.

Under the edict of Lincoln the "Germans and Irish must be annihilated, to make room for the negro." [14]

At the start of the Civil War the Wisconsin groups most eager to volunteer were, predictably enough, those most devoted to the Republican party and its ideals. Not only did Americans of Yankee heritage come promptly forward, but so, too, did foreigners of similar bent, such as Forty-Eighters from Germany and Haugeans from Norway. Germans formed the Ninth and Scandinavians, the Fifteenth Wisconsin Regiment. Irishmen made up most of the Seventeenth. "Two recruiting officers approached me last fall with the question why so few Catholics enlisted," an Austrian-born priest wrote in the summer of 1862. So far, only one of the state's regiments, the Irish Seventeenth, had a Catholic chaplain (the officers of each regiment chose its chaplain, and only the Seventeenth contained a majority of Catholics). Hence Catholics felt that the army discriminated against them. "According to my judgment," the priest said, "this accounts for the German Catholic reluctance to enlist." [15]

When drafting began in 1862, rioting broke out in several predominantly Catholic areas of Wisconsin. In Green Bay, Belgians marched on the home of a United States senator whom they blamed for the conscription law; he took to flight. In West Bend, Germans drove the draft commissioner away. In Port Washington, Luxembourgers attacked the commissioner, destroyed the boxes containing the names of those eligible for the draft, and went on a looting and wrecking spree. The next year in Milwaukee an Irishman hit an enrolling officer in the face with a spade, and several Irish women pelted the officer with stones. In heavily German Dodge County a secret assassin killed one of the enrolling officers.

14. Milwaukee *Seebote,* October 25, 1862, quoted in Mary D. Meyer, "The Germans in Wisconsin and the Civil War: Their Attitude Toward the Union, the Republicans, Slavery, and Lincoln" (unpublished master's thesis, Catholic University of America, 1937), pp. 45–46.

15. The priest, the Reverend Francis Fulleder of Port Washington, is quoted in Peter Leo Johnson, "Port Washington Draft Riot of 1862," *Mid-America,* new series, 1 (January 1930):219–222.

The pressure of the draft brought larger and larger numbers of reluctant foreigners into the Wisconsin regiments. When the first thirteen of these, all truly volunteer regiments, were formed in 1861, the immigrants constituted less than 27 percent of the membership. By the time the fifty-third had been organized in 1865, the overall proportion of the foreign-born came to 40 percent. The foreign-born, however, made up more than 50 percent of the state's men of military age (eighteen to forty-five). So their contribution to Wisconsin's soldiery was still comparatively low. Of course, many thousands of immigrants, including Catholics, served willingly and heroically. The fact remains that, proportionally, the Americans of Yankee stock made the greater effort—which, no doubt, they ought to have done, since on the whole they had more interest in the war aims, including emancipation.

Wisconsin's blacks had done their part in the war, and they expected to be rewarded with the right to vote. In 1865 a Negro suffrage proposition got the approval of the majority in twenty-four of the thirty-eight Republican counties but in none of the nineteen Democratic counties. It lost. Nevertheless, the state supreme court decided the next year that Wisconsin's blacks already had the franchise on the basis of the results, properly interpreted, of a previous referendum. Wisconsin's Indians, especially the Menominee, also had enlisted in proportionally large numbers. They made no apparent gain in status as a consequence.

In advocating Negro rights the Wisconsin Republican party pleased the devout among native Protestants, the 1866 state conference of Presbyterians and Congregationalists resolving that racial equality was an expression of righteousness. But the party continued to repel immigrant Catholics. It could hold on to its immigrant Lutheran following—and thereby hold on to its control of the state—only so long as it avoided nativistic and moralistic platforms. Unfortunately for Republican politicians, the same Puritan ethic that called for emancipation and equal rights called also for temperance, by legislative fiat if necessary. In 1872 the Republican-dominated legislature responded to reformers' agitation and passed a strict liquor-control law, another one making saloon keepers liable for damages due to the intoxication of customers. German leaders, among them the brewers Valentin Blatz and Joseph Schlitz, formed the Wisconsin Association for the Protection of Personal Liberty and accused the Republicans of having converted Wisconsin into a police state. The following year the legislature tightened instead of repealing the liquor act. In the state elections that November the German Lutherans abandoned the party in droves, and it fell from power in Wisconsin for the first time since taking over before the war.

Restored to power at the next elections, the Republicans held on without a break until 1890. They did so by keeping clear, once again, of evangelistic causes and also by appealing to the anti-Catholic convictions of Lutherans, whom they reminded of the long struggle against papal domination in Europe.

Native Protestants were coming more and more to fear a kind of papal domination in Wisconsin. Catholic voters multiplied faster than others, because of both the large immigration and the high birth rate of Catholics from Germany and Ireland. The church leaders became more aggressive than ever. They drew German Catholic children increasingly into parochial schools, as others were doing with German Lutheran children. In 1870 less than 1 percent of the state's total enrollment had been in church-run schools; by 1890 it was more than 15 percent. More than half (40,000 of 70,000) of the parochial pupils attended Catholic institutions. And the Catholic schools were demanding a share of the state's school funds.

Advocates of Americanization still believed that only public schools could facilitate the process, and the public schools only if they taught in English. Earlier laws had prescribed English as the medium of instruction, yet district schools in German districts continued to use German exclusively. Parochial schools of both the Catholic and the Lutheran Germans of course conducted all classes in German. Few church schools of any religion or nationality used English, and few attracted any Irish children.

Then, in 1889, the legislature passed and the governor signed the Bennett Law. This required all children of school age (seven to fourteen) to attend a school, either public or private. It specified further that the school must be one in which the basic courses—reading, writing, arithmetic, United States history—were taught in the English language. The bill's author, Michael Bennett, himself an Irish Catholic, had taken his draft from a model that out-of-state educational reformers were proposing as a means of making education compulsory and reducing the extent of child labor. Neither Bennett nor his fellow legislators anticipated any such uproar as the measure was to provoke. German Lutheran ministers joined with Catholic priests of all nationalities in denouncing the Bennett Law. Even Norwegian Lutheran clergymen attacked it; they had few full-time parochial schools, but they aspired to set up more of them and operate a comprehensive school system, with Norwegian as the language of the classroom.

Here was an imminent threat to the ascendancy of the Republicans. To stay in power they needed foreign votes. Barely 22 percent of Wisconsinites eligible to vote in 1890 were Americans of old stock. A much larger number, 39 percent, were of German background. The Scandinavians made up 13 percent, the British 9, and the Irish almost 9. The rest were of various national heritages, mostly Polish. Now, if the Republicans should uphold the Bennett Law, they could expect to lose most of their German Lutheran and much of their Norwegian Lutheran support. Still, they could hope to hold the German and Norwegian pietist and anticlerical vote and even to attract some groups that were habitually Democratic, not only Yankee Democrats but, considering the Irish-German ill will, even Irish Democrats.

The Republicans, under the leadership of Governor William D. Hoard, a New York native and a devout Methodist, chose to stand by the Bennett Law in the campaign of 1890. They made the "little red schoolhouse" their slogan and their symbol. Hoard on the stump talked of saving "poor German boys" from the evil influence of their pastors and priests, and he offered as the agency of salvation "that unrivalled, that invaluable political and moral institution—our own blessing and the glory of our fathers—the New England system of free schools.'' [16] In the election the Republicans did gain a few Democratic voters, including Irish ones, but they lost far more of their own than they had expected. For the Republican party it was a disaster as bad as that of 1873, or worse. The Bennett Law was soon repealed.

All this was a victory for Lutherans as well as Catholics. The Catholics won another victory in a contest over a statue—one to represent a distinguished and deceased citizen of Wisconsin in Statuary Hall in the nation's Capitol. Father Marquette was proposed for the honor, but the objection arose that he had been a citizen of France, never of Wisconsin. A more serious objection, on the part of many Wisconsinites, was that he had been a Catholic. This became clear enough when, in the 1890s, the Wisconsin members of the American Protective Association added their resistance to the Marquette movement, the A. P. A. being dedicated to combatting the ''diabolical work'' of the Roman Catholic Church. Only after a decade of effort by the adherents of Marquette did they finally get a place for him in Statuary Hall.

Germans of all shades of belief felt threatened by the Prohibition movement, which gained momentum with the founding of the national Anti-Saloon League in the 1890s. By 1907, more than seven hundred Wisconsin communities, exercising their right of local option under a state law, had eliminated saloons. Wisconsin brewers were growing desperate. They along with other brewers and distillers looked for help to the German-American Alliance, a federation of groups devoted to the preservation of German culture. Chartered in 1907 by Congress, the alliance by 1914 claimed more than a million members, the largest number in New York, the next largest in Wisconsin. The alliance took a stand against such infringements of personal liberty as prohibition laws. In this the Germans had the co-

---

16. Quoted in Richard Jensen, *The Winning of the Midwest: Social and Political Conflict, 1888–1896* (Chicago: University of Chicago Press, 1971), p. 129.

operation of the Irish, as the Ancient Order of Hibernians and other Irish organizations sided with the alliance. After the outbreak of war in Europe, the alliance advocated American policies favorable to the fatherland and American neutrality at least. American sympathizers with Great Britain and France charged that the alliance was a propaganda arm of the Kaiser's Germany. In fact the alliance was receiving generous subsidies—not from the imperial German government but from the American brewing industry.

Along with other German-Americans, those in Wisconsin received a shock when the United States entered the First World War. Most of them, whatever their attitude toward Kaiser Wilhelm II and his policies, were disinclined to renounce their German cultural heritage. Yet, if they did not publicly do so, they exposed themselves to the charge that they were Huns as bad as the Kaiser and his armies. "We have German enemies across the water," a Wisconsin Prohibitionist declared in 1918. "We have German enemies in this country too. And the worst of all our German enemies, the most treacherous, the most menacing are Pabst, Schlitz, Blatz and Miller." [17] Actually, there was little or no unpatriotic activity, no attempted obstruction of the draft, for example, such as there had been during the Civil War. Yet Wisconsin got the reputation of being both a German and an unpatriotic state. A speaker at a war rally in the east sneeringly proposed a federal expedition to rescue Americans interned in Wisconsin.

In the postwar reaction against things foreign, particularly German, the forces of nativism and moralism seemed triumphant in most of the country. The new Ku Klux Klan was riding high. The Eighteenth Amendment was the law of the land. In Wisconsin, however, Prohibition got little backing even from federal judges, drink flowed freely, and the state became known as one of the wettest of all the wet states. As for the Klan, it

17. Thomas C. Cochran, *The Pabst Brewing Company: The History of an American Business* (New York: New York University Press, 1948), p. 320, citing the *Milwaukee Journal,* February 13, 1918.

took upon itself such fatuous projects as cleaning out crime in the Italian quarter of Madison, but it was a rather halfhearted and ineffectual organization throughout Wisconsin. Wisconsinites of old Yankee stock were inclined to fear that they were continuing to lose the cultural contest. The war, one said, had "consolidated the spirit of revolt against the Yankee tradition." [18]

After the repeal of national Prohibition, drink ceased to be a divisive issue in Wisconsin. The Second World War had no such traumatic effect as the First. The old, old question of state aid to church schools was revived in 1946, when a referendum was held on amending the state constitution to permit public-school buses to transport parochial-school students. The fight over the amendment was as bitter as any political struggle in the state's history. With an organization of Protestant churches taking the lead, the opponents won. In another referendum nineteen years later, however, there was little organized opposition, and the amendment carried. By that time the subject of public busing to parochial schools was beginning to be less and less controversial, not only because of the general trend toward secularization but also because of the rapid decline in parochial school enrollments. In 1969 the state's parochial schools lost nearly 20,000 students while its public schools gained about 30,000. By the 1970s the traditional kind of ethnic and religious conflict in Wisconsin appeared to be a thing of the past.

But a different kind of conflict had recently arisen. Wisconsin's small minorities of blacks, Chicanos, and Indians were militantly demonstrating against their economic and social disadvantages. In Milwaukee the blacks, because of geographical propinquity, came most directly into confrontation with one of the newer European groups, the Poles. In Milwaukee and other Wisconsin cities the issue of busing again arose, but it was no longer a question of busing Catholics.

18. John Ballard, "The Revolt Against the Yankee," *Outlook,* 132 (November 1, 1922):366.

4

For many years Wisconsin was something of a living ethnological museum. This was unplanned. It was simply the natural result of immigration from a variety of countries, settlement largely in homogeneous groups, and attachment to inherited ways of doing things. People of each nationality—not all the people but large numbers of them—tried to preserve what they could of their dress, diet, arts, pastimes, and other folkways as well as their language and religion. Hence Wisconsin long remained, at least in part, a collection of ethnically distinct communities rather than a single, more or less uniform society.

The variegated gardens of exotic customs were set in a background of earlier American growth, the pioneers of New York and New England inheritance and their descendants being widely scattered over the state. Immigrants from England and Scotland generally lost their separate identity soon after their arrival, merging easily with the native Americans.

Some of the other English-speaking groups, however, retained much of their distinctiveness. In Mineral Point and other mining towns of the southwest the Cornishmen wore their peculiar low-crowned hats, ate their pasties (triangular meat-and-vegetable pies), and took their Saturday-afternoon ease in a kiddly-wink (a beer and soft-drink tavern). In mining settlements and elsewhere, as in the village of Cambria, many of the Welsh kept alive their *Eistedfodd* or singing festival and sang the Welsh national anthem, *"Hen Wlad Fy Nhadan,"* and other numbers in the old language of Wales. Some of the Irish remembered their Gaelic, and many maintained such traditions as fiddling and jigging at weddings and telling ghost stories at wakes for the dead. And of course the Irish celebrated St. Patrick's Day.

Of all the foreign-language communities, Milwaukee's "German town" was much the largest and most highly developed. "Here one sees German houses, German inscriptions over the doors or signs, German physiognomies," the Swedish novelist Fredrika Bremer wrote after her 1850 visit. "Here are published

German newspapers; and many Germans live here who never learn English, and seldom go beyond the German town." [19] Milwaukee early gained a reputation as *das Deutsche Athen,* the German Athens. It had its *Musikvereine* or music societies, its choruses, its instrumental groups, and its stock companies putting on German dramas and operas, which rivaled those of at least the lesser capitals of Germany itself. Brewers sponsored both beer gardens and opera houses. The Stadt Theater company, organized in 1884, moved in 1890 into the new Pabst Theater, which had a handsome bar where playgoers at intermission could quench their thirst with lager. Fine German restaurants abounded.

German food and German culture persisted in lesser cities such as Watertown and on farms throughout the German settlements, which were most numerous in the triangle that had its corners at Madison, Manitowoc, and Milwaukee. Around Watertown many of the farm wives and daughters kept up the ancient practice of stuffing geese to produce huge livers for making pâté de fois gras. Everywhere *Hausfrauen* set on the family table dishes of sauerkraut, cole slaw, dill pickles, hot potato salad, sour meats, hasenpfeffer, noodles, dumplings, black bread, bratwurst, and the like. Even in small towns, bakeries and delicatessens sold German pastries and other specialties. And, as a pastime, German men continued to prefer *Schafskopf* (sheepshead) to other card games.

In Green County and especially in New Glarus the Swiss settlers reproduced much of the life they had known in their native cantons of Switzerland. They early turned to making not only Swiss cheese but also Swiss-style laces, embroidery, and wood carvings. Farmers yodeled in the evening while herding and milking their cows. Yodelers wearing the Old Country costume entertained in taverns. Singing societies performed in the Swiss German dialect, New Glarus once boasting a *Maennerchor* of more than sixty voices. Annually, on the first Sun-

19. Fredrika Bremer, *The Homes of the New World: Impressions of America,* 2 vols. (New York: Harper and Brothers, 1868), 1:615–616.

day in August, the Wisconsin Swiss observed Swiss day, the anniversary of Switzerland's national independence.

The Norwegians, who had one or more settlements in almost every county of the state, celebrated their independence day, *Syttende Mai,* on May 17. They danced the *halling* at weddings, sang in the annual *sangerfest,* and feasted on *lutefisk* in the fall. The *lutefisk* dinners included not only the cured cod-like fish but also many other Norwegian delicacies, among them rice pudding with fruit, or sweet soup, and *lefse,* a pastry in thin, circular sheets that were buttered, sugared, and then rolled up. From 1848 on, one or more Norwegian-language newspapers were published in the state. Norway's great violinist Ole Bull, who married a Wisconsin girl and made Madison his home in the 1870s, both symbolized and promoted Norwegian culture. With Bull's support, Rasmus B. Anderson persuaded the University of Wisconsin to let him teach courses in the Norwegian language and then to establish the first enduring chair in Norse studies at any American university.

The less numerous Scandinavian groups shared much of the Norwegian way of life but also had cultural traits of their own. Swedes, concentrated particularly in the St. Croix Valley, enjoyed their meatballs, their rusk, and their afternoon coffee *klatschen.* Danes ate so much *kringle* that their section of Racine became known as "Kringleville." Icelanders on Washington Island caught and packed fish as they had done on their home island, and they subscribed to a Reykjavik newspaper. Settling in the cut-over timberland of the far north, Finns built their houses as in Finland, by squaring logs, fitting them tightly together, and dovetailing them at the corners. In back of each dwelling they put up a separate bathhouse, or sauna.

The Catholic Dutch and the Protestant Dutch lived quite apart from one another, yet preserved not only the same language but many of the same customs. In the valley of the lower Fox, in the Catholic settlements, many farmers wore wooden shoes at work, and the village of De Pere once was noted for its factories that made the shoes. Farmers did likewise in the Protestant area near Lake Michigan, to the south of Sheboygan. As late as the

1940s a cobbler near Oostburg was still carving shoes out of basswood blocks. Indoors, the wearers kicked off the shoes and went about in stocking feet.

French Canadians, along with descendants of the early French, remembered their folk songs and their folklore in the Green Bay area and in the north woods. The French village of Somerset, in St. Croix County, was notable for its frog farms and for the number of Old World customs it retained. Related to the French in language and culture were most of the Belgians. After losing their log buildings in the terrible forest fire of 1871, they reconstructed everything of brick they made from local red clay. "New Belgium took on the foreign look of Old Belgium." [20] The people went on holding, at each summer's end, their ancient harvest festival, or *Kermiss,* with dances and other activities every weekend for several weeks.

In South Milwaukee, in Stevens Point, and in other cities and rural areas the Poles maintained their *Sokols* for physical training and other societies to serve their religious, charitable, recreational, economic, and patriotic interests. Their market in the Stevens Point public square, with the Polish sausages and other national specialties on sale, was reminiscent of the market towns of Poland. Polish women in rural Wisconsin covered their heads with scarves or kerchiefs as they had done in the Old Country. Weddings among the Poles were drawn-out affairs, with as much as three days of ceremonies, feasting, and dancing. On the first Sunday in August the people sang the patriotic hymn that King Jan Sobieski and his troops had sung when they rescued Vienna from the Turks in 1683.

Smaller Slavic groups brought their ancestral ways to Milwaukee and other parts of the state. Russians had their *borscht,* their *kutia* (made of barley, nuts, honey, and poppy seeds), and their churches with an oriental-looking onion-shaped dome instead of a spire. Czechs, or Bohemians, presented plays in Czech and sang the national anthem *Kde Domov Muj* ("Where Is My Home?"). Slovakians in northwestern Dunn County,

20. Holmes, *Old World Wisconsin,* p. 163.

where they had their largest rural settlement in the state, cured their pork and beef with brine according to recipes they had brought from Slovakia. Serbs, mostly in and around Milwaukee, observed *Vivovdan,* the anniversary of a heroic but losing battle against the Turks, with church services, patriotic speeches, and traditional dances in traditional costumes.

In the Little Italy of Madison, housewives boiled big kettles of tomatoes to make *sarsa,* a relish for dishes of eggplant, macaroni, spaghetti, and other such ingredients. Housewives in the Italian sections of Milwaukee, Racine, and Kenosha did the same. Genoa, Wisconsin, a fishing village on the bluffs of the Mississippi River, recalled Genoa, Italy, especially in the architecture of the stone buildings. Wherever they were in the state, Italians celebrated saints' days as well as Columbus Day with noisemakers and fireworks.

Numerous and various—far more so than these examples suggest—were the Old World ways that survived the transit to Wisconsin. With the passage of time, however, the survivals became fewer and fewer, and those that persisted became less and less natural, more and more artificial. From the beginning the immigrants ran into some difficulties in trying to hold on to the familiar style of life. Norwegian women found, for example, that they had to discard their traditional dress and put on American clothes if they were to get jobs as servants with American families. So long as immigrants continued to arrive in large numbers, they repeatedly refreshed the Old World inheritance, but when immigration fell off, the younger generations were increasingly exposed to American influences. The automobile, motion picture, radio, and television had a standardizing effect. Eventually it took conscious effort to preserve, or to revive, the fading customs of the ancestral homelands.

By the early 1900s, Milwaukee was already losing its character as the German Athens and was fast becoming a less picturesque and more typical American city. The reason was not simply the arrival of large numbers of non-German immigrants but also the growing conformity of the German Milwaukeeans to

American patterns. While the afterglow of the German sunset lingered on in Milwaukee, German ways persisted longer in smaller cities like Watertown and in relatively isolated communities. Nevertheless, many Wisconsin Germans felt that, if not they themselves, at least their fellows were fast being stripped of their Germanic qualities. That was why so many joined the German-American Alliance, the primary aim of which was to preserve and promote Teutonic civilization. The national president of the alliance warned its Milwaukee members, in 1915, that they must keep themselves and their culture distinct or else "be prepared to descend to the level of an inferior culture." [21]

As early as the 1870s Rasmus B. Anderson and other Norwegians had been concerned about preserving Norway's civilization in Wisconsin—hence their campaign for Norse studies at the university. In the 1920s another son of Norway sought to achieve the same end by different means. Isak J. Dahle, a Chicago businessman, decided to construct a Norwegian village in the Mt. Horeb area, where his forbears had been pioneers. There, in Little Norway, Dahle set up a number of typically Norwegian buildings, including a fine replica of a medieval stave church, which the Norwegian government had put on display at the Paris exposition of 1889 and the Chicago fair of 1893. He filled the buildings with examples of *rosemaling* and other national handicrafts, some of them antiques, and put local craftsmen and craftswomen to work, making copies. The result was a museum, one well worth paying the fee to visit. It was not, however, a real pioneer village that had somehow survived in all its Norwegianness.

In the 1960s and 1970s there was an added attraction near Little Norway. During the summers a cast of people from the surroundings, with a star from New York, put on performances of the *Song of Norway,* based on the music of Edvard Grieg.

21. *Milwaukee Germania-Herold,* December 2, 1915, quoted in Clifton J. Child, *The German-Americans in Politics, 1914–1917* (Madison: University of Wisconsin Press, 1939), p. 176.

When, in 1975, the troupe entertained members of the State Historical Society of Wisconsin, meeting in Oshkosh, a spokesman explained that the singers had memorized the Norwegian words. None of them knew Norwegian.

The Swiss of New Glarus also had their ethnic revivals. From 1938 on, the townspeople and farmers re-enacted each autumn, in a hillside amphitheater, Johann von Schiller's eighteenth-century dramatic pageant *Wilhelm Tell*. New Glarus in 1938 was indistinguishable in appearance from any other midwestern farmers' supply town. To give the place a Swiss look, merchants began several years later to deck out the business buildings with false chalet façades. By 1975 an enterpriser who had recently come from Switzerland was planning an elaborate "Swiss Village" with additional tourist attractions and facilities. The mayor was quoted as saying: "We're trying to keep our heritage, but we're trying to make it a salable commodity, too." [22] This was not a case of the people clinging generation after generation to the customs and traditions of their ancestors. It was a case of promoters cultivating and exploiting ethnic nostalgia from motives of either sentiment or profit—or both.

Many of the re-creations and exhibitions were quite free from commercialism. Milwaukee in the 1950s and after was the scene of a Holiday Folk Fair at which, for two full days in the early winter, men, women, boys, and girls of three dozen national backgrounds presented their distinctive dances, handicrafts, and dishes before tremendous crowds. The State Historical Society in 1976 inaugurated an extensive outdoor (and indoor) ethnic museum, Old World Wisconsin, in the Kettle Moraine region of Waukesha County. Here, in authentic old buildings brought from various parts of the state, were to be displayed the architecture, artifacts, and activities of each of the state's nationality groups. The necessity for such a planned collection was in itself a sign that Wisconsin as a whole was ceasing to be the unplanned museum it once had been.

22. Calvin Trillin, "U.S. Journal: New Glarus, Wis. Swissness," *New Yorker*, January 20, 1975, p. 48.

5

In Milwaukee young "Anglo-American" (that is, Yankee) men sometimes took part in the German Sunday, the Swedish Miss Bremer reported as of 1850. They were attracted, she said, by the beer, music, and festivities and, quite "irresistibly," by the "strong, blooming German girls." [23] Maybe so, but at that time very few native American men anywhere in Wisconsin took German wives. For many years intermarriage between American men or women and immigrants of any nationality (except British), or between immigrants of different nationalities, remained extremely rare. Men and women were not likely to marry unless they at least knew the same language. Thus cultural assimilation, in some degree, had to precede physical amalgamation.

The merging of cultures and peoples went ahead faster in some circumstances than in others. The more nearly the same the language and religion, the more rapid the growing together, of course, was likely to be. Catholic and Lutheran clergymen generally discouraged the adoption of American traits. Old people of whatever religion or nationality were inclined to resist more than the young; Norwegian elders complained of children and youths picking up English and pretending not to be Norwegian. Immigrants who settled in communities of their own, especially isolated ones, were slower to give up the old ways than were those who settled among the Americans and other nationalities. For example, the Swiss in the compact ethnic settlements of Green County held on to their Swissness much longer than the Swiss in the ethnically mixed communities of Buffalo County, on the Mississippi. The public school was more effective as an Americanizing institution in a heterogeneous district, where children of different national backgrounds mingled in the same classroom, than in a solidly German or Norwegian neighborhood, where the pupils saw only their own kind and might not even learn English.

23. Bremer, *Homes of the New World,* 1:615–616.

Though politics divided one group from another, it also exerted an assimilating influence. Foreigners, some sooner than others, learned the American art of local self-government. In predominantly German-speaking Sauk City, for example, the second village election (1855) brought into office as president and trustees men with the names of Hantzsch, Halasz, Scharff, Deininger, Conradi, and Heller. Political parties brought the European-born and the American-born into co-operation in state campaigns. Foreign-language newspapers, like the German *See-bote* of Milwaukee, discouraged assimilation. Or, like the Norwegian *Emigranten,* they encouraged it. *Emigranten* announced its purpose in a special message in English (1852): "Through our paper we hope to hurry the process of Americanization of our immigrated countrymen." [24]

War experience, too, had an integrating as well as a divisive effect. If, in the Civil War, some of Wisconsin's foreign-born troops were segregated in companies or whole regiments of a particular nationality, others were intermingled with various immigrants and with the American-born. If some of the foreigners lacked enthusiasm for the war, others patriotically identified themselves with the Union cause. A Norwegian, lying seriously wounded on the battlefield of Stone's River, took pride in the confirmation of his American identity when the rebels came upon him and one of them said: "Here is a damn Yankee." [25] At the end of the war an Irishman rejoiced: "How glad that the sons of Erin's Isle have helped to save this our dear land." [26] Wisconsin soldiers of other nationalities expressed themselves similarly on the Civil War. Later generations acquired the bond

24. Quoted in Olaf H. Spetland, "The Americanizing Aspects of the Norwegian Language Press in Wisconsin, 1847–1865" (unpublished master's thesis, University of Wisconsin, 1960), pp. 12, 30.

25. Lars O. Dokken to his family, early 1862, quoted in Theodore C. Blegen, *Norwegian Migration to America: The American Transition* (Northfield, Minn.: Norwegian-American Historical Association, 1940), p. 396.

26. James Lockney to his parents, August 14, 1865, quoted in Elizabeth Ann Bascom, "Why They Fought: A Comparative Study of the Impact of the Civil War on Five Wisconsin Soldiers, with Selections from Their War Letters" (unpublished master's thesis, University of Wisconsin, 1941), p. 227.

of service as comrades in arms in the First and Second World wars.

Time itself was an important factor in the acculturation process. The more recent the immigrant or the immigrant group, obviously the less the exposure to the forces of assimilation. When some of the later arrivals appeared to resist the melting pot, certain historians and sociologists thought of them as "unmeltable ethnics." Those experts seemed to forget that the earlier groups also had been very slow to melt at first. Scholars specializing in ethnic studies talked of cultural pluralism as if its survival were both a noble goal and an inevitable fact. Complete assimilation would leave such scholars without much of a subject or a clientele. They had a vested interest in the maintenance of ethnic exclusivity, as some clergymen, journalists, professors, politicians, and others had had before them.

In the history of Wisconsin's older immigrant groups, the Second World War serves as a kind of dividing strip. Before that time many Germans and Norwegians, even those of the second or third or later American-born generations, continued to learn English as a second language, if at all, and to speak it with a very noticeable accent. As late as the 1940s movies in Norwegian dialogue were still being shown in the village of Westby. After the war, however, the Wisconsinites who understood German or Norwegian became fewer and fewer, and in a couple of decades they were downright scarce. The same is true of those who understood Dutch, French, Polish, Italian, or some other foreign language.

Statistics were lacking to show the extent of intermarriage, but there was reason to believe that, by the third quarter of the twentieth century, it was considerable. In Racine, for example, there lived in the 1970s a family whose children had ancestors, some Protestant, some Catholic, from England, Scotland, Ireland, Norway, Germany, and Poland. That family was not viewed as peculiar on account of its ethnic mix; there were many others comparable to it in Racine and throughout the state.

In Lake Delton there was a neighborhood of ten families of which five represented mixtures of two or more nationalities.

One couple consisted of a husband whose parents were Irish (Catholic) and Welsh (Methodist) and a wife whose parents were German and Norwegian (both Lutheran). Only one person in the neighborhood, a Hollander, was of foreign birth. Among the five couples of uniform ancestry, two were British, two were German, and one was Norwegian. The Norwegian family and one of the German families had Anglicized surnames, and the Norwegian family included a son with the Welsh name Gary. None of the people, except for the one Dutch-born, could speak an ancestral language other than English, and none spoke English with even the slightest foreign accent. Five of the families were Catholic, four were Protestant, and one couple (of British background) was half-and-half. In relationships among neighbors, there was no tendency toward cohesion or separation on the basis of either religion or ancestry. Indeed, the people were seldom conscious of any difference in national origin—except for one person of historical bent who had a professional curiosity about such matters.

Though pockets of separate ethnicity remained, Wisconsin as a whole had a fairly widely shared culture in the latter part of the twentieth century. Assimilation had not meant Americanization in the old, one-way sense in which nativists had advocated it. Wisconsin was not the Puritan Zion that early Yankee evangelists had desired. Neither was it a German state. Culturally it was a blend of native and foreign ingredients, mainly Yankee and Teutonic. The German Sunday prevailed among the people of British and Norwegian as well as those of German descent. Characteristic of Wisconsin were, among other things, beer, brandy, and brats (bratwurst). It consumed more per capita of each of these things than did any other state.

He was not far wrong—that Irish-born promoter of Wisconsin who, more than a century earlier, had predicted that the disparate elements would "jar for a moment, like different metals in the furnace," but would eventually combine to form a people quite unique and superior to any other that had ever appeared on earth.

3

America's Dairyland

$\mathcal{C}$HEESE and beer—when you think of either of the two, you think of Wisconsin. It came to produce more cheese than all the other states combined, and more beer per capita than any other state. Much more, in both cases. It produced so much milk and milk products of all kinds as to deserve the designation it proclaimed on its automobile license plates: America's Dairyland. But originally it had been a land of wheat, the great cash crop of the pioneers. Only when Wisconsin farmers could no longer make wheat pay, in competition with the harvests of the newer wheat-growing states to the west, did they turn to dairying. They also turned to other crops, such as potatoes, cranberries, cabbage, sweet corn, beets, and, above all, peas. Wisconsin became the nation's largest canner of peas and beets in particular and vegetables in general. So, even in its agricultural aspects, it was more than a dairyland. And it was more than a food-and-beverage state. It was a leader in the science of nutrition.

1

For farms, the early Wisconsin settlers preferred a combination of prairies and oak openings. With four or five yoke of oxen they could break two or three acres of prairie sod a day, and they could get needed timber from the oak groves. Yet many of the settlers took heavily forested land in cases where it was the only thing conveniently available to them or where it had advantages of location (nearness to a market, a lake port, or a railroad). A pioneer with such land might pardonably have been discouraged as he confronted the thick growth of pine, maple, beech, and basswood, many of the trees five or six feet in diameter and some of them over a hundred feet tall. In a whole year he and his family could clear no more than six or seven acres, and he would still have the task of breaking the land to the plow.

On a new farm the pioneer as a rule planted corn for his first crop, to feed himself, his family, and his oxen. But he intended to be a commercial farmer as soon as he could. He needed a cash crop, and his best bet was wheat (spring wheat). This he could not only be sure of selling but would also find comparatively easy to grow. After plowing and sowing, scattering the seed by hand, he could leave the field unattended till harvest time. True, harvesting was something of a problem, for with a scythe and cradle he could cut only two or three acres of the ripe grain a day. But he could take care of a much larger crop if he could afford to buy or rent one of the horse-drawn mechanical reapers that the McCormick company had begun to manufacture in Chicago in 1846. He could thresh the grain by swinging a flail, having oxen tread it out, or using a horse-powered threshing machine of the kind that Jerome I. Case was making in Racine.

Though wheat was the early Wisconsin farmer's favorite sale crop, it had its disadvantages and risks. It was hard on the soil, rapidly using up the nitrogen. The yield varied from year to year, depending on the vagaries of the weather. And the price fluctuated in response to international trends of demand and supply. Bad weather ruined much of the Wisconsin crop for three years in succession—1849, 1850, and 1851—while the price remained low because of a world glut. Then came several seasons of good harvests and high prices for Wisconsin farmers. Production in the older states was declining because of soil exhaustion and an insect pest—midge larvae or "little yellow worms"—that spread from Vermont to Ohio. Railroads, as construction advanced across Wisconsin, opened the markets of the world to more and more of the state's farmers. All this "revived their drooping spirits," as a contemporary remarked, "and placed them in comparatively affluent circumstances, which is visible in the number of shanties which are being replaced by comfortable and sightly frame dwellings in every part of the State." [1] So long as high profits continued, wheat growers had little incentive to diversify their crops or to worry about the depletion of their soil.

Year after year Wisconsin farmers planted more and more acres to the profitable grain. Another succession of rather poor seasons struck in 1857, 1858, and 1859 because of depression prices and a persisting drought. Even so, Wisconsin rose during the decade of the fifties from ninth to third among the wheat-growing states. Then came the "golden year" of 1860, with a mild winter, an early spring, and abundant rain. The Wisconsin harvest was almost twice as large as ever before, and the price was higher than at any time since the panic of 1857. As a wheat producer and exporter, Wisconsin now stood second only to Illinois.

Wisconsin wheat helped to win the Civil War. Southerners had been saying that cotton was king, and they expected King Cotton to win the war for them. They thought Great Britain and France, dependent as those countries were on the southern crop, would intervene on the side of the Confederacy to assure their supply of it. The time for intervention seemed to have arrived in the fall of 1861, when Great Britain and the United States were embroiled in a dispute over the Union navy's treatment of a British packet the *Trent*. But Great Britain needed American wheat as well as American cotton, and the Union also depended on the wheat trade, for grain exports from the northwest (that is, the Midwest of today) made up for the loss of cotton exports from the South in procuring foreign exchange to pay for necessary imports. "The farmers of the Northwest, in producing this

1. Gregory, *Industrial Resources*, p. 113.

surplus grain, have fought a battle for the Union of greater significance than any possible achievement of the Grand Army of the Potomac.'' So declared the Milwaukee newspaper *Daily Wisconsin*. ''Wheat is king,'' the *Milwaukee Sentinel* added, ''and Wisconsin is the center of the Empire.'' [2]

Milwaukee was the entrepôt for most of the wheat leaving Wisconsin and for much of that coming from Iowa and Minnesota. At first the grain dealers met the farmers arriving with their wagonloads at the outskirts of the city and bargained with them individually. As the railroads were extended and brought in vaster and vaster quantities, the trade became more impersonal and more systematic. Dealers organized a board of trade and a corn exchange, then combined them into the Chamber of Commerce and agreed upon a system for grading wheat and handling it in bulk. Two large steam-operated grain elevators were erected.

Sailing vessels picked up the wheat and carried it through the Great Lakes on its way to the millers of the eastern states and the rest of the world. Milwaukee's Daniel Newhall, reputedly the biggest single grain dealer in the west, had his own fleet of sixteen schooners, the Badger Line, and loaded as much as fifteen thousand bushels a day for delivery to Buffalo. From some of his profits he built the Newhall House, Milwaukee's finest, a show place among western hotels. Shipments by Newhall and others rose to a total of several million bushels a year. By 1862, Milwaukee had surpassed Chicago to become the world's largest primary market for wheat.

Large quantities of wheat remained in the state to be ground into flour in its own mills. Indeed, from the 1850s to the 1880s, flour milling was Wisconsin's most important industry. In 1860, Milwaukee had fourteen flour mills, and the rest of the state 285. A few were powered by steam, the rest by water. Most, quite small and primitive, turned the neighboring farmers' wheat into flour or grist for their own use and produced a small

---

2. *Daily Wisconsin,* November 1, 1861, and *Milwaukee Sentinel,* November 8, 1861, quoted in Merk, *Economic History,* pp. 16, 58.

surplus for local sale. Some, however, were large and modern. By 1866, Milwaukee had taken the lead in flour production from St. Louis and had made itself the Miller City of the west. Though it held the lead for only five years, it continued to be one of the nation's important milling centers for considerably longer.

Neenah-Menasha and other Wisconsin cities aspired for a time to rival Milwaukee. A Neenah miller, John Stevens, perfected in 1879 a chilled iron roller that would produce cleaner and more durable flour than the old-fashioned millstones. By then, both wheat growing and flour milling were moving on to the west and leaving Wisconsin behind. During the 1880s Minneapolis established itself as the flour-milling champion of the entire country. Its success owed much to a Wisconsinite, Cadwallader C. Washburn, who made good use of the new roller technology in his Minneapolis mills. Between 1898 and 1902 Wisconsin produced more flour than ever, but less and less thereafter.

Already, in 1873, Wisconsin had reached its acme as a wheat-growing state. While some of its fresher lands in the western counties continued to yield the grain on a paying basis, the older areas of the southeast suffered more and more from the effects of soil exhaustion and the inroads of rust and smut and finally the chinch bug. Ever since the poor wheat years of the early fifties, agricultural reformers had been calling for diversification. Some farmers did experiment with new products during the Civil War, when the supply of southern crops fell off and the scarcities resulted in abnormally high prices. To make up for the lack of cotton, sugar, molasses, and tobacco, Wisconsinites turned to the production of wool, flax, sorghum, sugar beets, and tobacco itself. After the war they tried out still other things.

For a time it looked as if hops would be the best alternative to wheat and all other produce. The price of hops shot up at the end of the war, when the hop louse drastically cut the harvest in New York and other hop-producing states of the east while beer sales over the country were steadily increasing. Suddenly Wis-

consin hop growers were enjoying a bonanza. By 1867, the
state's crop was more than fifty times as large as it had been in
1861. Sauk County alone accounted for a fifth of the entire nation's output, and Kilbourn City (Wisconsin Dells) was said to
be "the greatest hop depot in the United States—perhaps in the
world." [3] At harvest time the good pay brought young men and
women from near and far for merrymaking as well as for picking the ripe cones from the vines. Growers lived high, buying
pianos for their wives, silks and satins for their daughters, and
blooded horses and fancy phaetons for their sons, and even taking their families on trips abroad. What was left of their profits,
and whatever they could borrow, they sank in buying additional
acres and preparing them with poles to support more vines.
Many were left deeply in debt when the price collapsed and
Wisconsin's hop craze ended as quickly as it had begun.

Some farmers continued to supplement their income, as they
had been doing for some time, by gathering cash crops that
grew wild in various parts of the state. In shady places they
could find ginseng, a plant with a man-shaped root that had
unique medical properties in the belief of the Chinese, who
were willing to pay well for it. In sandy bogs the farmers picked
cranberries; some were beginning to cultivate them and produce
them on a fairly large scale. In maple groves they collected the
sap and made syrup and sugar. In the forests of the north they
trapped beaver and other animals for furs.

Much more important for the diversification of Wisconsin's
agriculture, farmers were growing larger and larger quantities of
corn, oats, and hay and using these to feed larger and larger
numbers of horses, pigs, cows, and especially sheep. During the
1860s the sheep in Wisconsin increased much faster than the
cows—sheep from 332,954 to 1,069,282; milk cows from
203,001 to 308,377. Wisconsin seemed on the way to becoming
a wool-producing rather than a dairying state.

Indeed, when the census takers made their rounds in 1870,

3. Kilbourn City *Wisconsin Mirror,* June 17, 1868, quoted in Merk, *Economic History,* p. 40.

only twenty-five Wisconsinites (out of a total of 159,687 who were engaged in agriculture) identified themselves as dairymen or dairywomen. A much larger number of men and women on the farms were making butter and cheese as sidelines, and fifty-four small cheese factories were in operation. Among the cheese-producing states, Wisconsin was already in sixth place, but it lagged far behind the leader New York with only three million pounds as compared with New York's hundred million. Wisconsin the dairyland—with its ubiquitous herds, its tremendous barns, and its towering silos—still lay in the future.

2

It was no accident, this metamorphosis of Wisconsin into the nation's foremost dairying state. It took thought and will. In the 1870s, when it really began, Wisconsin did not seem like the most obvious place for the development of a dairy industry. The state had no locational advantages; it was comparatively distant from the larger markets of the country and the world—too distant for the quantity shipment of fresh milk—and transportation difficulties and costs for cheese and butter would be much greater than for wheat. The industry would require heavy and risky outlays of capital for herds and barns, whereas wheat growing demanded a relatively small investment. Wheat farming, though back-breaking at harvest time, was unconfining for most of the year, and it necessitated no particular knack. But dairying was a seven-day-a-week, year-round operation that took both skill and attention to routine. Before they could succeed in the new industry, Wisconsin's independent and individualistic wheat farmers would have to force themselves to submit to its rigorous discipline.

Wisconsin did have the advantage of the presence of some experienced cheesemakers who could help to show the way. Swiss, Dutch, German, Scandinavian, and other immigrants had brought the knowledge of their various national specialties. More important for the future of Wisconsin, settlers from New York state retained the cheddar-making ability they had inherited from their English ancestors. Already commercial dairying was well established in New York, and migrants from there were to develop it in Wisconsin. Countless men and women, most of them New Yorkers, were to contribute to Wisconsin's rise to supremacy. One person, however, was to make a much bigger contribution than any of the rest.

That was William Dempster Hoard. Born the son of a Methodist minister in New York's Mohawk Valley dairy region, Hoard as a boy learned from one of his grandfathers something about caring for cows and making butter and cheese. In 1857, when he was just turning twenty-one, he went to Wisconsin. There he worked as a farmhand, a Methodist circuit rider, and a water-pump salesman, then served in the Civil War. Afterwards he made some money selling nursery stock, put his savings into hop culture, and was left, when the hop craze passed, with nothing but debts to pay and a wife and three small children to support. In 1870 he began to publish a four-page weekly newspaper, the *Jefferson County Union*. From the first, he urged his farm readers to turn from wheat growing to dairying to restore their depleted soil—"it is a story as old as the tribes of Abraham that wheat robs the soil and cattle drop fatness." [4]

Hoard had found his calling. For nearly half a century, until his death in 1918, he was to preach and promote with revivalistic fervor the cause of dairying in Wisconsin. In 1885 he started *Hoard's Dairyman*; by 1918, with a circulation of nearly 70,000, it was probably the most widely read of dairy periodicals. "Speak to a cow as you would to a lady" was one of the slogans he popularized. [5] His message was, in a word, specialization, not diversification. Concentrate on milk and milk products! Perfect your techniques of production and marketing! Hoard made his influence felt not only as a newspaper editor but also as a platform speaker, experimental farmer, organizer and

4. Quoted in Francis F. Bowman, *Why Wisconsin* (Madison: published by the author, 1948), p. 101.

5. Quoted in Jensen, *The Winning of the Midwest,* p. 129.

lobbyist, governor of Wisconsin (1889–1891), and president of the state university's board of regents.

From the 1870s on, the number of milk cows in Wisconsin rapidly increased, and by 1899 they were to be found on more than 90 percent of the farms in the state. By the 1930s they totaled two million, about 400,000 more than in New York, by then in second place. Wisconsin's herds had grown in quality as well as numbers. The pioneers had used their nondescript cattle more or less interchangeably for drawing plows and providing beef as well as producing milk. In the 1870s some farmers advocated dual-purpose meat-and-milk cattle. Hoard insisted upon single-purpose dairy cows and eventually won out. At first the Jersey was a favorite milking breed, but during the early 1900s the Holstein came to predominate, and later the Guernsey outnumbered the Jersey to take second rank.

Spread on the fields, the barnyard manure restored fertility to the soil. Also restorative were new feed crops that dairy farmers introduced to Wisconsin. At first the farmers were reluctant to try alfalfa, doubting whether it would grow well in the Wisconsin climate. In vacant lots in his hometown of Fort Atkinson, Hoard planted a hardy northern variety of Asian origin, one with a yellow instead of a purple flower. It grew splendidly. Soon Wisconsin fields were thick with yellow-blossoming alfalfa; eventually it became so common that people thought it must be native to the state. Along with clover and other legumes, which the dairy farmers also raised for feed, the alfalfa brought nitrogen back to the soil. No longer was the soil's goodness being sold away as it had been in the golden days of wheat.

If herds were to give milk in abundance and throughout the year, they needed something more than hay for winter feeding. The answer came in the form of ensilage. Since ancient times some European farmers had preserved green fodder by burying it and allowing it to ferment. In the nineteenth century, French and German husbandmen began to dig regular pits, or silos, for the fodder. In 1875 the United States Department of Agriculture issued a brief report on the practice of ensilage, and in 1877 a French agricultural scientist published a treatise on the subject, a work that was soon available to American farmers in an English translation. The honor of constructing the first silo in the United States is disputed, but Hoard—who of course quickly became an enthusiastic advocate of ensilage—claimed the honor for Wisconsin.

One of his fellow citizens of Fort Atkinson, Levi P. Gilbert, in the summer of 1877 dug a trench six feet wide by six feet deep by thirty feet long and filled it with alternate layers of rye straw and chopped green cornstalks. That was Wisconsin's first silo. Three years later Dr. H. S. Weeks of Oconomowoc built one something like a deep swimming pool—of stone and concrete, twelve by twelve by thirty—with a wooden superstructure. It was the first in the state to be partly above ground. Later other Wisconsinites built above-ground structures of a variety of materials and of rectangular shapes. Toward the end of the century Franklin H. King, professor of agricultural physics at the University of Wisconsin, developed the round silo. Only gradually did it rise to a towering height.

And only gradually, at first, did silos spread over the state. A count in 1904 came to a mere 716. Then, during the next twenty years, they rose in tremendous numbers. A tally in 1915 showed 55,992, and by 1924 there were more than 100,000. This amounted to one each for about two-thirds of all Wisconsin farms. The silos took ensilage from half of the corn grown in the state.

Under nineteenth-century conditions, milk itself could not be sold in large quantities and at great distances. Cheese, more compact and less perishable, was easier to ship. Yet cheese was difficult to make at home in good and uniform quality. The factory, with an expert concentrating on the one task and producing comparatively large amounts, had the advantages of both skill and scale. From the 1870s on, cheese factories multiplied in Wisconsin. Some were co-operatives, the dairy farmers themselves being the owners, but most belonged to separate enterprisers, whose demand for rich milk at a low price conflicted with the interest of the farmers. Though the output included Swiss and Limburger, much the largest part of it consisted of "American" cheese, or Cheddar, and after 1885 also an original Wisconsin variant of Cheddar, milder and moister, known as Colby. By 1899, Wisconsin was producing more than a fourth of all the country's cheese; by 1909, nearly a half; by 1919, almost two-thirds.

In the beginning the Wisconsin producers had run into difficulty in trying to dispose of their cheese. They soon had a surplus on their hands, and they were desperate to find markets both in the United States and abroad. After 1865 they could ship by through "fast" freight from Chicago to New York in a week, but they had to pay such high rates that they could hardly complete with eastern cheesemakers. To deal with problems of shipping and marketing, Hoard proposed that the state's producers organize, and they did so in the Wisconsin Dairymen's Association in 1872. The association sent Hoard to Chicago to get lower freight rates, and he persuaded the railroads, in 1874, to reduce them to less than half. Commission merchants had been buying Wisconsin cheese at a discount, labeling it "New York," and selling it at a good price. To reach eastern buyers directly, the association set up a dairy board of trade in Watertown, Wisconsin.

Wisconsin producers early found an outlet in England, where during the 1870s they exported as much as half of their cheese. They found the English market such a good thing that they took unfair advantage of it. Along with those from New York, Illinois, and other states, the Wisconsin cheesemakers began to adulterate their product by using skim milk and adding lard or oleo. Cheese from Wisconsin and other states acquired such a bad reputation in England that exports fell in the 1880s as fast as they had risen in the 1870s.

To save the cheese industry, the state and federal governments had to step in. As early as 1881 the Wisconsin Dairymen's Association persuaded the state legislature to pass a law requiring that "skim" or "filled" cheese be labeled as such. But the law was not enforced. While he was governor, Hoard induced the legislature to provide for a state food and dairy commissioner with authority to prosecute anyone who adulterated or counterfeited dairy products. Later, in 1895, the legislature prohibited the manufacture and sale of skim cheese within the state. The next year the federal government began to tax such cheese and to compel its labeling. By 1912 the Wisconsin dairy commissioner could report that, to his knowledge, no filled cheese had been made or sold in the state for at least a decade. Meanwhile, the domestic market had expanded enough to take Wisconsin's entire output, though the foreign market never recovered.

Butter lagged behind cheese, and creamery butter behind the homemade, in the early years of Wisconsin dairying. Between 1880 and 1891 the number of creameries grew from fewer than forty to approximately 265, and their annual output from less than a half million to more than fourteen million pounds. Still, it was yet to overtake the farm production of butter, which meanwhile rose from about thirty-three million pounds to more than forty-six million. Farmers who kept cows for butter—whether it was churned at home or at a creamery—generally raised hogs as well. Such farmers preferred to sell only the cream and to use the skim milk for feeding the young pigs. Butter, then, was a product of corn-and-hog farming.

In the interest of butter makers the state of Wisconsin early declared war on the nation's manufacturers of oleomargarine. Oleo was the invention of a French chemist, who had started out with the interesting notion that he could somehow transform an udder's fatty tissue into butter. His perfected process—much more sophisticated than that—received an American patent in 1873. Soon oleo factories sprang up in New York and other states, and sales rapidly increased, even in Wisconsin. Its dairymen complained that oleo was being sold as genuine butter, and they demanded protection both for themselves and for consumers.

The 1881 law against misbranding dairy products was intended to discourage out-of-state manufacturers of oleo as well as Wisconsin makers of oleo-filled cheese. Lobbyists representing the dairy interest in Wisconsin and other states obtained in 1886 a federal act heavily taxing manufacturers, wholesalers, and retailers of oleo and requiring the manufacturers to pack it in wooden tubs. Governor Hoard demanded that still more be done "for the protection of the interests of the people . . . against such iniquity" as the oleo business, and the legislature banned from the state all products made in "imitation of yellow butter." [6] In 1902 the United States Supreme Court ruled that state laws (there were then more than thirty states with them) against the sale of colored oleo were constitutional so long as they did not interfere with interstate commerce in colored oleo. That same year, Congress imposed on colored oleo an additional tax of ten cents a pound.

How much effect the state and federal laws against oleo had, it is impossible to say. Certainly they did not prevent a steady rise in oleo sales throughout the country, nor did they prevent the persistent decline in butter consumption that began after the First World War. At last the oleo interests got the upper hand, politically, over the dairy interests. Congress in 1950 repealed the 1902 act taxing colored oleo. One by one the states removed their discriminations against the product. By the mid-1960s, only Wisconsin was still holding out. It was the last of the states to let colored oleo compete with butter. By that time, butter was far less important than it once had been for Wisconsin's dairy industry.

While, since 1900, a smaller and smaller proportion of Wisconsin's milk (or rather its cream) had been going into butter, a larger and larger proportion had been reaching the market in other forms—dried, condensed, or pasteurized. In 1876 the English-born and English-educated William Horlick began to experiment with dried milk in Racine. Eleven years later Horlick combined dried milk with an extract of malted wheat and barley to produce what he trademarked as Malted Milk. It was

6. Quoted in Eric E. Lampard, *The Rise of the Dairy Industry in Wisconsin: A Study in Agricultural Change, 1820–1920* (Madison: State Historical Society of Wisconsin, 1963), pp. 259–260.

an instantaneous success. Horlick's Food Company (later to be known as Horlick's Malted Milk Company) built new plants in Racine and set up a branch office in New York City and another in England. The birthplace of the "malted," Wisconsin remained its principal home till after the Second World War, when the English branch took control of the company.

Condensed milk, which had originated in New York in the 1850s, did not appear among Wisconsin products until 1889, when Gail Borden's New York company set up a condensery in Monroe. By 1920 there were sixty-seven plants in the state, and they produced almost a fourth of the nation's condensed and evaporated milk. Condensation and evaporation represented the "epitome of industrial revolution in the dairy industry," as the Wisconsin industry's historian has written. "From the first introduction of the milk to the vacuum pan to its final passage into cans automatically sealed, labeled, wrapped, lithographed, and cased by machine, the condensery product was exposed to neither hand nor air." [7]

Less hygienic, for many years, was the distribution of fresh milk. Its sales increased rapidly after 1900, with improvements in refrigeration and transportation and with the growth of urban markets in and around Milwaukee, lesser Wisconsin cities, and Chicago. Some dairy farmers were eager enough to sell their whole milk to urban consumers, but were reluctant to go to the trouble of pasteurizing it or making sure it did not come from tubercular cows.

Wisconsin led the nation in the campaign against bovine tuberculosis. After studying in Germany with Robert Koch, the discoverer of the tubercle bacillus, Harry L. Russell in 1893 joined the staff of the Wisconsin Agricultural Experiment Station and introduced Koch's tuberculin test in this country. Hoard, promptly having his own cows tested, enthusiastically supported Russell's testing program. But farmers generally opposed it. When, in the early 1900s, the Milwaukee department of health undertook to require it, the farmers prevented it by

7. Lampard, *Dairy Industry,* pp. 241–242.

threatening to strike. Not till after the First World War did the testing of cattle and the pasteurization of milk come to prevail, even in America's Dairyland.

Dairyland it certainly was by that time. Wisconsin agriculturists engaged in other lines, such as corn-hog, grain-cattle, specialty, and truck farming, but the majority concerned themselves mainly with dairying. They accounted for more fluid, condensed, and evaporated milk as well as more cheese than did the dairymen of any other state.

Dairymen from all over the country gathered in front of the Wisconsin College of Agriculture's main building, in 1922, for the dedication of a bronze statue of William Dempster Hoard. The statue, the work of Gutzon Borglum, was to stand above a marble frieze depicting the history of agricultural progress. Here the living Hoard once had stood to welcome farmers' sons arriving in search of agricultural knowledge. He then pointed toward Bascom Hill, the site of the university's liberal-arts college and law school. "My young friends," he began, "over on yonder hill they are wont to speak of this 'cow college' in terms of derision, but I want to say to you that the business of farming is the greatest vocation of all." He concluded: "You speak of the great men of the world, the lawyer, the preacher, and the doctor. Who and what are they when compared to the man who feeds the world?" [8]

3

Agricultural scientists in Wisconsin strove to enhance the quantity and quality of milk and milk products. They studied, among other things, the diet and digestion of cows. Their efforts to improve bovine nutrition led to the improvement of human nutrition as well.

These scientists had a distant forerunner, a pioneer who experimented directly with the stomach of a living man. William Beaumont, an army physician from New England, made the

8. Quoted in Bowman, *Why Wisconsin,* pp. 98–99.

most of a rare opportunity. While stationed at Fort Mackinac, Michigan, in 1822, Dr. Beaumont was called upon to treat a young French Canadian voyageur, Alexis St. Martin, who had been accidentally shot in the side. St. Martin's wound eventually healed in such a way as to leave a hole with a valvelike flap that covered it. By pushing in the flap, Beaumont could look right into the man's stomach. He could also insert a tube and draw out samples of the gastric juice and of partially digested food. No sooner had the doctor begun his experiments, however, than his subject left him and went home to Quebec. After being transferred to Fort Crawford, near Prairie du Chien, Wisconsin Territory, Beaumont managed to get St. Martin back and resume the tests, which he carried on at this fort from 1829 to 1831.

On the basis of his studies of St. Martin in Wisconsin and elsewhere, Beaumont wrote a book, *Experiments and Observations on the Gastric Juice and the Physiology of Digestion,* which he got published in 1833. Among the fifty-six experiments at Fort Crawford, Beaumont described the occasion when St. Martin "breakfasted on *fat pork, bread* and *potatoes*" at nine in the morning and his stomach's contents were analyzed at one in the afternoon. They were "of a milky, or rather thin, gruel-like consistence, and considerably tinged with yellow bile," St. Martin having been in a "violent anger" at the time the sample was taken. "This experiment shows the effect of violent passion on the digestive apparatus." [9] Besides revealing the influence of emotion on digestion, Beaumont made a number of other lasting contributions to physiology, among them the first accurate descriptions of the gastric juice, the motions of the stomach, and the comparative digestibility of various kinds of food. Indeed, he did more for the understanding of the digestive process than any other experimenter until the Russian physiologist Ivan Petrovich Pavlov made his famous discoveries almost a century later.

9. William Beaumont, *Experiments and Observations on the Gastric Juice and the Physiology of Digestion,* facsimile edition (1833; New York: Peter Smith, 1941), pp. 153–154.

A contemporary of Pavlov (born six years before him, in 1843), the agricultural chemist Stephen Moulton Babcock arrived in Madison from New York state in 1887, to serve on both the faculty of the university and the staff of the experiment station. Here he continued the investigations he had previously begun of the digestive process of dairy cows.

Temporarily Professor Babcock turned from these to attack a problem of immediate concern to the dairy industry—how to ascertain quickly and cheaply the richness of milk. Neither producers nor processors of milk were satisfied with the existing method of evaluation. Farmers were simply paid on the basis of weight, and some watered their milk, yet received as much for it as those who delivered the purest. The best practical indicator of quality was the butterfat content. To measure this, Babcock in 1890 came up with a device that was simplicity itself. A centrifuge whirled a bottle containing a sample of milk into which sulphuric acid had been put to release the fat. The percentage could then be read directly from a scale on the bottle's neck. The Babcock tester—which the inventor made no attempt to patent—eventually went into use throughout the world. It had extraordinary consequences in the improvement of dairy breeds and dairy products.

Since the Babcock tester did not measure casein content, it was a less-than-perfect indicator of milk's suitability for making cheese. Babcock and other scientists at the experiment station, therefore, concentrated on casein, and they devised the "Wisconsin curd test" in 1895. With one of his colleagues, Harry L. Russell, Babcock ascertained that the curing of cheese must be the work of an enzyme. Experiments with milk, curds, and rennets and with curing, salting, and packing brought visible results in the rising quality of Wisconsin cheese. For three years in a row, 1909, 1910, and 1911, the state's producers, in competition with the best from the rest of the country and abroad, won the top three prizes in practically every category of cheese exhibited at fairs in Milwaukee and Chicago.

Babcock had not lost his interest in the alimentary process of cows, and in the early 1900s he was still experimenting with them, feeding certain ones nothing but corn, others nothing but wheat. He noticed that the corn-fed cattle thrived and the rest did not. There must be something in the corn, some mysterious X, he concluded, that accounted for the difference. He had learned there was a "hidden hunger" that allows people, as well as cattle, to starve even though they have plenty to eat. And he was on the track of an even greater discovery—the discovery of precisely what was lacking in cases of nutritional deficiency. "This man," an admirer was to say, "is the father of the vitamines." [10] More accurately, he was the grandfather. The actual discovery was left to one of his assistants, Elmer V. McCollum.

Dr. McCollum, of the experiment station, was investigating the nutritional qualities of milk. He succeeded in isolating vitamins A and B. Vitamin A he found in butterfat and eggs, and he demonstrated that it was the growth factor. Animals fed on butter far outdid those fed on oleo—a fact that Hoard in 1917 broadcast to the world in a special issue of his dairy newspaper. McCollum went on to discover the "fat soluble vitamine D," which proved capable of curing or preventing rickets. Perhaps as many as half of the children in the United States at that time were suffering to some extent from vitamin D deficiency, but the most readily available source of the vitamin, cod-liver oil, was both distasteful and expensive.

Another of Babcock's one-time assistants, Harry Steenbock, who had grown up on a northern Wisconsin farm, hit upon a way to get vitamin D in an abundant and inoffensive form. It was already known that sunlight discouraged rickets; there must be some connection between the sun and the "sunshine vitamin." In 1923, as a young biochemist at the University of Wisconsin, Steenbock discovered the link. For years he had been experimenting with rats. He finally found that, if he exposed casein and millet seed to sunlight or to artificial ultraviolet light and then fed the mixture to undernourished rodents, they quickly lost their rickety symptoms and rapidly gained in

10. Paul de Kruif, *Hunger Fighters* (New York: Harcourt, Brace and Company, 1928), p. 297.

weight. He had "trapped the lifeguarding X of the sun's rays." [11] The next step was to infuse vitamin D into human foods such as milk, cereals, bread, and oleo by the simple process of ultraviolet irradiation.

The process was worth millions, but Steenbock had no desire to make money for himself out of it. He wanted a foundation to take out a patent, manage it, and use the proceeds to support future research at the university. Harry L. Russell, then dean of the College of Agriculture, and Charles Sumner Slichter, dean of the Graduate School, appealed to alumni for immediate funds to get the program started. The upshot was the Wisconsin Alumni Research Foundation (WARF). In 1927 Steenbock transferred his rights in the irradiation process to WARF for the consideration of ten dollars. By 1945, when the patent expired, it had brought in more than eight million dollars in royalties. Its use had eliminated rickets as a major health problem.

With earnings from the Steenbock process, from other patents assigned to WARF, and from gifts and investments, the foundation financed projects in many scientific fields. In the field of nutrition it made possible such additional discoveries as a preparation of copper and iron for relieving anemia, a method of stabilizing iodine in table salt, the treatment of pellagra by nicotinic acid, and new developments in the hybridization of corn.

4

With the decline of wheat growing in Wisconsin, the state's farmers took up as an alternative not only dairying but also other lines that they could pursue in conjunction with it. One of these was the raising of hogs. Another was the cultivation of vegetables, especially peas. In consequence, the state became notable for its meat packing and still more for its vegetable canning.

Not that Wisconsin ever turned into a corn-and-hog country comparable to Iowa or Illinois. Its swine remained subordinate

11. DeKruif, *Hunger Fighters,* p. 301.

to its milk cows, its pork subordinate to its cheese. But farmers could slop their pigs with whey left over from cheesemaking as well as with buttermilk left over from churning. They brought more and more hogs to slaughter, as many as two and even three million of them a year. By the 1940s the porkers accounted for a fifth of the state's farm income.

Almost a century before that, with the coming of the railroads in the 1850s, Milwaukee firms had entered the business of butchering hogs, preparing hams, bacon, lard, and salt pork, and sending the products to eastern markets. One of the pioneers in the business was Philip D. Armour, a native of New York state, who had tried his luck in the gold fields of California, then in a soap factory and a wholesale grocery in Milwaukee. Armour got into meat packing after he found he could make money by selling pickled pork to migrants on their way west. In 1863 he joined in a partnership with Delaware-born John Plankinton, who was already well established as a Milwaukee packer. The Civil War created a brisk demand, and Plankinton and Armour gained handsome profits by putting up mess pork in barrels for the Union army. In the one year 1865 they reputedly cleared $1,800,000 and made themselves the wealthiest packers in the entire country. Milwaukee as a whole did not keep pace with Chicago or even Cincinnati. Still, by 1870, with a total of seven firms busily at work, Milwaukee had emerged as the nation's fourth largest meat-packing center.

Investing their war profits wisely, Plankinton and Armour opened branches in Chicago and several other cities. In 1875 Armour left Milwaukee to take charge of the Chicago branch. The tail wagged the dog when, about a decade later, Armour got control of the entire organization, to go on and develop it into one of the greatest meat businesses in the world. Meanwhile, back in Milwaukee, Plankinton formed a new company with Patrick Cudahy as his partner. Cudahy, brought from Ireland as a baby, had risen from butcher's boy to superintendent of Plankinton and Armour's Milwaukee plant. Before long, Cudahy's brother John bought Plankinton's interest, and in 1893 the Cudahy Brothers Company moved outside of Milwaukee, to the south, where they founded the industrial city of Cudahy.

Meat processing eventually rose to importance in other Wisconsin cities also, among them Sheboygan, Green Bay, Jefferson, and especially Madison, the site of an Oscar Mayer and Company plant. Oscar Mayer, a German immigrant, reversed the Wisconsin-to-Chicago movement of Philip D. Armour. Mayer's business, which he had started with a butcher shop in 1883, was well established in Chicago when, in 1919, the company opened its Madison branch. This grew into one of the largest packinghouses in the Midwest.

Vegetable canning got a later start in Wisconsin than meat packing, but eventually overtook it. Indeed, commercial canning amounted to little anywhere till after 1874, when there appeared the first pressure cooker for processing the cans or jars in which the food was to be preserved. This device was crude, and for some time the processing remained a hit-or-miss affair. Such it was when, in the early 1880s, Albert Landreth tried his hand at canning peas in the kitchen of a small Manitowoc hotel. Landreth had arrived in the Manitowoc area as the representative of a Philadelphia seed company to supervise the growing of pea seeds. Already the lakeshore north of Milwaukee was known as good land for peas, the pea-eating immigrants from Germany, Holland, and other countries having long planted them for their own tables. In 1887 Landreth set up in Manitowoc a small canning plant, in which he installed the primitive equipment then available. Three years later he built another factory in Sheboygan.

Things did not always go well for Landreth. From time to time the cans exploded, scattering a vile green substance that stank up the warehouse where they awaited shipment. In 1894 Landreth appealed to the dean of the College of Agriculture, and the dean sent him Dr. Harry L. Russell, then a twenty-eight-year-old assistant professor of bacteriology. After experimenting with Landreth's equipment, Russell worked out a table of temperature, pressure, and exposure time, which, if followed, would assure the safe canning of peas. Science had come to the rescue of the young and faltering industry.

By 1900 there were twenty small canneries in the state, and after that the number steadily increased. Most of them concentrated on peas, but some took sweet corn and other produce. Dairy farmers were glad to contract for planting some of their acres to peas when they saw that these fit in well with both crop rotation and cattle feeding. The plants, as legumes, restored nitrogen to the soil, and the vines made good ensilage. Corn husks, cobs, and stalks also helped to fill the silos. More and more sweet corn was grown in the state as the College of Agriculture developed hybrids that would mature well despite the short growing season.

Every canning season brought something of a crisis in the early years. An entire crop ripened within a very short period, and all of it had to be got to and through the cannery in a rush. A great deal of the work had to be done by hand. This meant long hours for cheap labor. Boys, girls, and women from the locality were not enough; migrant workers were brought in for eighteen-hour shifts. Cries of exploitation caused the legislature to limit the hours, and then it was the canners' and farmers' turn to protest. They complained that they could no longer stay in business. With the First World War the demand for canned goods rose to unprecedented heights, and the lure of high profits and high wages, together with the call of patriotism, stilled the dispute. Already, in 1913, Wisconsin had canned more peas than any other state. In 1918 it canned as much as all the others put together.

After the war, consumption remained high, the American people having got used to eating food from cans. In Wisconsin, farmers planted more and more acres to vegetables, enterprisers set up more canneries, and these operated with more labor-saving machinery. A mechanical pea viner—made in Kewaunee, Wisconsin, and in only two other places in the country—shelled more peas in an hour than a hundred people could do in a day. A canning machine filled and sealed as many as four hundred cans a minute. An automatic system carried the sealed cans in a continuous flow through a pressure-cooking tank, from which they emerged ready to be stored or shipped. The industry, spreading inland from the Lake Michigan shore, came to be concentrated mainly in the south-central part of the state.

Canning in Wisconsin reached a new peak of production in 1945, in an effort to meet the needs of the armed forces during the Second World War. In that year the state's canneries turned out some 15,000,000 cases of peas, 5,700,000 of corn, 3,409,000 of beets, 2,000,000 of beans (green, wax, and lima) and carrots, and lesser quantities of sauerkraut, asparagus, and tomatoes. After the war, 150 canneries or so continued to operate. They still produced annually more peas than those of any other state, and in some years more sweet corn. They produced a fifth of the nation's supply of canned vegetables and red cherries. All in all, Wisconsin was the leader in the canning industry.

5

Even in the early years of statehood, some Wisconsin farmers could supplement wheat, as a cash crop, with hops or barley. These found a market among the brewers who set up their establishments in Milwaukee and other places in the state. The pioneer breweries were necessarily small and scattered, since their product could not be kept long or transported far. But times were changing. Milwaukee was to produce much more beer than could be sold in the city or in the entire state, and the beer Milwaukee made was, quite literally, to make Milwaukee famous.

The state's first brewers were not Germans but Englishmen and Welshmen, and they turned out not lager beer but ale, porter, stout, and English-type "strong beer." Even the Germans, who were soon to dominate the business, at first produced beer of the same general type. This was top-fermentation beer, made with a yeast that floated to the top and had to be skimmed off. Though giving a good alcoholic kick, the stuff was quite perishable. By the 1840s, brewmasters in Bavaria were making, by a bottom-fermentation process, a different kind of brew, a lager beer, that had much better keeping qualities. Germans prepared the way for Milwaukee's brewing greatness when they brought over the new yeast and the new process.

The biggest breweries of Milwaukee began as family businesses. Arriving in 1844, Jacob Best persuaded a brother and a son, who were already on the ground and operating a vinegar works, to join him in making beer. Frederick Pabst married the brother's daughter and, with another son-in-law, eventually took over the firm. John Braun started a brewery in 1846. When Braun died, his foreman Valentin Blatz bought the business; later Blatz married Mrs. Braun. The Schlitz story was similar. August Krug went into brewing in 1849. After Krug's death his bookkeeper Joseph Schlitz succeeded him, wed his widow, and ran the enterprise in co-operation with his (Krug's) nephews August, Henry, Alfred, and Edward Uihlein. In time the Uihlein brothers became the sole owners of the Schlitz brewing company.

Even before the Civil War, Milwaukee could boast fourteen or fifteen breweries, among them those of Frederick Miller and Adam Gettelman. As early as 1852, beer was "exported" from the city, that is, shipped to other parts of the country, a total of 645 barrels being recorded for that year. After the war the national consumption rapidly increased because of rising German immigration and also a growing American taste for beer, which was hit less heavily by war taxes than whiskey was, and which, unlike whiskey or rum, could be safely drunk by workingmen on the job. Milwaukee's production increased much faster, multiplying twenty-six times during the four decades after 1870.

By 1900, Wisconsin stood fourth in the output of malt liquors, after New York, Pennsylvania, and Illinois. New York that year had a total more than three times as large as Wisconsin's (9,946,968 barrels to 3,205,265). Yet, per capita, Milwaukee produced more than three times as much as New York City, and more than five times as much as Philadelphia or Chicago. The breweries of most other cities sold in a local, a state, or at most a regional market; those of Milwaukee sold in a national and even an international one. Two of the nation's three largest breweries were located in Milwaukee—Pabst and Schlitz. Pabst was half again as big as the second-place company, Anheuser-Busch of St. Louis.

Milwaukee had risen above all the rest of American cities as an exporter of beer (exporting it both to other states and to foreign countries). Why? There were skilled German brew-masters also in St. Louis, Cincinnati, and elsewhere. But Milwaukee had some advantages. It had a cool climate and an abundance of natural ice, both factors of crucial importance in the days before artificial refrigeration (which spread during the 1880s but did not prevail till after 1900). It had cheap cooperage at a time when beer was shipped in wooden kegs. And it had a disadvantage that worked to its benefit—a comparatively small population, hence a limited local market, and hence a necessity to push exports harder than its metropolitan competitors did. Its brewers met the challenge with great promotional as well as technical ability. And they had the benefit of a bit of luck.

As judged by the value of the product, brewing was the first industry of Milwaukee in only one year—1889. Earlier it had ranged as high as second or third; later it was to fall to fifth. Yet the brewers succeeded in identifying Milwaukee with beer. They also identified Milwaukee beer with the highest quality.

As early as 1862 a German-language newspaper of Louis-ville, Kentucky, commented: "Yesterday our neighbor received some Milwaukee beer of which it is impossible to drink but one glass. One must exert great effort to stop with the second glass. We assert that no one can ever drink too much of it, even when one does drink too much of it." [12] The great Chicago fire of 1871, a severe blow to Chicago brewers, many of whom it ruined, was a boon to Milwaukee brewers. It enabled them to increase their sales by 44 percent the next year, as thirsty Chi-cagoans looked northward for relief from the local drought. The Milwaukee Chamber of Commerce showed municipal pride as it reflected that, by 1872, the "relatively small city of Milwaukee had overtaken such great brewing centers as New York, Phila-delphia, and St. Louis as the greatest beer exporting center in the nation." [13]

12. *Louisville Anzeiger,* reprinted in the *Milwaukee Sentinel,* June 11, 1862, and quoted in Cochran, *The Pabst Brewing Company,* p. 53.

13. Quoted in "Milwaukee Beer—It Made a City 'Famous,' " *Wisconsin Then and Now,* 14 (February 1968):3.

With Blatz leading the way, Milwaukee brewers began to bottle their beer in 1875. At first they used earthenware bottles, polygonal rather than round. Brand names were more conspicuous with bottled than with barreled beer.

In their advertising, the brewers stressed both their individual labels and the Milwaukee connection. Already familiar by the 1890s was the slogan "Schlitz, the Beer that Made Milwaukee Famous." Schlitz had bought the phrase from a small brewery for five thousand dollars. Pabst replied with this: "Milwaukee Beer Is Famous—Pabst Has Made It So." As the producer of the biggest selling brew (which the company sold under the label "Best" until 1889), and as the most active promoter of the beer-and-Milwaukee theme, Pabst had the better claim to such a slogan. Nevertheless, in 1898, Pabst abandoned it when Schlitz objected on the ground of its similarity to the Schlitz version, which had the advantage of prior use. And Schlitz beer was indeed acquiring attention, both for itself and for Milwaukee. It was sent to the Philippines for Admiral George Dewey after his glorious victory in Manila Bay. It went along with ex-President Theodore Roosevelt on a safari in Africa.

Besides advertising their brand names and their slogans, the big Milwaukee beer companies encouraged sales in other ways. At home they sponsored beer gardens, beer halls, and other outlets for their own brands. The Schlitz Hotel and Palm Garden rose in 1889. Pabst controlled hotels and restaurants not only in Milwaukee but also in Chicago, Minneapolis, San Francisco, and New York. The company hired celebrities of the stage to visit bars and treat the customers to rounds of Pabst Blue Ribbon. Pabst and its competitors lured conventions to Milwaukee by offering free beer and lavish entertainment. They exhibited their products and won prizes at world's fairs.

They had a big investment in the word "Milwaukee" as well as in their respective brand names. From time to time they had to take legal action in order to protect their stake. In 1900, Pabst, Schlitz, and Blatz obtained from a federal circuit court separate but identical injunctions requiring New York brewers to desist from labeling their bottles "Milwaukee beer." The three Milwaukee companies used the decree itself as an advertisement, publicizing it in a circular they sent to dealers throughout the country.

By the early 1900s, brewmastery and salesmanship had brought Milwaukee its greatest fame. Soon came the catastrophe that brewers had been dreading—national Prohibition. Wartime food controls brought beer production to an end in 1919, and then the Eighteenth Amendment went into effect in 1920. As applied by the Volstead Act, the amendment prohibited the manufacture, transportation, or sale of beverages with an alcoholic content of more than a half of one percent. So it ruled out beer and light wines along with hard liquors.

Wisconsin's smaller breweries simply went out of business, but Milwaukee's big ones had too much invested in their physical plant, business organization, and good will to do the same. They kept their equipment going by adapting it to the manufacture of different products. Among these were processed foods, candies, ''near beer'' and other soft drinks, and malt extracts, which were used for medicinal purposes and also for baking and home brewing. Some breweries converted to entirely new lines, such as the manufacture of machinery.

After thirteen years of illegal and inferior beer, legitimate brewing came back to life with the repeal of the Volstead Act. On New Beer's Eve, April 6, 1933, crowds waited at bars and breweries for midnight, when beer could again be legally served. Even small breweries reopened sooner or later, and during the 1930s it seemed as if, once more, practically every Wisconsin town had at least one of them. Most of them were quite hospitable. In Reedsburg (population about four thousand), for example, a stranger could get out of the summer heat by taking a brewery tour, during which he received his fill of the still cloudy brew, direct from the cool vats.

All but a few of Wisconsin's small breweries eventually gave up again, or else they were taken over by larger, consolidating corporations. Not many pioneers were in business a hundred years after their original founding. One of those outside Milwaukee was the J. Leinenkugel Brewing Company, which Jacob

Leinenkugel had started in 1865, and which a century later was producing in Chippewa Falls a local beer that appealed to fanciers even outside the state. Another was the G. Heileman Brewing Company, which Gottlieb Heileman had established in La Crosse in 1858. By the 1970s Heileman owned and operated breweries in several states and put out beer under various names besides its own, one of them being Blatz. The big Milwaukee brewers—Schlitz, Pabst, and Miller—had similarly expanded. Milwaukee and its beer were still famous, but the city was no longer distinguished as an exporting center, since so much of its beer was going to consumers from breweries scattered over the country.

4

The Arm and Hammer

HERE is this Wisconsin of "bucolic *Gemuetlichkeit*"? a Racine advertising man asked in 1949. "Industry," he contended "is the true Wisconsin colossus—the veritable symbol of the state—for it is in industry that more Wisconsin people make their livings and it is through industry that Wisconsin very largely prospers." [1]

Industry did have a place, though by no means an exclusive one, in Wisconsin's official symbolism. The state seal, dating from 1851, contained a shield on which were pictured a plow to represent agriculture, a crossed pick and shovel for mining, an anchor for navigation, and an arm and hammer for manufacturing. These were the economic activities that had seemed actually and prospectively important at that early time. Little foresight would have been needed to add an ax and a saw for lumbering and sawmilling. Greater prophetic power would have been necessary to include an arrangement of wheels and gears for symbolizing the complex and gigantic machinery that was to become one of Wisconsin's most characteristic products.

It was also true, as of 1949, that manufacturing, including

1. Louis Sidran to the editor, *Holiday,* 6 (October 1949):5. Sidran was commenting on Mark Schorer's article "Wisconsin," which had appeared in *Holiday,* 6 (July 1949):34–53.

food processing, yielded a larger return for Wisconsinites than did farming. The state's manufactured goods were worth almost twice as much as its agricultural products. This meant a higher proportion of industrial to agricultural output for Wisconsin than for its neighbors to the west, but a lower proportion than for Ohio, Indiana, Illinois, or Michigan. Within Wisconsin the concentration of industry was heaviest in the east, along the lakeshore from Two Rivers, Manitowoc, and Sheboygan through Milwaukee, Racine, and Kenosha. Yet factories were widely scattered over the state.

Wisconsin was notable for the diversity of its industrial products, no one line being predominant, not even machinery. It was notable also for the mechanical inventiveness of its people and for their innovative spirit. It certainly contributed its share, if not more than its share, of the impetus to the industrialization of the United States. Given the economic resources of the state, some of its contributions were perhaps to have been expected, but others were rather surprising. The typewriter, of all things, originated in Wisconsin.

1

The world's first practical writing machine was developed in Milwaukee between 1867 and 1873. Several men took part in its development, but the two who had the most to do with it were the pioneer Wisconsin newspapermen Christopher Latham Sholes and James Densmore. These two had first met in Madison during an editors' convention in 1853. At that time they hardly seemed likely partners. Sholes was tall, tubercular, dreamy-eyed, gentle, whimsical. Densmore had a huge muscular body, a bold red face, and an aggressive, argumentative spirit. Yet, opposites though the two men were, their lives already had run parallel in significant respects.

Born in Pennsylvania, of English stock, Sholes had come to the wilds of Wisconsin in 1837 as an eighteen-year-old journeyman printer. Soon he started his own paper, the weekly *Southport* (later Kenosha) *Telegraph*. Through its columns he preached a gospel of salvation on earth through works of reform. He demanded an end to capital punishment, among other wrongs, and as a member of the state legislature he helped to bring it about. Progress, he believed, required that human minds and hearts be brought closer and closer together, and so he carefully noted the signs of improvement in penmanship, shorthand, telegraphy, and the entire art of communicating thought. He even interested himself in communicating with the other world. When spiritualism became a national fad in the 1850s, he attended seances where he listened to weird rappings and felt chairs and tables float in the air.

Occasionally editor Sholes reprinted the observations of editor Densmore, founder and publisher of the first newspaper in Oshkosh, the *True Democrat*. Densmore, a year younger than Sholes, had been born in western New York and had been raised there and in western Pennsylvania. Until the age of twenty-eight he traveled about the countryside peddling the clothespins and other woodenware that his father turned out. Then, in 1848, after studying law on his own and passing the Pennsylvania bar examinations, he left for the brand-new state of Wisconsin. In his weekly *True Democrat* he expressed views similar to Sholes's on Free Soil and other matters. He, too, showed an interest in improving communication; he wanted to begin by reforming the alphabet. A vegetarian, he accepted advertisements from butchers, but he recommended "flesh" only to the "carnivorously inclined" among his fellow townsmen.

After their first meeting, Sholes the spiritualist and Densmore the vegetarian soon came together in support of their shared principles. For a year the two co-operated in publishing a Kenosha daily, which they filled with "news by lightning," with telegraphic reports from the Associated Press. They could not make a go of it, however, and so they parted, the best of friends.

About a dozen years later, in 1867, Sholes was living in Milwaukee, making a living for his large family as collector of the port, and spending most of his spare time at Kleinsteuber's machine shop. Charles F. Kleinsteuber and his German employees made models, castings, and metalwork of various kinds. Amateur inventors frequented the place. Sholes already had invented two machines, one for addressing newspapers to subscribers by mail and another for numbering or paging ledgers, tickets, coupons, and the like. A fellow habitué of Kleinsteuber's shop, Carlos Glidden, suggested to him one day that, having produced a numbering machine, he ought to try his hand at a writing machine. A little later Sholes read in the *Scientific American* an account of a newly invented device of that kind. "The subject of type writing is one of the interesting aspects of the near future," the magazine commented. It predicted that "the weary process of learning penmanship in schools" would sooner or later be "reduced to the acquirement of the art of writing one's own signature and playing on the literary piano." [2]

Sholes set to work with the assistance of Glidden and another amateur inventor, Samuel W. Soule, and also one of Kleinsteuber's men, a former builder of tower clocks in Germany, Mathias Schwalbach. They proceeded along lines quite different from those of the invention the *Scientific American* described. In two months they had a model ready, one that certainly looked like a "literary piano." It had a pianolike keyboard, with letters in alphabetical order, which was attached to the side of an old kitchen table. Over a hole in the table top was a flat frame holding a sheet of tissue paper. Above the paper an inked ribbon passed under a small metal plate, or platen. The types struck from underneath and pressed the paper against the ribbon and the metal surface, thus causing the letters to appear on top of the paper. This had to be thin enough that the types could make their impression *through* it.

Nevertheless, Sholes and his associates thought they had finished the job, and they looked for someone to buy the invention or finance its manufacture. They could find no one with sufficient confidence and capital. So Sholes turned to his old newspaper partner, sending Densmore a letter, typed on tissue paper,

2. *Scientific American,* n.s. 17 (July 6, 1867):3.

in which he described the invention and then suggested its profit-making possibilities with a quotation from Shakespeare (*Julius Caesar,* Act III, Scene 2):

> *There is a tide in the affairs of men*
> *Which, taken at the flood, leads on to fortune.*

Densmore was ripe for that Shakespearean hint. He had returned to western Pennsylvania in the hope of getting rich from the oil boom and had failed, though he had managed to get and hold on to miscellaneous assets of some potential worth. Now, immediately captivated by the typewriter idea, he replied with an offer to buy a share in it. As soon as he could get away, in 1868, he went to Milwaukee and took charge of the enterprise. He secured the first patents on the machine and in Chicago undertook to have it manufactured. It proved to have many faults in addition to its basic one, its inability to write on paper of ordinary thickness. After having only fifteen units made, Densmore gave up on this particular model.

During 1869 Sholes redesigned his machine to meet Densmore's demands. In its new version it had a cylinder to hold the paper, a cylinder that rotated to space the letters and moved longitudinally to change the lines. That is, the types wrote *around* a revolving drum. The paper, wrapped around the drum and clipped to it, could be as thick as cardboard, though it could be no longer than the drum was. "I am satisfied the machine is now done," Sholes proudly wrote to Densmore on the latest model.[3]

Though highly pleased with Sholes's new, "axle" machine, Densmore was determined not to rush it into production. He was going to wait until the thing was really perfected. So he instructed Sholes to have Schwalbach put together a few of the machines in Kleinsteuber's shop. These he sent to stenographers for them to test. He relayed the typists' complaints and sugges-

3. Sholes to Densmore, September—, 1869, quoted in Richard N. Current, "The Orginial Typewriter Enterprise, 1867–1873," *Wisconsin Magazine of History,* 32 (June 1949):397. The original is in the possession of Priscilla Densmore, Marquette, Michigan.

tions to Sholes and insisted on changes in the design. Sholes impatiently complied, adding one improvement after another.

By the summer of 1870, even Densmore was convinced that the typewriter (as he named it) was ready for manufacture. When he heard that the Atlantic & Pacific Telegraph Company might be interested in it for recording telegrams, he exhibited a model in New York City. But he learned that the telegraph people wanted a machine that would type on a continuous roll of paper. The job of invention, he had to conclude, was not finished after all, and he set poor Sholes to starting over again.

By early 1872, Sholes had produced a third basic model. On this one the cylinder moved lengthwise to space the letters and rotated to change the lines. It would accommodate paper of any desired length. Still, Densmore could find no capitalist willing to take a chance on it. So, that summer, he decided to try his own hand at manufacturing. In Milwaukee he rented a wheelwright's shop, a rough stone building equipped with water power. He hired a few laborers and Schwalbach as their foreman, mustered a meager outfit of secondhand tools, and accumulated a supply of raw materials and ready-made parts. Schwalbach and his workmen kept turning out new typewriters and remodeling old ones all summer and fall. Each unit of the output was a little different, if not a little better, than the one before it.

Before the end of 1872 the writing machine, as produced in that makeshift Milwaukee plant, had assumed a form essentially the same as that of all standard typewriters a century later. Even the keyboard had taken the familiar pattern—q w e r t y u i o p, etc.—that it was to keep. Only two really basic improvements remained to be made: the addition of a shift, for typing in lower- as well as upper-case letters; and the arrangement of a front stroke, for making each line visible as it is being typed. The Milwaukee machines gave good service, as testimonials from users indicated. But the business was yielding no profit. Densmore concluded he must have facilities for manufacturing more efficiently and more economically.

At the end of the year he received a visit from G. W. N. Yost, a Pennsylvania implement manufacturer who employed him as a lawyer. Yost suggested that an ideal place to get typewriters made would be the gun factory of E. Remington & Sons in Ilion, New York. In the spring of 1873 he and Densmore went to Ilion and made an agreement according to which they would pay the Remingtons to make typewriters for them. A year later Densmore and Yost received their first Remington-made machines to sell. These were better looking and better constructed but in all essentials the same as the latest models that Densmore had manufactured in Milwaukee.

No sooner were the handsome new typewriters ready for the market than the panic of 1873 struck, bringing on the worst depression yet in American history. Mark Twain bought one of the new-fangled things and was enthusiastic about it, but sales were slow for several years. Not till the 1880s did the typewriter become a fixture in business offices, and at first the word "typewriter" often referred not only to the machine but also to the person who operated it—usually a young woman. To women it brought new opportunities for respectable employment. Eventually it helped make possible both big business and big government.

Densmore, before he died in 1889, was beginning to realize a small fortune from his typewriter interests. Sholes, by that time, no longer held an interest. Despite Densmore's advice, he had sold his rights in bits and pieces because he had little faith in the future of his own invention. "Whatever I may have thought in the early days, of the value of the typewriter," he said in 1888, "it is very obviously a blessing to mankind, and especially to womankind. I am very glad I had something to do with it." At times Sholes felt that Densmore had stolen the invention from him; at other times he took a quite different view. "It is possible I have done something toward the enterprise, and it is quite possible, had it not been for me there would have been no enterprise," he once wrote to Densmore. "But while this is only possible, in my case, it is very certain that there would have been no enterprise, had it not been for you.'' [4] In truth, it was the combined effort of both of these men—the inventive genius of the one, the promotional drive of the other—that gave America and the world the typewriter.

2

The industrial future of Wisconsin had looked very bright when, on June 5, 1848, the new state's first governor, Nelson Dewey, gave his maiden speech to the legislature. Governor Dewey was a rather small and unimpressive man, with no gift for public speaking, yet he grew almost eloquent as he referred to the industrial and commercial along with the agricultural prospects. "It is under the most favorable auspices," he concluded, "that the State of Wisconsin has taken her position among the families of States." [5]

Wisconsin, its early boosters thought, was blessed with natural resources not only in the fertility of its soil and the abundance of its forests but also in the richness of its mineral deposits. Lead had long been coming from its mines, and iron was expected to come from veins already known and yet to be discovered. True, there was no anticipation of finding coal within the state, and indeed there was none to be found (nor was there petroleum or natural gas). Still, the plentiful wood could presumably be counted upon to serve adequately and indefinitely as fuel. And the many streams with their steady flow would surely provide more than enough water power.

In that day, when water was the element of transportation as well as power, one of Wisconsin's greatest potential advantages seemed to be its location on the map. The state lay directly between the nation's two vast natural systems of inland transport.

4. The two quotations are from Richard N. Current, *The Typewriter and the Men Who Made It* (Urbana: University of Illinois Press, 1954), pp. 126–127. Originals are in the possession of Priscilla Densmore.

5. Quoted in *History of Sauk County,* p. 54.

One of these led eastward to the Atlantic Ocean by way of the Great Lakes and the Erie Canal or the St. Lawrence River. The other led southward to the Gulf of Mexico by way of the Mississippi and its tributaries. And one of these tributaries, the Wisconsin, ran close by the headwaters of the Fox, which flowed in the opposite direction, emptying into Lake Michigan. If the Fox and the Wisconsin could be connected and properly improved, a grand thoroughfare of domestic and foreign commerce would pass right through the state. Commercial and industrial greatness, it seemed, must surely be Wisconsin's geographical destiny.

Trying to help fate along, pioneer industrialists and their friends urged Wisconsinites to patronize home industry, to give their own mechanics and manufacturers the preference. Such promoters often talked as if the state were a separate country, one that lost money by paying for imports and that stood to gain by making itself economically self-sufficient. If comparable to an independent country, however, Wisconsin at first was like an underdeveloped one, shipping most of its raw materials away for manufacture. The Milwaukee Chamber of Commerce complained in 1871:

> At present we are sending our hard lumber east to get it back as furniture and agricultural implements, we ship ore to St. Louis and New York, to pay the cost of bringing it back as shot, type, pipe, sheet lead, white lead, paint, etc., we ship away our wool crop and import cloths, carpets, blankets and other fabrics; we give rags for paper, and hides for boots and harness, and iron ore for stoves—and our consumers all the while are paying the double costs of this unnecessary transportation.[6]

The lag in industrialization showed that early Wisconsin had handicaps as well as advantages for manufacturing. Most serious was a lack of capital. Funds from the outside went largely into land speculation, which promised quicker and more

6. Milwaukee Chamber of Commerce, *Report*, 1871, p. 16, quoted in Merk, *Economic History*, p. 124.

dazzling profits. Also inadequate was bank credit and currency. Indeed, the state constitution completely prohibited banks in the beginning.

Even the supposed advantages of Wisconsin proved, in some cases, to be more or less illusory. Its lead production, already declining in the year of statehood, was never to recover its former importance. Wisconsin's iron mining amounted to little until the opening of the Gogebic Range, along the Michigan border in the far north, in the 1880s. Even then, most of the good ore turned out to be on the Michigan side. With the exploitation of the vast and rich surface deposits of Minnesota's Mesabi Range, from the 1890s on, Wisconsin's deep mining became less and less economic. In the late 1960s the last of the state's iron mines closed. Already, in the 1920s, iron smelting had ended in the state when the fires of the blast furnaces at Bay View—first lit in the 1870s—finally went out. Wisconsin was never to be a great producer of iron or steel, but with cheap freight on the Great Lakes it suffered from no lack of material for its metal-fabricating industries.

Waterpower did much for the development of Wisconsin's manufacturing, but not as much as had been expected. State law encouraged the construction of milldams. On a stream not navigable a dam could be built without an official permit and without the consent of property owners whose land might be flooded by the resulting pond; they would have no legal recourse except to sue for damages. On a navigable stream no dam could be erected without the permission of the state legislature, but such permission was freely granted. By 1870 the census takers could report 1,288 waterwheels in the state, as compared with only 926 steam engines. Already, however, the steam engines were putting out very nearly as much horsepower as the waterwheels, and before long the engines, steadily increasing in number and size, were to account for the greater share of the horsepower. They could be fueled with wood so long as it remained abundant and cheap. Eventually, most of them would have to have coal.

Hydroelectric power promised to lessen the dependence on

fuels, and Wisconsin pioneered in its development. After improving the incandescent lamp to the point of practicality, Thomas A. Edison set to building, in the city of New York, a steam plant for generating electricity. He also licensed three Appleton businessmen, one of them a personal friend of his, to use his generating and lighting system in the Fox River Valley. The New York plant began successful operation on September 4, the Appleton plant on September 30, 1882. The one in Appleton, however, was different: It was run by waterpower instead of steam. Here was the world's first hydroelectric central station.

At the start one residence and two paper mills in Appleton were wired for lighting. The *Appleton Post* reported that "the lamps produced a beautiful soft white light absolutely steady and constant, and equal in intensity or exceeding, if desired, the illuminating power of a gas jet of the best quality. The electric light is perfectly safe and convenient, and is destined to be the great illuminating agent of the near future." [7] But the lights were little used between dawn and dusk; the Appleton Edison Electric Company needed a daytime demand for electricity. It found one in the electric streetcar. Experiments had been made with such cars in a few cities in 1885, but the first permanent line was installed in Appleton (and another in Mobile, Alabama) in 1886.

As time passed, electricity provided more and more of the power that turned the wheels of industry, in Wisconsin as in other states, but the large-scale production of hydroelectric power had to wait till after the successful harnessing of Niagara Falls in 1896. In the early 1900s, fairly big dams and dynamos appeared on the Wisconsin River at the Dells and near Prairie du Sac. By 1934 more than four hundred dams in the state were converting waterpower into electric power. Still, they accounted for only a third of the state's electricity; the larger part of it was generated by coal-fired steam plants. Even in Wisconsin, stream

7. *Appleton Post,* October 5, 1882, quoted in G. W. Van Derzee, "Pioneering the Electrical Age," *Wisconsin Magazine of History,* 41 (Spring 1958):211.

flow was not steady enough to be depended upon for a year-round electricity supply. By 1968, less than a tenth of the state's supply came from hydroelectric generators. The rest was soon being derived not only from fossil fuel but also from nuclear fission. In 1973, three nuclear power plants were under construction or already functioning in the state.

By that time, Wisconsinites had been repeatedly disappointed in their hopes of industrial benefits from the improvement of transportation. An early disappointment was the projected Fox-Wisconsin waterway. This, together with the Welland Canal and other improvements, was expected to give the state's farmers and manufacturers access to the markets of the world. As a birthday gift to the new state, the federal government had bestowed upon it a grant of land for financing the work. The state transferred the land to a private corporation, which constructed dams, locks, and channels on the lower Fox and a canal at the portage between the upper Fox and the Wisconsin, but failed to complete the desired through route for large vessels all the way from Lake Michigan to the Mississippi River.

Already railroad construction was drawing attention away from the Fox-Wisconsin project. Farmers, even more than manufacturers, expected to benefit from the extension of rails to and through the state. Indeed, the farmers were so eager that they gladly mortgaged their farms and exchanged the mortgages for railroad stock. The mortgages were passed on to eastern investors as security for the railroad bonds they bought. When the companies went bankrupt in consequence of mismanagement and the panic of 1857, the eastern bondholders took them over and threatened to foreclose. Several thousand Wisconsin farmers were in danger of losing their farms. To protect the farm mortgagers, the state legislature enacted a series of stay laws. Sooner or later, the state supreme court threw these out, but not soon enough to keep Wisconsin from getting a bad name as a repudiating state. Eastern capitalists became less willing than ever to lend to Wisconsin enterprisers, and the state's industries suffered from an even worse capital scarcity than usual.

The spread of railroads caused Wisconsin to lose the locational advantage its early boosters had counted on. There was little to gain from being situated on a great potential inland water route after water transport had begun to be superseded by rail. By water, Milwaukee had been ninety miles closer to eastern markets than Chicago; by rail it was ninety miles farther away. Once Chicago had become the nation's great rail center, Wisconsin was off the beaten path.

At the end of the Civil War, two railroad companies dominated shipping across the state—the Chicago and North Western and the Chicago, Milwaukee, and St. Paul. The two co-operated in setting rates, and the rates were generally high. To break the railroad monopoly, Governor Lucius Fairchild and other Wisconsinites revived the idea of a Fox-Wisconsin waterway and appealed to Congress for funds. Year after year, Congress included the project in its annual rivers-and-harbors bill, but the money just seemed to disappear in the mud and sand of the Fox and the Wisconsin. Meanwhile reformers turned to the state legislature for a law to control railroad rates, and Wisconsin along with some of its neighbors became noted for the presumably rigorous and agrarian "granger laws" of 1874. Actually, the Wisconsin measure was ineffective and it was soon repealed.

Rate fixing by the federal government was no more effective when the Interstate Commerce Commission was first set up, in 1887. When the ICC acquired real powers a couple of decades later, it did not use them for the benefit of Wisconsin industry. As of 1940 the commission-set freight rates from Wisconsin points to New York were 5 to 15 percent higher than those from equally distant Illinois points to New York. The charge for shipments to Liverpool was $1.60 per hundred pounds from Wisconsin, 94 cents from New Orleans. "The State derives little advantage as a gateway to the West, for manufacturers find it cheaper to ship to the Pacific Coast via New York and Panama, or, if rail is to be used, to freight through favored Chicago," a Wisconsin economist pointed out. "This is perhaps the greatest single handicap to further industrial development in Wisconsin." [8]

Something had to be done about it, and Wisconsin boosters again preoccupied themselves with an old, old dream, the dream of an improved water route that would make Wisconsin, in effect, a coastal state. The St. Lawrence Seaway—this was the up-to-date version of the project. Such a seaway would enable ocean-going ships to ply the Great Lakes. By means of it, Wisconsin could get around its transportation obstacles and thus could maintain and enlarge existing industries and attract new ones. After the Second World War the governments of the United States and Canada began construction of the seaway as a co-operative undertaking. The city of Milwaukee installed the very finest dock facilities in preparation for its metamorphosis into an ocean port.

"Already the St. Lawrence River-Great Lakes route permits 16 foreign lines to pick up choice Wisconsin items and distribute them to markets all over the world, from Liverpool to Bremen, from Istanbul to Rio de Janeiro," an editor of the *National Geographic* wrote in 1957. "When the billion-dollar seaway and power project is completed in 1959, ships of 25 foot draft, rather than 14, will be able to move through the deepened channels." [9] Then, the writer predicted, the cargoes would rise to several times their existing tonnage.

Once again, Wisconsinites were doomed to disillusionment. After the completed seaway had been in use for a decade, the *Wall Street Journal* summed up its fortunes in a headline: "St. Lawrence Seaway, Completing 10th Year, is Awash in Problems: Its Traffic is Off, Debt is Up And It is Getting Obsolete; Some Ships Curtail Runs." [10] During the next decade the seaway continued to have difficulties as ships were discouraged by

8. Writers' Project, Works Progress Administration, *Wisconsin: A Guide to the Badger State* (New York: Duell, Sloan and Pearce, 1941), p. 76.

9. Beverley M. Bowie, "Wisconsin, Land of the Good Life," *National Geographic Magazine,* 111 (February 1957):144.

10. Quoted in Robert C. Nesbit, *Wisconsin: A History* (Madison: University of Wisconsin Press, 1973), p. 503.

the shortness of the navigation season (only eight months), the expense of the tolls, and the length and inconvenience of the lake voyage. In the 1970s, only a small proportion of the goods manufactured in the Milwaukee area was being shipped from the Milwaukee port.

Wisconsin's industry had been receiving little stimulus from the federal government's defense spending, the Wisconsin share being microscopic in comparison with that of such favored states as California, Texas, and Washington. Nevertheless, Wisconsin in 1970 ranked eleventh in the value of its manufactures, though only sixteenth in the size of its population. A study in 1975 predicted that in the decades ahead the industries of Wisconsin—except for dairying and food processing—would grow less rapidly than those of the rest of the country. But Wisconsinites had no need to resign themselves to an industrial decline. In the past they had achieved industrial successes in spite of economic handicaps, and they had done so largely through their ingenuity and enterprise. In the future they could do the same.

3

Circumstances favored Wisconsin as a lumbering state. It was the right place at the right time. Before 1848, when most pioneers were making homes in heavily forested country, they had little occasion to buy lumber; they simply cut what they needed from their own trees. Now that they were emerging to settle the prairies and plains, however, they were beginning to exert a seemingly insatiable demand for the products of the sawmill. In the states to the east—New York, Pennsylvania, Michigan—the more accessible pine forests were rapidly yielding to the ax and the saw. Wisconsin was next.

It was as if God had designed this area for the lumberman. Here, in the northern two-thirds of the new state, mixed in varying degrees of concentration with hardwoods, were some of the finest stands of white pine ever to be found anywhere in the world. The supply seemed as limitless as the demand. And here were watercourses cunningly arranged for carrying logs to sawmills and lumber to market. The St. Croix, Chippewa, Black, and Wisconsin rivers led to the Mississippi; the Wolf, to Lake Winnebago; and the Oconto, Peshtigo, and Menominee, to Green Bay and Lake Michigan.

The early lumbermen were interested only in the pine. It was in demand, being easy to work and resistant to rot. Besides, it could be floated down the streams; the oak or maple or beech would sink. Most of the Wisconsin lumbermen came from the pineries of the eastern states or the Maritime Provinces and brought their practiced techniques with them. Steadily they increased their output. By 1870, Wisconsin had reached fourth place among the lumbering states. During the 1890s it kept ahead of all others in the production of white pine. Lumbering, instead of flour milling, was now Wisconsin's most important manufacturing industry as judged by the value of the annual product.

At first, logging was a seasonal activity. Every fall the red-shirted lumberjacks gathered in camps to prepare for the winter's work. Some were experienced woodsmen who had learned the trade in the east and who stayed at it year after year. Others were farmers or farm laborers, many of them newly arrived immigrants, who had free time and needed money. For most of these men, one winter in the north woods was enough. The pay was hardly worth the long hours, the monotonous routine, the back-breaking exertion. The crews had to chop the trees, trim the fallen timber, cut the logs into suitable lengths, load them on ox sleds, drive these over runways of ice or packed snow to a stream bank, and pile the logs on the edge of the frozen stream.

In the spring, with the thawing and the flooding, the log drive got under way. Downriver went the logs, to be caught and stored in booms, or reservoirs, which were enclosed by strings of timbers. The drive might be held up by a log jam, especially in times of low water. One of the worst jams occurred in 1869, when a boom above Chippewa Falls broke and let go such a rush of logs that they could not clear the rapids. With the passage obstructed, other logs were caught. Finally the accumulation rose, in places, as high as thirty feet, and it backed up for fifteen miles.

At a boom the logs were sorted in accordance with log marks—very similar to cattle brands—indicating ownership. The logs might go to mills in the immediate vicinity, or they might be consigned to mills farther downstream. In the latter case they would usually make the rest of the trip in the form of rafts. Those heading down the Mississippi would (after 1865) be combined into larger rafts on reaching that river and would be towed the rest of the way by steamboat.

Sawmills appeared along all the state's logging rivers, but sawmilling came to be most heavily concentrated in Chippewa Falls, Eau Claire, La Crosse, Oshkosh, and Fond du Lac. Other mills taking Wisconsin logs were located along the Mississippi River in the states of Minnesota, Iowa, Illinois, and Missouri. In the early days the Wisconsin mills produced mainly rough lumber. The output per mill increased with improvements in machinery. Steam engines, becoming larger and more powerful, used sawdust for fuel. In the late 1860s, mill men on the Chippewa River developed a steam-powered system for carrying the sawdust automatically from the saws to the boiler. The gang saw, with several blades moving up and down together in a frame, sliced a log into several boards at once. Circular saws were fast, but cut a wide and wasteful kerf; in the 1880s they began to be replaced by band saws.

From the mills along the rivers emptying into Green Bay, ships carried the rough-sawed lumber to yards in Milwaukee, Racine, and especially Chicago for finishing and marketing. From the mills along the tributaries of the Mississippi, the lumber floated in rafts, each of them consisting of several cribs and each of these consisting of twelve to twenty layers of boards. On the Mississippi the lumber rafts—like the log rafts—were combined to form larger ones, and these, too, were towed by steamboats. The combinations of floating lumber grew bigger and bigger until, by the 1870s, a single one of them might cover as much as three or four acres.

Rafting lumber was hazardous work, as was driving logs.

Raftsmen risked both the lumber and their lives. Especially dangerous was the Wisconsin River with its sinuosities, its shifting sands, its rapids, and its narrows. The worst stretch of all was the Little Bull Rapids at Mosinee, where for half a mile the water plunged and swirled through a rocky gorge only thirty feet wide. Here a raft was completely submerged and, at times, so was the crew. Dams added to the peril. A dam on a driving or rafting stream was required by law to have a chute over which logs or rafts could slide. The chances of a raft's going over intact were so slim in some places that people waited below to salvage and sell, for a living, the boards that scattered from broken cribs. Not content with the unavoidable hazards of their occupation, drivers and raftsmen willingly ran unnecessary risks for sport. One game was to stand on a log and ride it through a chute.

Log drivers and log raftsmen, loggers, timberland owners selling timber, sawmillers along the Mississippi who bought the logs—all had an interest in seeing that log driving and rafting were facilitated on such rivers as the Chippewa. Sawmillers upriver on the Chippewa itself had no such interest. In 1866 those of Chippewa Falls and Eau Claire bought land at Beef Slough and secured from the legislature a charter giving them exclusive rights there. Beef Slough was one of the channels at the Chippewa's mouth; it was the only good place to sort logs and prepare them for rafting to the downriver mills. The object in getting control of the channel was not to use it but to prevent others from using it.

The upshot was the Beef Slough war. Some Mississippi River mill owners organized the Beef Slough Manufacturing, Booming, Log Driving & Transportation Company and started a campaign to get a charter that would give them the right to construct and operate a boom at the slough. They succeeded by means of legislative trickery. The Chippewa River mill owners and their employees then armed themselves and threatened to fight, thus discouraging the company from going ahead with its plans. When the company fell into bankruptcy, the Chippewa forces appeared to have won the war. The real victory, however, was eventually to go to the Mississippi River lumbermen, who in 1870 leased the Beef Slough company's rights and set up a new firm, the Mississippi River Logging Company, to exploit them.

The railroads began to change the lumber industry when, in the 1870s and 1880s, they penetrated the north woods. Thereafter log driving and rafting declined slowly, and lumber rafting much faster. Logging became a year-round activity, and loggers got at stands of pine that had survived because of distance from logging streams. Lumbermen increasingly removed the hardwoods in addition to the pine. And Wisconsin mills and factories turned out larger and larger quantities of finished lumber and wood products, shipping them to market by rail.

It was high time for Wisconsin to elaborate its lumber manufacturing. "We should continually bear in mind," the *Oshkosh Journal* had urged in 1869, ". . . that the greater the quantity of skilled human labor which is added to a given quantity of raw material, the greater will be the wealth of the people." Eventually the pine would disappear, the editor argued. Then sawmill centers, even such a growing and prospering one as Oshkosh, would "be taking the back track" unless new industries were developed. There should be factories to work up the hardwoods still left in the forest.[11]

Already there was some sophisticated woodworking in Oshkosh and other mill towns. As early as 1851 the Wisconsin exhibit at the Crystal Palace Exposition in London had featured a machine for shaping and grooving staves for tubs or barrels. With this machine, the invention of a Milwaukeean, seven men could make four hundred tubs in a single ten-hour working day. In 1852 a storekeeper from Rhode Island bought a tub and pail factory in Menasha. Soon he was employing seventy-five workers, and eventually his business was to become the largest of its kind in the United States.

By the 1880s, Oshkosh had risen to be the country's biggest

---

11. *Oshkosh Journal,* November 6, 1869, quoted in Richard N. Current, *Pine Logs and Politics: A Life of Philetus Sawyer, 1816–1900* (Madison: State Historical Society of Wisconsin, 1950), p. 119.

manufacturer of every one of the following: doors, window sashes, blinds, matches, wagons, carriages. It also produced trunks, other luggage, and furniture. The state's furniture industry, however, was being concentrated mainly in the Lake Michigan port towns. From Kenosha, during the 1890s, came Simmons wooden (later steel) beds; from Port Washington, McLean patent swing rockers; from Sheboygan, kitchen chairs—six thousand of them a day. Fond du Lac was famous for its iceboxes. These and other cities were making Wisconsin one of the foremost furniture-producing states. Its planed lumber, millwork, woodenware, and other wood manufactures were bringing in more money than were its logs and rough lumber. Most of its woodworking industries, however, could not long survive its lumber industry, and the great forest was going fast.

Lumbermen saw no reason to conserve the forest. Waste, to them, meant leaving timber uncut. "We have no right to waste this rich material," Joseph G. Thorp of Eau Claire told the National Lumbermen's Association in 1876, ". . . by adopting a policy of indifference, or by failing to use all the means available to so manufacture and use it as to accomplish the greatest good to the greatest number." [12] So far from asking the federal government for conservation, the speaker was demanding that the government speed up deforestation by providing better facilities for the lumber business.

The federal government did assist the lumbermen in their pursuit of profit. It sold timberland cheap, and it spent money on river and harbor improvements. The state government also helped. It conferred special favors in acts of incorporation, acts that gave lumber companies practically the rights of eminent domain within specified areas. Thus the state government encouraged the formation of monopolies, and neither it nor the federal government did anything effective to restrain them.

No wonder Wisconsin lumbering became a big business.

12. *Eau Claire Free Press,* September 28, 1876, quoted in Robert F. Fries, *Empire in Pine: The Story of Lumbering in Wisconsin, 1830–1900* (Madison: State Historical Society of Wisconsin, 1951), p. 227.

WISCONSIN

A photographer's essay by Don Getsug

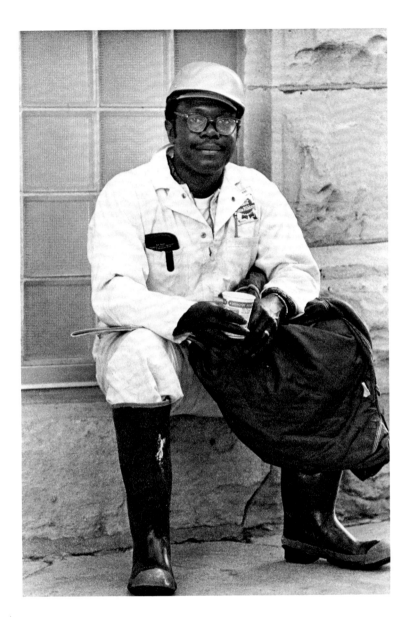

Photographs in Sequence

House near La Crosse.
Horses near La Crosse.
Farm buildings near La Crosse.
Brewery worker, Milwaukee.
Welder, Star Prairie.
Main Street, Dennison.
Cafe, Dennison.
Farm near Dodgeville.
House at La Crosse.
Strong's Bank, Dodgeville.
First Wisconsin Building, Milwaukee.
Lobby of Pfister House Hotel, Milwaukee.
Milwaukee Art Center.
Children in Martin Luther King Park, Milwaukee.
Route 90 near La Crosse.

Knapp, Stout and Company of Menomonie was said to be, even in the early 1870s, the largest lumber corporation in the world. It was highly integrated. It not only operated sawmills but also owned pine lands, cut and rafted logs, maintained wholesale and retail lumberyards, sold general merchandise to lumberjacks, and ran farms and flour mills to provide food for the men and feed for the animals. But the Weyerhaeuser syndicate, which emerged in 1880, functioned on a much vaster scale than did Knapp, Stout and Company. Frederick Weyerhaeuser, born in Germany, had gone into the lumber business in Rock Island, Illinois. He headed the group of down-river mill men who in 1870 formed the Mississippi River Logging Company and got control of Beef Slough. After a ten-year struggle with the Chippewa Valley mill men, he brought them to terms and ended the Beef Slough war. The two groups combined and, together, monopolized the lumbering in the area.

As the forest disappeared, the fortunes of the successful lumbermen grew. By 1900, when he died, Philetus Sawyer of Oshkosh had accumulated four or five million dollars. Forty-four years earlier he had come to Wisconsin from New York state with his life savings of $2,200. He had little education, but it was not true, as some wit said, that he always signed his name "P. Sawyer" because he could not spell "Philetus." After becoming wealthy he liked to surprise his daughters on their birthdays with $25,000 checks under their dinner plates. Isaac Stephenson of Marinette, who had arrived from Maine in 1845, was reputedly worth more by 1900—twenty-five or thirty million.

Younger lumbermen had been hedging against the disappearance of timber in Wisconsin by acquiring forested land in the southeast and the northwest. In the early 1900s, Weyerhaeuser moved his operations to Minnesota and on beyond the Rocky Mountains. The Weyerhaeuser company, once the mammoth of the Midwest, was to be a far bigger giant on the Pacific Coast. Lumbering in Wisconsin did not cease entirely. It was to continue, with the aid of tree farming, but the annual cut was to be only a fraction of what it had been at its peak in 1892.

The lumber bonanza was over for Wisconsin. Once-booming sawmill towns had to find new occupations. Memories remained of sawdust cities where the whine of saws slicing into pine was continually heard, where sawdust and slabs accumulated in huge piles and were used to fill bogs and pave streets, where the smell of fresh pine constantly filled the air.

Stories of the long-gone logging camps were told and re-told—stories of Paul Bunyan, who tied a rope to his ax handle, whirled the ax around his head, and cut down forty acres of pine with every stroke; stories of Babe, Paul's blue ox, the tips of whose horns were so far apart that lumberjacks strung clothes-lines from one tip to the other and hung out their clothes to dry. Apparently few if any of the Paul Bunyan tales originated with the actual lumberjacks. Most were the creations of an imagina-tive advertising man and other comparatively recent authors of instant folklore. It is an authenticated fact, however, that Paul Bunyan was buried in Wisconsin. The grave is near Wausau. Obviously, Paul was a fairly large man, for the dirt on his grave made a pretty high pile. It formed Rib Mountain.

4

Lumbering and woodworking prepared the way for other in-dustries, which rose to prominence as the earlier ones declined. The connection between wood and wax was quite direct. In the 1880s a parquet-flooring salesman, Samuel Curtis Johnson, bought the business and began to manufacture the flooring in Racine. To enable his customers to preserve their fine floors, Johnson went into the production of floor wax as a sideline. Before long he was selling more polish than parquet. Eventually S. C. Johnson & Son, Inc., was supplying the world with wax and related products not only from the Racine plant but also from branches in Canada, England, France, Brazil, and Austra-lia.

The transition from lumbering to papermaking seems natural if not inevitable, though in fact there was a lag. The relation between woodworking and the manufacture of aluminum ware is much less obvious, but it nevertheless exists.

The first paper mills in Wisconsin did not depend on the forest; they used rags rather than wood pulp for raw material. Not till after the Civil War did the pulp process come to the United States from Germany, where it had been developed a quarter of a century earlier. In 1872 Wisconsin's first pulp-using mill went into operation in the Fox River Valley. Here was an abundance of water both for powering the mill and for processing the paper, and not far away was plenty of hemlock, balsam, and spruce, trees that previously had been neglected or wasted but now could be utilized for making pulp. Within a decade, twenty companies were operating mills in Neenah, Menasha, Kaukauna, and Appleton, and two thousand men were working in the mills. Papermaking had already become the leading business along the Fox River.

In that part of the state the new industry was a successor to flour milling rather than lumbering. John A. Kimberly had been a lumberman and Charles B. Clark a hardware dealer, but Kimberly had also been a flour miller, and so had almost every other early Fox River paper entrepreneur. As the nation's wheat-growing and flour-milling centers moved westward, the Fox River millers looked for a promising enterprise to which to transfer their accumulated capital. The manufacture of paper seemed the best bet.

Later, as the choice pine timber began to grow scarce, some lumbermen hedged against its ultimate disappearance by investing a part of their profits in pulp or paper plants. The industry now developed in the Wisconsin River Valley, whence it spread over much of the northernmost reaches of the state. Before long, more than sixty mills and six thousand workers had been added to Wisconsin's paper industry. Some of the companies failed and others were combined. By 1910, only fifty-seven mills remained in operation, but these were so large and productive that they put Wisconsin in third place among all the states manufacturing wood pulp and paper.

Some Wisconsin mills still used the original method of making pulp, a rather simple grinding process. Others employed more recent chemical processes, either the sulfite or the sulfate. These made possible the more complete utilization of wood of various kinds. The sulfate process also flavored the breeze with a stench that, when the wind was right (or wrong), told the stranger he was approaching a papermaking town. Most of the Wisconsin paper was of rather coarse varieties, and half of it consisted of newsprint, forty-two carloads a day, which fed the daily presses of much of the Midwest.

In 1911 the state's thriving pulp-and-paper industry faced a crisis when Congress approved a trade agreement that would have allowed the duty-free importation of cheap Canadian newsprint. Few mills in Wisconsin could have competed with those in Canada. The emergency passed when the Canadians themselves turned down the agreement, but a long-range threat of destructive competition remained. For the Wisconsin mills were losing their competitive advantage as their nearby sources of low-cost pulpwood disappeared. It looked as if pulp- and papermaking might go the way of flour milling and lumbering in Wisconsin.

The state's paper industry saved itself through ingenuity. Its chemists and engineers turned from the concentration on kraft paper and newsprint to the development of an amazing variety of paper specialties. And "light weight papers, tissue papers, glazed papers, glassine papers, serum-resisting papers, machine marked papers, parafilm, toilet tissues, absorbent wadding, crepe wadding and insulatings all arose in their time like Arabian jinni [sic] from the fumes of the Wisconsin test tube." [13] The Kimberly-Clark Company, one of the nation's largest paper manufacturers, contributed a household word as well as a household convenience in Kleenex.

To encourage further research, leaders of the Wisconsin industry arranged in 1929 for the founding of the Institute of Paper Chemistry as an adjunct to Lawrence College in Apple-

13. Bowman, *Why Wisconsin,* p. 167.

ton. The institute accepted its first students in 1930. It received financial support not only from companies in Wisconsin but also from others throughout the country. Its staff and students promptly began to contribute to paper technology, discovering, for example, means by which even the previously worthless aspen could be used in making paper.

Between 1910 and 1929 the papermakers of Wisconsin doubled the number of people they employed and tripled the quantity of pulpwood they consumed. They had to look farther and farther afield for wood and pulp—to Michigan, Minnesota, Oregon, Washington, Canada, and finally Sweden and Finland. From distant places they also brought in other locally unavailable raw materials, such as sulphur, lime, rosin, salt, and a special kind of clay. Papermaking became Wisconsin's second largest industry, and Wisconsin became the second largest papermaking state.

Even more spectacular, though on a smaller scale, was the rise, during the same period, of Wisconsin's aluminum-cookware industry. In 1910 the state's manufacturers accounted for less than 5 percent of the nationwide sale of aluminum pots and pans. By the 1920s they were producing more than 50 percent. That is, Wisconsin was responsible for more of the product than all the rest of the states together. Wisconsin was to lose its majority share of the market during the Great Depression but was to recover it after the Second World War.

The growth of aluminum manufactures in Wisconsin could hardly have been predicted. After all, the state had, and has, never yielded so much as a pound of bauxite. The manufacturers had to buy their aluminum from a distance and at a monopoly price, and they had to sell their finished product in a comparatively remote market. In the beginning they had no pool of skilled labor to draw upon. Yet they succeeded in winning national pre-eminence.

All the Wisconsin producers were located within an eighty-mile strip near the eastern edge of the state, a strip extending from Kewaunee, Two Rivers, and Manitowoc in the north to Kewaskum and West Bend in the south. The development of the industry in this particular area, though unpredictable, was not entirely accidental. Once covered by a thick pine and hardwood forest, the area had supported sawmills, tanneries, sash-and-door factories, and other offshoots of lumbering. As the timber receded, the people looked for new businesses to provide employment. They found one in aluminum manufacturing.

The Wisconsin aluminum story begins in Two Rivers. There, in 1872, Joseph Koenig, an immigrant youth from Germany, took a job in a woodworking plant. Koenig soon left, to spend twenty years in one state after another while he made a living as a painter, lawyer, factory manager, land speculator, and school-teacher. In 1893 he acted as legal representative for a German firm that exhibited aluminum novelties at the Chicago world's fair. Afterwards he bought the exhibit and sold all the items at a very profitable markup. He decided to manufacture more of them.

While casting about for funds and facilities, Koenig went back to Two Rivers to visit relatives. In Two Rivers he happened to meet James E. Hamilton, a prominent local business-man, the manufacturer of wooden type (for printing posters) and various kinds of specialized furniture. Hamilton offered him the free use of a bit of factory space, with the privilege of taking power from an overhead shaft. Here, for nearly two years, Koenig developed machines for mass-producing aluminum novelties, such as combs, key fobs, cigar cases, salt and pepper shakers, and ash trays. Then, in 1895, Koenig and Hamilton joined to form the Aluminum Manufacturing Company. To it the city of Two Rivers contributed $2,000 to keep it in town as an employer. Soon the company was selling $125,000 worth of novelties a year.

Wisconsin firms making aluminum articles multiplied by a kind of cell-division process. Employees of Koenig left him to found new companies, and men associated with these broke away to start still others. By 1907 Koenig's most serious competitors were the Manitowoc Aluminum Novelty Company and a New Jersey company with a similar name. In the wake of the panic of 1907, to stop the ruinous competition among its largest customers, the Aluminum Company of America (Alcoa) brought about a merger of the three novelty manufacturing firms and the formation of what was to become the Mirro Aluminum Company.

At that time the novelty manufacturers took much the greater part of the output of aluminum, which was still a comparatively unfamiliar metal and a very expensive one. For some years an Alcoa-owned firm had been making aluminum cookware and selling it—at a much higher price than iron or copper utensils— by means of a house-to-house campaign, with home demonstrations. As late as 1914, however, cookware absorbed only a third of the aluminum supply. The First World War temporarily reduced the supply while permanently increasing the demand, as all kinds of new uses for the metal were discovered. Afterwards a smaller proportion of the total output but a larger and larger absolute amount was used in the production of kitchenware.

A Wisconsin company had begun to specialize in such ware in 1908, when one of Koenig's foremen, Adolph Kummerow, went into business on his own. "He manufactures exclusively aluminum baking pans and cooking utensils," the *Two Rivers Chronicle* optimistically reported, "and the special adaptability of this metal for this purpose ensures the success of his enterprise." [14] But Kummerow had to depend on imported aluminum, and when the war came, he could no longer get it. He now had no choice but to sell out to the Mirro combine.

Kummerow's brother-in-law and business associate Herman Wentorf decided to start a new, competing firm. Two of Wentorf's brothers left Mirro to join him. With the aid of a youthful wizard of finance, B. C. Ziegler, the Wentorf brothers founded the West Bend Aluminum Company. At first the company had only a small plant, with a draw press for stamping out various

---

14. *Two Rivers Chronicle,* July 7, 1908, quoted in James M. Rock, "A Growth Industry: The Wisconsin Aluminum Cookware Industry, 1893–1920," *Wisconsin Magazine of History,* 55 (Winter 1971–1972):95.

kinds of utensils and with a half-dozen or so employees. The factory grew fast as sales boomed, the Sears Roebuck mail-order house accounting for nearly half of the sales.

At the end of the war, only West Bend and Mirro were manufacturing aluminum cookware in Wisconsin, and Mirro was responsible for more than 80 percent of the state's product. Then in 1919, five other Wisconsin companies went into the business, three of them successfully. Two shifted over from the manufacture of novelties, one of the two to produce exclusively for the F. W. Woolworth stores. The third successful firm converted to aluminum manufacturing from grain malting, the wartime food-control act having stopped the production of beer and thus ended the brewers' demand for malt.

A twofold theme runs through the story of the rise of Wisconsin's aluminum-cookware industry. German names keep appearing; they reflect the dominant role that German immigrants played. And evidences of technological skill and business acumen stand out; they show that the industry's success was a triumph of inventiveness and entrepreneurship.

5

The human factor seems decisive also in the rise of what became, in the aggregate, Wisconsin's largest industry: the fabrication of iron and steel and the manufacture of machinery. Certainly Wisconsin had no advantage in the production of the metal itself, since most of it (and eventually all of it) was both mined and smelted outside the state.

Foundries and machine shops appeared quite early in the state's history, an example being Kleinsteuber's Milwaukee shop in which Sholes had his first typewriter models put together. As far back as the 1850s these establishments were making stoves, boilers, miscellaneous castings, mill gears, steam engines—practically everything from kettles to locomotives. A century later the factories of Wisconsin were turning out an even more diversified array of metal and mechanical products, including tools and other hardware, plumbing equipment and supplies, farm implements, gasoline engines, electric motors and generators, turbines, pumps, hoists, ore crushers, concrete mixers, refrigerators, automobiles, motorcycles, tractors, and precision instruments. Wisconsinites could boast of having built the world's largest mine hoist; seventy-seven of the 107 steam shovels that dug the Panama Canal; the three largest American-made diesel engines, for use on the canal; outboard motors, flashlights, batteries, radio equipment, and marine engines for Donald B. MacMillan's 1924 Arctic expedition; machinery for the construction of Boulder Dam; and the first automatic assembly line, for manufacturing automobile frames.

Originally the immediate demand for machinery came from the exploitation of Wisconsin's own natural resources—from lead and zinc mining, wheat growing, flour milling, and lumbering. Encouraging Wisconsin foundrymen to supply this demand was the cost of transporting heavy machines from the older, more highly industrialized states. The transportation cost had much the same effect as a protective tariff would have had. Also favoring the local enterprisers was the abundance of hardwood, an essential material in the construction of much of the machinery. Once they had got their businesses well established, some of the machine makers were able to survive and expand even after the original advantages had ceased to exist.

Wisconsin inventors and manufacturers contributed significantly to the mechanization of the American farm. The wheat harvest, requiring as it did a sudden increase in manpower, gave an urgency to the invention and production of labor-saving devices. Among Wisconsinites who responded to the need were George Esterly, Hiram Moore, and John F. Appleby, all three of old Yankee stock.

While farming near Janesville, George Esterly in 1844 began to devise a succession of new or improved horse-drawn machines: a harvester, a mowing machine, a reaper, a sulky cultivator, and a seeder. From 1858 to 1892 he manufactured mowers and other implements in his own Whitewater plant.

While living in Michigan, Hiram Moore had designed, built, patented, and put into use a contrivance that sixteen horses pulled to harvest and thresh a grain field in a single operation—the world's first combine. After moving to Wisconsin and settling in Green Lake County he made improved models, which he used on his own and his neighbors' farms. For efficient combining, the fields needed to be planted in such a way that the wheat would grow and ripen uniformly. So Moore developed and in 1860 and 1861 patented a "force feed" grain drill. It planted in straight rows and at an even depth.

While working as a youth on his stepfather's Iowa County farm, John F. Appleby experimented with a knotting device for binding grain. As a Civil War soldier he invented a breech-loading, repeating "needle gun," which the Union government turned down but the Prussian army adopted and employed with great effect. After the war he set up, in Mazomanie, the Appleby Reaper Works and manufactured implements while he resumed his knotting experiments. Finally, in Beloit in the late 1870s, he perfected the twine binder.

Appleby in Mazomanie and Esterly in Whitewater were only two of many enterprisers who, in towns large and small throughout Wisconsin, manufactured farm implements during the early years of statehood. Even the tiny village of Delton (now Lake Delton) was once noted for its fanning mill—a machine which, mounted on and powered by a moving wagon, separated the chaff from the grain. Most of the businesses, as a result of improvements in transportation, sooner or later succumbed to the competition of larger and more efficient manufacturers. One that more than held its own, one that eventually became the largest of its kind in the world, was the J. I. Case Company of Racine.

Jerome Increase Case got his start by bringing with him from New York state six threshing machines (which he had bought on credit), selling five of them, and using the sixth to thresh for Wisconsin wheat growers. He purchased patent rights and made improvements of his own, developing a "sweep" model (powered by horses moving in a circle) and a "tread" model (powered by horses on a treadmill). As early as 1850 he was manufacturing one hundred machines a year in what was said to be the "largest establishment of its kind in the West." By 1857, after adding a foundry and a machine shop, he could advertise: "Every article connected with the threshing machine is made on the premises." [15] Meanwhile he found customers in Indiana, Illinois, and Iowa as well as Wisconsin. Through all these states he traveled in person to demonstrate machines, make repairs, and collect debts from buyers to whom he had extended credit.

By the 1870s the Case company had begun to substitute steam power for horsepower. At first the engines were stationary, then self-propelled though horse-guided, and finally self-steering. These steam tractors could pull plows and other implements as well as activate threshers. Improvements were constantly made. In 1898 the rear axle was placed behind the boiler rather than under it, so as to overcome the machine's tendency to rear up when pulling hard. One model represented a dubious improvement; it was a twenty-three-ton behemoth intended for hauling ore from mines, logs from lumber camps, and other heavy loads over rough terrain.

By the early 1900s the Case company could proclaim: "There is not a spot in the civilized world where grain is grown that is not touched or can[not] be quickly reached by the departments of our organization." [16] The company had sixty-three branches in twenty-nine states, Puerto Rico, Canada, Mexico, and South America. It had ten thousand dealers in the United States alone. It sent out circulars it printed on its own presses, which had a capacity of fifty thousand a day, and it advertised widely through the *American Thresherman* of Madison, Wisconsin, and through other farm journals. It demonstrated its traction engines at state and county fairs, running them up a 45-degree slope and stopping and starting again to show they would not tip over backward. And it gave a fancy nickel-plated model to a circus

15. *Wisconsin Farmer,* February 1, 1850, and J. I. Case handbill advertisement, Racine, April 25, 1857, both quoted in Reynold M. Wik, "J. I. Case: Some Experiences of an Early Wisconsin Industrialist," *Wisconsin Magazine of History,* 35 (Autumn 1951):5–6.

16. Reynold M. Wik, *Steam Power on the American Farm* (Philadelphia: University of Pennsylvania Press, 1953), p. 155.

on the condition that the machine be used conspicuously in the circus parades.

Case's engineering and advertising paid. After 1900 the company took the lead in the manufacture of steam traction engines as well as threshing machines. These threshers it now made exclusively of steel. Sales of the engines peaked shortly before the First World War, and sales of the threshers shortly after it. The market for both disappeared during the 1920s, as gasoline tractors and modern combines began to take over. Case was prepared for the transition. The company was already producing gasoline tractors and a variety of other machines, including automobiles.

A number of Wisconsin firms began with agricultural machines and supplemented or superseded them with other products. One was the Eclipse Windmill Company of Beloit. It was set up to manufacture the 1867 invention of Leonard H. Wheeler, a Massachusetts-born Congregational missionary who since 1841 had been teaching Wisconsin's Chippewa Indians how to farm. Soon Eclipse windmills were drawing water from wells all over the prairies and the plains. Charles H. Morse thought it worth while to buy an interest in Eclipse; his Fairbanks, Morse & Company was a Vermont-based manufacturer and worldwide merchandiser of scales. Fairbanks Morse became the general sales agent for the windmill. Eventually the Vermont firm got control of both the windmill factory and a Beloit engine works. It combined the two to form the nucleus of what was to become its largest manufacturing unit. Another example of a departure from the farm-implement business is the Kohler Company, one of the world's greatest producers of plumbing fixtures. This company traces its origins to Austrian-born John Kohler, who in Sheboygan in the 1880s turned from making plows to making enameled cast-iron washbasins and bathtubs.

The biggest of the giants among Wisconsin machinery manufacturers got its start by equipping flour and grist mills. Established in Milwaukee in 1847, the Reliance Works branched out from the making of millstones to the manufacture of milling machinery and shipped its products as far as California. Indeed, the firm overexpanded, and it went broke after the panic of 1857. Here was an opportunity for Edward P. Allis, a graduate of Union College, Schenectady, New York, who after graduation had come to Wisconsin intending to go into law but instead had gone into the leather business and had dabbled in real estate, grain, and railroads. In 1860 he borrowed money and bought the Reliance Works at a sheriff's sale.

Edward P. Allis and Company immediately grew and prospered as a result of the entrepreneur's (and sole owner's) combination of shrewdness and daring, his readiness to take on new products, his talent for finding able engineers—and his good luck. His business profited from the Civil War boom. Afterward he acquired the Bay State Iron Manufacturing Company and began to manufacture sawmill machinery, including the newly invented band saw. He built a pipe foundry and, underbidding eastern firms, provided the pipe as well as the pumps for the Milwaukee waterworks. Then, after the next financial panic struck, in 1873, his luck took a turn. He was forced into bankruptcy in the midst of the ensuing depression.

Losing none of his buoyancy, Allis managed not only to hold on to the firm but also to expand its operations. In the very year of his bankruptcy, 1876, he hired a Scottish-Canadian millwright, who set to work designing new roller-mill machinery and enabled the company to construct the "New Process" flour mill for C. C. Washburn in Minneapolis. Also in 1876 the Centennial Exposition in Philadelphia featured, among other mechanical marvels, the gigantic Corliss steam engine that Edwin Reynolds had helped to perfect in Providence, Rhode Island. The next year Reynolds accepted Allis's invitation to become his general superintendent, and for thirty-two years after that he made improvements in the Reynolds-Corliss heavy, low-speed engine and in all kinds of mining machinery. The Allis company was already world-famous for such equipment when, in 1889, Allis died. The firm became a corporation in 1890; this was merged with manufacturers of heavy machinery in Chicago and Scranton to form the Allis-Chalmers Company in 1901. Allis-Chalmers was operating a busy complex of factories covering ninety-seven acres under roof in West Allis, a suburb of Milwaukee, on the day in the 1950s when the *National Geographic* editor visited there. Some fifteen thousand workers were

> . . . making everything from light tractors to a 300,000-kilowatt steam turbine–generator unit. In the cavernous foundry, fires flickered from casting ladles, and molten metal pouring in a bright arc from the cupolas gave off showers of fiery particles like Fourth of July sparklers. A 2,500-ton hydraulic press in the forge shop smashed down on a great white-hot ingot. At a smaller steel hammer, a man making axle shafts pounded a white-hot lump of steel into a monstrous collar button and then—to impress a passing girl—picked up a piece of discarded trim in his tongs and lit his cigarette with it.[17]

Wisconsinites pioneered in the development of automobiles as well as heavy machines and farm implements. As early as 1873 a Methodist clergyman and physician of Racine, John W. Carhart, drove his own invention, a light, steam-powered buggy, over the city streets.

Inspired by what the appropriately named Dr. Carhart had done, the legislature in 1875 made the Wisconsin government the first anywhere to subsidize the automobile. The legislature did so by sponsoring the first automobile race, hoping thus to encourage the search for a "cheap and practical substitute for the use of the horse and other animals on the highway and farm." [18] The prize was to be $10,000. The winner would have to cover the two hundred miles from Green Bay to Madison at an average speed of at least five miles an hour. At starting time the next summer only two entries, both steam powered, were on hand. One, a seven-ton monster, foundered soon after starting out. The other made it to Madison in a week, averaging better than six miles an hour while on the road. Still, the legislators

---

17. Bowie, "Land of the Good Life," p. 144.
18. Quoted in Harold L. Plummer, "The State Highway Commission of Wisconsin," *Wisconsin Magazine of History,* 37 (Winter 1953–54):75.

were not sure they had found a replacement for the horse or even the ox. They awarded only $5,000 to the winner.

Wisconsin scored other firsts in automobile history. In the early 1900s Otto Zachow and William Besserdich produced in Clintonville the first successful four-wheel-drive vehicle. Arthur P. Warner invented the speedometer in Beloit. Clarence A. Shaler, brought up on a farm in Green Lake County, devised a tire-patching kit that enabled motorists, in the early days when flats were frequent, to fix their own. The state (in 1918) set an example for the rest of the country by numbering its highways. And the A. O. Smith Corporation in Milwaukee, to mass-produce car frames, created the automatic assembly line.

Arthur Oliver Smith, Wisconsin-born, had begun by manu-facturing bicycle frames; he added automobile frames in 1903. Upon his death ten years later, his son Lloyd R. Smith took charge of the company. The younger Smith, like other indus-trialists, was impressed by Henry Ford's arrangement for assem-bling cars in his Detroit factory, with lines of workers adding components as the work moved past them. Smith was also fa-miliar with time-and-motion studies, which aimed, in the inter-est of "scientific management," to reduce the workers' move-ments as nearly as possible to mechanical efficiency. It occurred to Smith, in 1916, to take the next logical step, that is, to sub-stitute machines for men on an assembly line.

Four years later, Smith's transformed car-frame plant was ready. In it, one machine inspected and straightened strips of steel as they came in. Other machines cut, punched, and shaped the strips as these went by on conveyors. Still other machines clamped together the appropriate pieces and guided them past "rows of automatic riveters with enormous jaws like the heads of mythical birds." [19] The process took an hour and a half from the arrival of a strip of steel to the storage of a completed, cleaned, and painted automobile frame. One was added to the

19. Siegfried Giedion, *Mechanization Takes Command* (New York: Oxford Univer-sity Press, 1948), p. 121.

pile every ten seconds. A million or more could be made in a year. All together, fifty million had been produced by 1955. And that was only a part of the output of the A. O. Smith Corporation, which also manufactured a great diversity of other products, from glass-lined tanks and silos to oil-well casings and large steel pipe for oil and gas lines.

Though by no means the first or the largest, Wisconsin became one of the leaders among the car-manufacturing states. Dozens of makes came from Wisconsin at one time or another. Among those that were nationally familiar during the 1920s were the Case, the Mitchell, the Vixen, the Kissel, the Nash, and the FWD, a four-wheel-drive truck, a make that had given much service in France during the First World War.

The Kissel Kar was a classic. From the beginning, in Hartford in 1906, the German-born Louis Kissel and his son George insisted on custom-made quality. They had a feeling for style and a boldness in innovation. One of their cars won a road race from Los Angeles to Phoenix in 1910. They introduced a detachable top in 1922. Their sport model, the Gold Bug, was, in the later, nostalgic judgment of *Road and Track* magazine, the "niftiest, raciest, and classiest American production car ever to hit the highways." [20] But Louis and George Kissel could no longer compete with mass production when the crunch of the Great Depression came, and they went out of business in the 1930s.

The Nash did not appear until 1917, but its predecessor, the Rambler, goes back to 1900. In that year the Chicago bicycle manufacturer Thomas B. Jeffery, who had been born in England, moved to Kenosha, bought a bicycle factory there, and began with his son to convert it into an automobile plant. Two years later they turned out their first cars, fifteen hundred of them, which qualified the Jefferys as mass producers for that time. After the father's death the son sold the plant to Charles W. Nash, formerly the president of Buick and of General Mo-

---

20. Quoted in "Wisconsin Played a Pioneer Role in Development of Automobiles," *Wisconsin Then and Now*, 21 (March 1975):5.

tors, who had quit both organizations over policy differences. Nash now had a free hand with what he renamed the Nash Motor Company, and he made it an instant success. He set up branch plants in Milwaukee, Racine, and Pine Bluff, Arkansas. By 1926 the Nash, though not a low-priced car, was a large seller, the seventh largest among all the numerous makes then on the market. In 1954, six years after Nash's death, the company was in difficulties, and to strengthen itself it merged with the Hudson firm, of Detroit, to form American Motors. More than twenty years later, still producing cars in Kenosha, American Motors was Wisconsin's largest employer.

5

Circuses and Such

I N your hotel room you find a copy of the Bible, the King James version, placed there for you to read. You find it not only in the United States but also in eighty-nine other countries, or any of them you may have a chance to travel in. Glancing at a recent copy, you learn it is one of more than a hundred million that the Gideons International, an association of Christian business and professional men, have distributed to hotels, motels, hospitals, prisons, schools, and other institutions. You may be led to wonder how and where the Gideons got their start.

The place—you guessed it—was in Wisconsin. It was, to be precise, Room 19 on the second floor of the Central House in the village of Boscobel. The time was the night of September 14, 1898. Sharing the double room (the hotel being full) were a traveling salesman from Janesville and another from Beloit. One of them took a Bible from his valise to read his nightly chapter before retiring. They fell to talking of the scriptural solace that lonely, God-fearing travelers needed. Maybe there should be some kind of organization. To make plans for it, the two met the next spring in the Janesville Y.M.C.A. building, where a salesman from Wild Rose joined them. He suggested naming the society after the Old Testament hero Gideon.

Wisconsin, the home of the Gideons, was also the home of a great many others whose mission it was to enlighten or at least to lighten the people of America and the world. Consider the variety and virtuosity in a partial list: More circuses than originated in any other state, and the greatest of all, the "Greatest Show on Earth." A professional football team unique in the annals of American sport. The country's once most widely read and beloved poetess—or poetaster. One of the founders of naturalism in American literature. The most influential American historian who ever lived. And a world-famous architect, the most creative of his time.

1

No sooner was the state itself born than it began to give birth to circuses. In the late 1840s Ed and Jerry Mabie of Brewster, New York, brought their Grand Olympic Arena and United States Circus to a farm they had purchased near Delavan for their winter quarters. Summer after summer they traveled with their wagons, tents, wild animals, and performers, while the business grew and prospered. As it did, several of the Mabies' employees—a bareback rider, an animal trainer, and others— broke away one by one to start shows of their own. They kept their headquarters in the same area, and the village of Delavan was transformed into an important circus center.

To Delavan came performers and promoters from other parts of the country. One of them was the trim and neatly bearded William Cameron Coup, a Hoosier who had made his way from roustabout to manager of a sideshow. Another was Dan Costello, an old-time Irish-American clown. Coup and Costello joined to organize a circus that toured out of Delavan for several seasons. Aspiring to something grander, they paid a visit one day to Phineas T. Barnum, who was resting on his laurels as the world's greatest showman, a reputation he had gained chiefly through exhibiting such curiosities as the midget Tom Thumb in his New York museum. The two lesser showmen from Wisconsin persuaded Barnum to emerge from his semiretirement and do something he had never done before—sponsor a traveling tent show. Theirs!

With Barnum's advice and financial aid, Coup and Costello

took their modest outfit from Delavan and converted it into the P. T. Barnum Circus, the most imposing yet. When it opened in Brooklyn, New York, on April 10, 1871, its promoters boasted that it had a larger tent and a larger number of men and women, horses, and wild animals than any before it in Europe or America. Going on the road, the new show traveled the first season like older ones, by horse and wagon (some of the older ones went by river or lake boat). For the next season, however, Coup readied a string of special railroad cars, and the Barnum Circus set another precedent when it made its annual tour by train. By the 1880s James A. Bailey instead of Coup was running the business, it was known as Barnum & Bailey, and its posters described it as the "Greatest Show on Earth."

The departure of Coup and Costello had been a loss to the circus colony of Delavan, and an even greater loss occurred when the colony's founders, the Mabie brothers, sold out to an up-and-coming Philadelphia circus owner, Adam Forepaugh, who later was to sell out to Barnum & Bailey. While Delavan declined as Wisconsin's circus capital, a number of other Wisconsin communities rose to the status of at least one-circus towns, among them Portage, Beaver Dam, Watertown, Janesville, Burlington, Evansville, Whitewater, and Wonewoc. None of these came close to matching Delavan as it had been at its height, and not even Delavan had ever known anything like the glory that was to fall upon Wisconsin's greatest circus city— Baraboo.

A harness maker, who had left Germany as August Ruengeling, arrived in Baraboo in 1855 as August Ringling. He opened a harness shop but had bad luck with it, so with his wife and three small sons he moved on to McGregor, Iowa, in 1860. After a dozen years there, he recrossed the Mississippi River and took a job in a carriage factory in Prairie du Chien. By 1876 he was back in Baraboo with another shop of his own. His fortune had not grown much, but his family had. It now consisted of seven sons, the oldest twenty-four, and a daughter just two years of age.

Al (Albrecht) Ringling, the oldest, had had the circus in his blood for several years, ever since the day in 1870 when a circus showboat docked at McGregor. He and four of his brothers watched the parade and the performance; he was inspired to rig up an amateur circus that also paraded and performed for the local citizenry. After the family's return to Wisconsin, Al pursued his interest by working summers in a shop in Brodhead and traveling winters as a juggler and ropewalker with a professional troupe. His specialty was an act that apparently no one else ever attempted: He would take a plow by the handles, swing it point-upward above his head, lower it until the rod between the handles was centered on his chin, and then balance it there. He had dexterity as well as a huge body and a powerful physique.

In 1882, having rejoined the family in Baraboo, Al, now thirty, organized his own variety show, the Carnival of Fun. He and the four brothers nearest him in age doubled as singers, dancers, comedians, acrobats, and band musicians. During the winter they made their way from one small-town stop to another in Wisconsin, Iowa, Dakota Territory, and Minnesota. The next winter they went out again. Though they got snowed in and had other troubles, they cleared enough from the two tours that they could do what Al long had wanted them to do. They could start a circus, a real circus.

The sky over Baraboo was a bright blue that afternoon, May 19, 1884, when the Yankee Robinson and Ringling Bros. Circus and Caravan gave its first show, on the grounds in front of the Sauk County jail. Yankee Robinson was the retired owner of a very well known circus; the Ringlings had hired him in the hope of gaining instant recognition through the use of his name. In reality, their new enterprise could not remotely compare with his old one, to say nothing of the great and growing Barnum & Bailey. The Ringlings themselves—with all their hired hands and other performers, including Al's wife, Louise, the snake charmer—numbered only twenty-one. Their tent accommodated no more than six hundred. Still, it was filled twice on that opening day, and the spectators seemed enthusiastic enough.

After the evening performance the weary troupe loaded ten

rented farm wagons and, after midnight, rode out of Baraboo. The caravan, with a lantern swinging under the rear of each wagon to light the way for the next one, wound its way up the steep sandy road over the Baraboo Hills. At dawn the dozing travelers reached Sauk City, where two more performances awaited them that day. Ahead the same week lay Black Earth, Mt. Horeb, Mt. Vernon, and New Glarus. The show was on the road.

Plowing their summer's profit back into the business, the Ringlings offered a bigger and better spectacle the next spring when they opened again in Baraboo. Ringling Brothers' Great Double Shows: Circus Caravan and Trained Animal Exposition they now called it, old Yankee Robinson having died. They had not only the "Most Gigantic and Tremendous Aggregation of Acrobatic Equestrians, Performing Feats of Breathless Wonder," as the advance posters proclaimed, but also the beginnings of a menagerie in a single mangy beast, a "Hideous Hyena—Striata Gigantium." When, after another successful season, the Ringlings left Baraboo for their third circus tour, the *Baraboo Republic* commented: "The boys are on the road to fortune." [1]

So they were. Year after year they enlarged their tent and put it up in more distant and more populous cities, undeterred by the hazards of rain and mud and, still worse, the threat of rival circus men who tore down posters and tried to disrupt performances. The Ringlings kept adding wagons, animals, performers, acts. After six years they were able to convert their circus into a railroad show, leaving Baraboo on May 2, 1890, in a train of eighteen cars. Compared to several other railroad shows of the time, theirs was still small, with only one ring, but it was growing faster than ever. In a year it expanded into a three-ring circus, and the year after that it got to the Atlantic coast, at Norfolk, Virginia, for the first time. It was now, in name, the Ringling Brothers' World's Greatest Shows, and it was well on the way to becoming the greatest in fact.

---

1. Quotations from Alvin F. Harlow, *The Ringlings: Wizards of the Circus* (New York: Julian Messner, Inc., 1951), p. 114.

By 1895 it was too big to open in Baraboo. Instead, it opened in Chicago, for a three-week stand, and then played in St. Louis, Boston, and other major cities. By 1901 it was ranging throughout North America, from Boston to San Diego, from Montreal to Yazoo City. It no longer had an equal or even a serious rival except for Barnum & Bailey. Barnum was already dead, and Bailey died in 1906. Bailey's widow, hard pressed financially by the panic of 1907, sold the Barnum & Bailey Circus to the Ringlings for a mere $410,000, and the brothers operated it in 1908. "Its profits in that one season were greater than the price they had paid for it." [2] They continued for the next decade to run Barnum & Bailey as a separate show, with its winter quarters in Bridgeport, Connecticut.

The winter quarters of Ringling Brothers remained in Baraboo, even though the Ringlings' circus no longer played there. Another circus also was based in the town—the small wagon show of the Ringlings' cousins the Gollmar brothers—and this one opened locally each spring. The Gollmars' operation meant something to the life of the little city, but the Ringlings' meant much more. Theirs was a big operation. Along the Baraboo River they had extensive brick barns to shelter the animals (dozens of menagerie creatures, including the first baby elephant ever born to a captive mother, and a thousand horses). Outside, huge piles of manure accumulated, to attract countless sparrows and flies. Besides the animal barns, the Ringlings had a building for the storage of costumes and shops for shoeing horses, forging wagon tires, and repairing railroad cars and other equipment. Quite a few Baraboo residents found jobs with the circus as hostlers, roustabouts, ticket sellers, bookkeepers, even performers. Boys enjoyed the privilege of hanging around the quarters and, possibly, turning a hand now and then—without pay. In addition to the circus establishment itself, there was the ancillary business of the Moeller brothers, who built the parade wagons, ornate and colorful, for the Ringlings.

For years the Ringlings themselves had lived modestly in

2. Henry Ringling North and Alden Hatch, *The Circus Kings: Our Ringling Family Story* (Garden City, N.Y.: Doubleday & Co., Inc., 1960), p. 126.

Baraboo while they saved their earnings and reinvested them in the circus. By the early 1900s they felt free to spend, and spend they did. They bought themselves a private railroad car, regal in its appointments. Al had a costly mansion of brownish red stone built near the site of the humble cottage where he and Louise had lived when they were newlyweds. Two of his brothers saw to the construction of houses as large as his but, less pretentiously, of wood. None of the brothers was so devoted to Baraboo as Al was, and John, the next to youngest, frankly disliked the "Baraboobians," as he dubbed them. John and others began to pour money into the confection of palaces in Florida, into the purchase of exotic art objects to fill the palaces, and into speculations in Oklahoma oil lands and other schemes for making yet more money. Al, instead, paid for the erection of a Baraboo opera house, a near-replica of Marie Antoinette's Versailles theater. He intended to donate this exquisite little building to the city, but before he got around to signing the deed of gift he died, on January 1, 1916. His surviving brothers decided not to go through with the gift.

For three more springs the departure of the great circus for its summer tour continued to be an exciting Baraboo event, with the hustle and bustle of getting the show ready and then the spectacle of the long, brightly colored train pulling out. Finally, in 1918, the train left and did not return. Instead, it went for the winter to Bridgeport, Connecticut. It now ceased to be a separate operation; it was merged into the Ringling Brothers and Barnum & Bailey Combined Shows. More than ever, the Ringlings could boast of the "Greatest Show on Earth," with as many as a hundred garishly painted cars going out each year. In 1927 the great circus abandoned Bridgeport and set up its winter quarters in Sarosota, Florida.

For its fiftieth season, on April 8, 1933, the circus opened in New York's Madison Square Garden—a far cry from the Baraboo lot of the first season's opening. In recognition of the show's origin, the Circus Fans of America held their annual meeting in Baraboo, and to climax the program the great circus itself performed there, on August 3, for the first time in almost forty seasons. It was an event such as Baraboo had never seen even in the days when Baraboo was the circus's home. The crowd was so large that people had to look for lodging as far away as Wisconsin Dells, nearly fifteen miles from Baraboo. Circus notables and other notables from all over the country were on hand. None of the Ringling brothers was there; all were dead except John, and he was too ill to attend. But one member of the original troupe was much alive and conspicuously present. That was Louise Ringling, Al's widow, now seventy-eight. She "thoroughly enjoyed every minute of it," she said of her visit to her old hometown.[3]

There was a great past, but not much of a future, for the familiar kind of circus, with its gaudy wagons and noisy calliope parading down Main Street and its vast canvas-covered arena rising like magic in a field on the edge of town. As the "modern" circus became old-fashioned and began to disappear, its past seemed more and more worth preserving—at least to John M. Kelley, who had long served as attorney for the Ringlings. In 1950 Kelley suggested the establishment of a museum, and the logical place for it was Baraboo. The city, its service clubs and other local organizations, and the State Historical Society took up the idea. In 1959 the Circus World Museum held its grand opening. There, on the same site and in some of the very same buildings that once constituted the Ringlings' winter quarters, people summer after summer could gaze at circus memorabilia and watch live circus acts.

2

The circus got its name from the Circus Maximus of ancient Rome. This was a huge stadium in which the Romans, as many as two hundred thousand at a time, watched chariot races, wrestling matches, and other athletic contests. One mid-twentieth-century American equivalent of the ancient Roman circus

3. Gene Plowden, *Those Amazing Ringlings and Their Circus* (Caldwell, Idaho: The Caxton Printers, Ltd., 1967), p. 128–129.

was professional football, and nowhere did it have followers so zealous as those who, autumn after autumn, filled the stadium at Lambeau Field in Green Bay.

Lambeau—that, to the early fans, was the great name in the history of the locality. True, in 1634 Jean Nicolet had arrived as the discoverer, and in 1745 Augustin de Langlade had founded the settlement with his trading post. But in 1919 Earl Louis Lambeau had organized the football team.

Curly Lambeau, son of a Belgian-born Green Bay building contractor, had played briefly for Knute Rockne at Notre Dame. Home again, working for the Indian Packing Company, he got together a group of players and persuaded his employer to pay for uniforms. With Lambeau as both coach and star player, the new Green Bay Packers proceeded to demolish their first ten opponents, running up a total score of 565 to 6 against such powers as Marinette, Sheboygan, Racine, and Oshkosh in Wisconsin and Menominee and Ishpeming in Michigan. The Packers were ready to claim a championship of some kind when, in the final game of the season, they lost 0–6 to the Beloit Fairbanks Morse team (the Fairies). For his season's efforts, each of the Packers got $16.75 as his share of what had been collected when the hat was passed at home games, the local field being as yet unfenced.

After another good season as an independent, the Green Bay team in 1921 joined the year-old association that in 1922 became the National Football League. The packing company put up the $50 that Lambeau needed to buy the league franchise, but he had to pay most of the expenses out of his own pocket. Even though he was now selling tickets for home games, he soon ran up a $2,000 debt. A group of five local businessmen bailed him out. Then in 1923, to give the team a financial cushion, they formed a corporation and sold a thousand shares of stock at $5 a share to Green Bay citizens. The team was now a community enterprise.

On the gridiron the Packers for a time fully justified their hometown support. They had a winning season during each of their first eight years in the National Football League and then, in 1929, 1930, and 1931, won three league championships in a row.

But disaster struck in 1933. The team, for the first time, lost more games than it won. A spectator fell from the Green Bay bleachers and sued. And the Great Depression lay heavily on professional football as on everything else. Other small-town teams in the league—there had been several of them—failed to survive the depression. In 1933 the only one of them that remained, besides Green Bay, was Portsmouth, Ohio. Though good enough to beat Green Bay in their final encounter, Portsmouth was unable to return to the league the following year. The citizens' corporation supporting the Packers went bankrupt, but again the Green Bay businessmen came to the rescue, reorganizing the company and selling more stock.

There followed another period of success and then another crisis. The Lambeau-led Packers were champions in 1936, 1939, and 1944, and they had no losing season from 1934 through 1947. But they won only three games in 1948 and only two in 1949, finishing last in the league. As a coach (he had not been a player since 1929), Lambeau faced insoluble problems. He was a master of the single-wing attack, but that was being replaced by the T-formation, and he never got used to the T. With his small budget, he could no longer sign up the best new players as their salaries soared in response to the competitive bidding of the newly organized All-America Conference. But the Packer board of directors blamed Lambeau, interfered with his conduct of the team, and forced him to resign.

Meanwhile the directors once more reorganized and refinanced the club, raising more than $100,000 from 1,698 purchasers of stock in a new corporation, Green Bay Packers, Inc. The investors expected no monetary return; they explicitly agreed that no dividends should be paid and that, if the corporation should ever be dissolved, its assets should go to the local American Legion post. All that the stockholders wanted was a winning football team.

This the directors were not able to produce for some time. During the 1950s they kept on trying to run the team by com-

mittee, and a succession of frustrated coaches accumulated a
much larger total of defeats than Lambeau had ever suffered in a
period of the same length.

Yet the fans remained faithful, even fanatical (as, of course,
real fans always should). An amazed sportswriter from out of
the state reported after visiting Green Bay: "Nearly 50,000
wild-eyed maniacs make up its population today and they know
more about football than any other 50,000 people on the face of
the earth." Followers of big-city teams, teams that at home
played to near-empty stands, would "get a tremendous thrill by
traveling to this picturesque town in upper Wisconsin on a zero
day, when snowbanks line[d] the Packers' field waist deep."
They would find a "sell-out crowd rooting their heroes"—"one
of the most heartwarming pictures in the world of American
sports." [4] The taxpayers of Green Bay in effect granted a subsidy to the Packer club when, in 1957, they voted to build a
million-dollar stadium to replace the rickety wooden stands that
had served since 1925. The team itself now had a new look,
having shed its original colors, gold and blue, and put on the
more appropriate gold and green. What would be the enthusiasm of the fans if only the team should have a winning season!

Instead, in 1958, the Packers had their worst season ever,
scoring only a single victory. Even the corporation's executive
committee realized, at last, that committee rule must give way
to strong, unified control. The executives looked for salvation to
a Brooklyn meatcutter's son, Vincent Thomas Lombardi. Then
forty-five and a New York Giants' assistant, Lombardi had had
experience playing at Fordham University, where he was one of
the legendary linemen, the "Seven Blocks of Granite," and
coaching at a high school and at Fordham and West Point. Except at the high school, he had never been a head coach. Now
the Packer executives made him both head coach and general
manager, and they gave him a free hand.

Lombardi more than vindicated their trust. He proceeded to
revitalize the team by means of his driving spirit, strict dis-

---

4. Roger Treat, *The Encyclopedia of Football: The Official Encyclopedia of the National Football League* rev. ed. (New York: A. S. Barnes & Co., 1959), pp. 1, 4.

cipline, and close attention to details. One of his relentlessly driven players said: "He treats us all alike—like dogs." [5] Testified another, who had done poorly before but was transformed into one of the Packers' most brilliant stars: "Lombardi has given me confidence in myself." [6] Lombardi himself believed: "Football is not a subtle game. It is two things: blocking and tackling. The winner is the team which blocks and tackles best." [7] And winning to him was not the main thing; it was the only thing. In 1959, his first year at Green Bay, with essentially the same players as the losers of the previous season, he produced a winning team, with a 7–5 record.

That was only a beginning. During the nine years 1959–1967 the Lombardi-coached Packers won 141 games, lost thirty-nine, and tied four, for a .783 average. Five times they were champions of the National Football League. In 1967 they met the champions of the rival American Football League in the first "super bowl" game, in the Los Angeles Coliseum. There they beat the Kansas City Chiefs by a score of 35–10, while an estimated sixty-five million television viewers looked on—the largest number that had ever watched a sporting event. The next year, in the second super bowl, in Miami, the Packers defeated the Oakland Raiders, 33–14.

The Packers' fame cast a refulgence on the city of Green Bay, the heart of "football country." The location in turn reflected additional glory upon the team. Green Bay, even with its population approaching ninety thousand, was still tiny in comparison with Kansas City or Oakland, to say nothing of Chicago, the home of the Bears, the Packers' oldest and most bitter rivals. So it seemed to be David against Goliath, and the Packers were sentimental favorites with many viewers throughout the country—even though the Packers drew fans from the

5. Harold B. Meyers, "That Profitable Nonprofit in Green Bay," *Fortune,* 78 (November 1968):142.

6. Paul Hornung, as quoted in Dick Schaap, "The Rough Road Ahead for Paul Hornung," *Pro, Pro, Pro: Stories of Pro Football's Greatest Stars,* edited by John Lowell Pratt (New York: Franklin Watts, Inc., 1963), p. 144.

7. Tex Maule, *The Official Picture History of the National Football League* (New York: Random House, 1963), pp. 120–121.

entire state and regularly played three of their seven "home" games in Milwaukee.

After a half-century of professional football, the distinctions of Green Bay (both the town and the team) were impressive. This, the smallest city in the sport, was also the oldest: It had continuously fielded a team longer than any other. The team was the only one whose ownership was widely distributed among the residents of the community it represented. And it was the all-time champion, the holder of the largest number of first-place trophies.

With success came prosperity for Green Bay Packers, Inc. Its league franchise, which Curly Lambeau originally had bought for $50, could now have been sold for $8,000,000 or more. The nonprofit corporation was making a considerable profit, chiefly from the sale of television rights. Its net income rose from $37,300 in 1958 to $1,514,000 before taxes and $827,000 after taxes in 1966 (the taxes were federal, not state). The company gave some of its annual receipts to charities, but of course it paid no dividends to the stockholders. It put its yearly surpluses into a reserve fund—against the possible return of hard times.

The prospects might become bleak if Lombardi should depart. "I think I'll always be loyal to Green Bay," he was quoted as saying, "but I don't have to be here to be loyal." The Packers would stay on in any case. "But, without Lombardi," concluded one student of the situation, "neither Green Bay nor the team could ever be quite the same again." [8] In 1969 Lombardi left, and the Packers soon began to lose more games than they won.

Oh, well, the Packers had gone through long losing spells before.

3

Ehrich Weiss, a rabbi's son from Hungary, a resident of Milwaukee and of Appleton, started out as a circus trapeze art-

8. The quotation of Lombardi and the succeeding quotation, expressing Meyers' own point of view, are both from Meyers, "Profitable Nonprofit," p. 195.

ist, took up magic, and, as the great Harry Houdini, amazed theater audiences throughout the world with his ability to escape from locked trunks and from confinement of practically any kind. Natives of Wisconsin—Fred Bickel (Fredric March), Spencer Tracy, Agnes Moorhead, Alfred Lunt, and many others—went out to gain fame as performers on the stage or screen. But perhaps the state's most distinctive contributions to popular entertainment and popular culture (aside from the contributions of its circuses and its professional football team) came from its song writers, its newspaper humorists, its outstanding cartoonist, and its beloved mistress of sentimental verse.

At least a thousand published songs were written by Joseph P. Webster, a Boston-trained concert singer who, after losing his singing voice, moved in 1859 to Wisconsin and, in Elkhorn, devoted himself to composition. His were both the words and the music of "Lorena," which he intended for the Union soldiers but which the Confederates adopted and adapted—and which was to form a recurring theme in the movie *Gone with the Wind*. He also composed the tune for a hymn that became a favorite, "In the Sweet Bye and Bye."

Far more successful than Webster, if not also more prolific, was Charles K. Harris, a native of Poughkeepsie, New York, who arrived in Wisconsin as a youth of fourteen in 1879. Several years later Harris was operating, in Milwaukee, his own music-composing and music-publishing shop. He manufactured songs to order for confirmations, engagements, weddings, funerals, and any and all occasions, working out the melodies on a banjo; he could neither read nor write music. From attending Milwaukee's most interesting social event, the annual brewery workers' masked ball, he got the idea for a sad song about two lovers parting forever as the result of a misunderstood kiss between the girl and another man at the dance (how could her sweetheart have known that the other man was only her brother?). Published in 1892, "After the Ball" was an instantaneous and unprecedented hit. Soon the sheet music was bringing in $25,000 a week, and after twenty years the sales had totaled more than ten million copies. Meanwhile, in the early 1900s, Harris moved his shop from Milwaukee to New York and kept on turning out saleable tunes. He was the real pioneer of tin-pan alley.

Better known than Harris and almost as successful was Carrie Jacobs Bond, a native of Janesville. In the 1890s, an impecunious widow in her thirties with a boy to support, Mrs. Bond tried writing songs for a living. No musical illiterate like Harris, she was a talented and trained pianist. Still, she could not sell her compositions, not even the one she titled "I Love You Truly"—which eventually was to be almost *de rigueur* at weddings. So she moved from Janesville to Chicago and ran a boardinghouse for a while, then borrowed money and herself published a collection of her songs, including "Just A-Wearyin' for You." These sold so well that she wrote more and set up her own publishing firm in Chicago, the Bond Shop. She promoted her sheet music by playing and singing it on concert tours throughout the country. By the time of the First World War she was a wealthy woman and a national figure, and her recent number "The End of a Perfect Day" stood high among the country's best sellers.

Though never on any best-seller list, the most widely and enduringly popular tune ever to be associated with Wisconsin (or with any other state) was the university's "fight song." As of 1909 the university already had a yell, the oldest of all college yells, "U Rah Rah Wis-con-sin," but it had no football march. An aspiring Chicago song writer, William T. Purdy, was planning to enter his composition in a University of Minnesota contest that fall. A Wisconsin undergraduate, a friend of Purdy, persuaded him to change the words from "Minnesota! Minnesota!" to "On, Wisconsin! On, Wisconsin!" In Madison, the university's new football song was an immediate winner, though its football team was not, losing to Minnesota by 6–34. Schools and colleges all over the United States took the melody and set new words to it (at West Junior High School in Colorado Springs the students sang "On, West Junior!"). In 1959, with verbal alterations, it became Wisconsin's official state song. On any football Saturday in the 1970s, many more bands across the country were playing the melody of "On, Wisconsin!" than were playing any other university's tune.

By that time the stories of Wisconsin humorist George W. Peck were long forgotten, but they once had been familiar far beyond the state's borders. Born in New York state, Peck was only three when, in 1843, his parents brought him to Wisconsin Territory. At fifteen, as a printer's devil, he began his journalistic career, which took him from paper to paper and from town to town until, in the 1870s, he was publishing his own weekly, *Peck's Sun,* in La Crosse and then in Milwaukee. He brightened the *Sun* with witty comments and funny fiction, most notably a serial about Hennery, a mischievous lad who played tricks on his father, like putting cod-liver oil in the syrup pitcher. *Peck's Bad Boy and His Pa* (1882) led off a series of widely read volumes in which the Hennery stories were collected. A master of the political as well as the comical art, Peck served two terms (1891–1895) as governor. Also something of a political philosopher, he once remarked: "When the affairs of taxation are adjusted so that all will pay taxes with a smile instead of a frown, an ideal state will exist." [9]

Bill Nye, with a somewhat more sophisticated humor, reached an even wider audience than Peck. Not quite two when, in 1852, he came from Maine to Wisconsin with his parents, Edgar Wilson Nye grew up on a farm near River Falls. At twenty-six he went west to Wyoming Territory. There he founded a newspaper, the *Laramie Boomerang,* which again and again struck some target of his satire. At thirty-three, already something of a celebrity with three books of collected pieces to his credit, he was back in Wisconsin, living with his wife and son in a house he had bought in Hudson, contributing to various newspapers and magazines, and lecturing. For several years he toured with the Hoosier wit and poet James Whitcomb Riley as half of a hilarious lyceum (prevaudeville) team. Meanwhile, at thirty-six, he became a denizen of New York City, to write a weekly humorous column for the *New York World.* When the *World* began to syndicate his work and told him he could live where he liked, he made his home in the mountains of North Carolina. There, at forty-five, he died.

9. *Wisconsin Then and Now,* 14 (July 1968):5.

Bill Nye's History of the United States (1894) continued to sell for years, but his newspaper sketches most entitled him to a high rank among the common people's jesters, the lesser Mark Twains, of his time. Much of his humor reflected his Wisconsin experiences. Of the 1884 tornado that touched down in the state and injured him among many others, he wrote: "My brother and I were riding along in the grand old forest, and I had just been singing a few bars from the opera of 'Whoop 'em Up, Lizzie Jane,' when I noticed that the wind was beginning to sough through the trees. Soon after that, I noticed that I was soughing through the trees also. . . ." Once, to get command over a noisy audience at the exclusive Clover Club in Chicago, he told of the time his brother, a "red hot Republican," had tried to address a crowd of Irish Democrats in Erin Prairie, Wisconsin. These people, with their booing and heckling, were about as courteous as the members of the Clover Club. He said:

> But there was one kind-hearted Irishman in the crowd—the man who swept up. When the others had gone and my crestfallen young brother prepared to shake the dust of that inhospitable town from his shoes, the old janitor comfortingly remarked: "Niver mind, Mr. Nye. This aggregation wasn't riprisintitive of Erin Prairie. They was nothing but the rag tag and bob tail of the town, they was. *Ivry man who had a damn bit of sense shtayed to home.*" [10]

The syndication of columns like Bill Nye's—and later of cartoons like Clare Briggs's—owed its origin to another Wisconsinite. During the Civil War the editor of the *Baraboo Republic,* Ansel Nash Kellogg, had been unable to put together a full weekly edition after the enlistment of his hired hands. So Kellogg filled the inside with two pages of ready-printed articles that he bought from the Madison *Wisconsin State Journal.* Soon he was distributing the "patent insides" to other small-town papers in the state. After the war he set up a syndicate in Chicago and began to sell pages of news and advertising to papers throughout the country. The next step was the syndication of

10. Frank Wilson Nye, ed., *Bill Nye: His Own Life Story* (New York: The Century Co., 1926), pp. 126, 258–259.

features through the sale of publishing rights rather than printed matter.

Clare Briggs, once a Reedsburg boy, originated the comic strip in its familiar form as a series of drawings that appear daily and tell a story with a continuing cast and with dialogue in "balloons." The first was Briggs's "A. Piker Clerk," a strip that followed the fortunes and misfortunes of a racetrack tout in his repeated schemes to raise a stake. It ran for part of the year 1904 in William Randolph Hearst's *Chicago American*. Briggs gained his greatest fame and following, however, with the panel cartoons (individual drawings as distinct from strips) that he did for the *New York Herald Tribune* between 1917, when he joined its staff, and 1930, when he died. His widely syndicated cartoons appeared under one or another of several headings, among them "Mr. and Mrs.," "When a Feller Needs a Friend," "The Old Swimming Hole," and "Ain't It a Grand and Glorious Feeling?" These commented with honesty and insight on the little trials and triumphs of ordinary life. "Childhood days are rich in comedy as well as in pathos and sentiment," Briggs once said. "I have tried to recapture some of this. . . ." [11] That old swimming hole was actually back home—in the Baraboo River not far from Reedsburg.

The Wisconsin background was also a key to the remarkable career of Ella Wheeler Wilcox, though in her it inspired little if any nostalgia. Her parents, Sarah Pratt and Marcus Hartwell Wheeler, had made the trek from Vermont to the new state in 1849, a year before her birth. Her father, a violin teacher, struggled in vain to realize the economic promise of the frontier. Her mother, a frustrated author, never reconciled herself to the hard and tedious role of a pioneer housewife. She was determined that her daughter, the first of four children growing up in a humble house on the prairie north of Lake Mendota, should do better than she herself had done. So she eagerly encouraged the talent that Ella began to show while yet a little girl.

11. Clare Briggs, *How to Draw Cartoons* (1926; Garden City, N.Y.: Garden City Publishing Co., 1937), pp. 17–18.

An amazing talent it was. Ella seemed to think, to feel, in rhythm and rhyme; verses flowed from her pen as if of their own accord. After vainly sending off one effusion after another, she finally made a sale—to the *New York Mercury.* She was fourteen. The sale was the first of many to eastern newspapers and magazines. Soon she was contributing heavily to the support of the Wheeler family. When old enough, she enrolled in the university on the other side of the lake, but she quit at the end of the year. She felt ill at ease among the girls in Madison, what with their fashionable clothes and their city ways. Besides, she wanted to write, not to study. She dreamed of an easy life and expensive things and the world's applause.

While yet a teenager she sold, for fifty dollars, a series of rhymed tirades against alcohol to the National Temperance Publishing House in New York, which brought them out as *Drops of Water,* her first book. Her next volume, a collection of miscellaneous verse under the title *Shells,* she dedicated to the People of Wisconsin, from whom she had "received so many words of praise and encouragement," and to whom she was "indebted for so many marks of appreciation." [12] Certainly her early neighbors appreciated her. The Town of Westport boasted that it was not only the location of a former governor's farm: "It is also the home of Miss Ella Wheeler, whose poems are becoming known, for their sweet and tender heart strains, from the Atlantic to the Pacific." [13] She herself was becoming known at least from Milwaukee to La Crosse. Wealthy people of both cities invited her to their literary circles and their homes. "These visits increased my ambitions and my necessities. I saw how other people lived and dressed, and my desire for *money* exceeded my love for art," she was later to admit. "Yet I loved and gloried in my work. It was an ecstasy to me." [14]

12. Ella Wheeler, *Shells* (Milwaukee: Hauser & Storey, 1873), p. 1.

13. *Madison, Dane County, and Surrounding Towns* (Madison: Wm. J. Park & Co., 1877), p. 303.

14. Ella Wheeler Wilcox, "Literary Confessions of a Western Poetess," *Lippincott's Monthly Magazine,* 37 (May 1886):540.

Ecstasy, indeed, could be felt in the rhymes and rhythms of her thirties. Not so much in the stanzas which the *New York Sun* printed early in 1883 and which contained, of all her many thousands of lines, the only two that were to be long remembered:

> *Laugh, and the world laughs with you;*
> *Weep, and you weep alone. . . .*[15]

But later that year a Chicago publisher brought out a book of pieces she had selected from her scattered contributions to magazines, a book to which she herself had given the title *Poems of Passion*. One of the poems raised the question "How does Love speak?" The reply:

> *. . . in the warm*
> *Impassioned tide that sweeps through throbbing veins,*
> *Between the shores of keen delights and pains;*
> *In the embrace where madness melts in bliss,*
> *And in the convulsive rapture of a kiss—*
> *Thus doth Love speak.*[16]

The author was still a virgin, according to the later testimony of the man she married the following year. In any case, the poetess of prohibition had become the poetess of passion.

Some Chicagoans were as shocked as if Miss Wheeler had become a purveyor of pornography, but Milwaukeeans sprang to the defense of Wisconsin's "talented, hard-working, cheerful little song-bird." Her Milwaukee literary friends held a meeting in her honor. The chairman, handing her a $500 award, proclaimed: "Wisconsin is proud of Ella Wheeler, proud of her history, her courage, her talent, and her promising future, and by words of commendation and more substantial aid the Commonwealth has encouraged and will encourage her daughter." [17] She really did not need the money. The morals con-

15. Ella Wheeler, *Poems of Passion* (Chicago: W. B. Conkey Co., 1883), p. 131.

16. Wheeler, *Poems of Passion,* p. 11.

17. Jenny Ballou, *Period Piece: Ella Wheeler Wilcox and Her Times* (Boston: Houghton Mifflin Co., 1940), p. 91.

troversy was selling her book—sixty thousand copies in two years.

Nor did Miss Wheeler longer need the aid or encouragement of her mother state. She was, by now, well launched on her way to wealth and fame. In 1884, after a Milwaukee wedding, she and her bridegroom, the silver salesman Robert Wilcox, left for his home in Connecticut. Her life was only half over, and the most glorious part was yet to come.

The new Mrs. Wilcox could not content herself with mere housewifery. She had to have a public and be in constant communication with it. Eventually she was thrilling to the moods and needs of millions of people, whom she reached regularly through the Hearst newspaper chain and irregularly through magazines and books. One of the first syndicated advisers, she counseled her readers in verse and prose on love, morality, work, and etiquette. She enjoyed luxury, traveled throughout the world, met important and charming people. In 1913 she was presented to the King and Queen of England.

In 1916 she was widowed and in 1919 she died at her Connecticut home. The *Daily Telegraph* in faraway London declared that, if she were not the most universally read poet of the time, she at least possessed "devoted readers almost beyond number, in her own country, here in England, and everywhere." But closer to home the *Brooklyn Eagle* disposed of her immense vogue as due merely to "journalized genius." And the *Philadelphia Inquirer* said: "It will hardly be claimed by her sincerest admirers that Ella Wheeler Wilcox is to be admitted to Parnassus." [18]

4

Though Ella Wheeler Wilcox failed to gain admittance to Parnassus, that mythical home of great poets, several other Wisconsin writers succeeded in achieving some measure of greatness in the field of *belles-lettres*. These writers drew inspi-

18. All three newspapers are quoted in the *Literary Digest* (November 22, 1919):32.

ration from their feeling toward the state, the best of them from a feeling of ambivalence. Whatever their mood of the moment, whatever the mixture of love and hate, Wisconsin was in their blood, and it found its way into their art.

The first and greatest was Hamlin Garland. Even Garland was not to rank among the giants of American literature, but he was to be well remembered for some of his writings—his down-to-earth short stories and his sensitive family chronicles—and even more for his advocacy of a new and true-to-life approach to fiction. If he did not fully realize his naturalistic idea in his own work, at least he helped to prepare the way for others, for the great realistic novelists of the twentieth century. He was a literary pioneer.

He was the son of farming pioneers. Two westering families, the Garlands from Maine and the McClintocks from Maryland, had come together in Wisconsin, at West Salem, and there he was born in 1860. When he was only a few months old, his parents moved several miles farther west to a farm near La Crosse. When he was not quite nine, they pushed on beyond the river and into Iowa. When he was nearly twenty-one, his father started out again in pursuit of the western horizon, taking the weary mother with him to Dakota Territory.

Instead of going along to Dakota, young Garland took the trail back to Wisconsin and then, reversing the route of his ancestors, on back to Boston, the nation's literary capital. He was determined to make himself into a writer. Trying his hand at short stories, he inevitably placed most of them in the Wisconsin setting of his boyhood. "Green's Coulee not far from Onalaska . . . my earliest recollections are of this lovely little valley and its wooded hills which seemed very high and remote to me then," he was to reminisce long afterward. "The birds, flowers, animals, and people of this time and place are the ones I most vividly recall." [19]

After nearly a decade of hard work in Boston and New York,

19. Hamlin Garland, *Prairie Song and Western Story* (1928; Freeport, N.Y.: Books for Libraries Press, 1971), p. xi.

Garland at the age of thirty-three was making his mark in the literary world. He had in print a collection of his published stories, *Main-Travelled Roads* (1891). Fresh and striking tales they were, starkly contrasting the harshness of rural and small-town life in his home country with the gentle beauty of the scenery. Garland was working on a novel, *Rose of Dutcher's Coolly* (to be published in 1895), in which he was to trace the sexual awakening of a country girl, her university experiences in Madison, and her search for a career in the big city of Chicago. He was also assembling some of his essays and lectures to embody his literary creed in a book that he titled *Crumbling Idols* (and that was to come out in 1894). In it he repudiated the "crumbling idols" of past literature, called for a "veritism" dealing honestly with the quotidian realities of life, and pointed to the Midwest as the source and center of the great writing of the future.

As good as his word, in 1893 he located in Chicago, hoping to help make it a new literary capital—and hoping also to re-establish ties with his parents and with his birthplace. By rail it was only eight hours from Chicago to West Salem. There, with profits from his writings, he bought a cottage, and in it he presided over a family reunion that Thanksgiving. For years he had revisited Wisconsin at every opportunity. Now he thought he was home at last and home forever.

The cottage provided a shelter for Garland's mother until her death in 1900 and for his father until Garland brought home his bride, Zulime Taft (sister of the famous Chicago sculptor Lorado Taft), and his father found other quarters in West Salem. In the cottage the first of his two daughters was born. To it he returned summer after summer, to spend several months at a time and rest from his lecture tours, his sight-seeing travels, his conferences with New York publishers.

Visiting Garland in West Salem, a friend once told him he ought to do for Wisconsin what Thomas Hardy had done for Wessex. Instead, Garland after 1900 looked away to the Rocky Mountains and the Great Plains for his scenes, to strong men for his characters, and to heroism and adventure for his themes, with scant regard for his proclaimed principle of veritism. Eventually he turned back again to the people and places of his own earlier life, but he began to see them through a nostalgic haze. There followed *A Son of the Middle Border* (1917), the first of four fine "middle border" volumes in which he recounted three generations of his family's wanderings, from his father's going west as a frontiersman to his own and his daughters' moving east as "back-trailers" to New York and London.

While more and more willing to forgive the Wisconsin of the past, Garland felt increasingly estranged from the Wisconsin of the present. When in 1912 the West Salem cottage burned down, he could not stand to lose his "family altar"; he had it rebuilt. But after his father died in 1914, he decided to make his residence summer as well as winter in New York state. Still, he could not bring himself to sell the cottage, though he told himself it was not really home, for home was only a "realm remembered," a region to which one could return "only on the wings of memory or of dream." He did return to the cottage from time to time, and he felt a "sense or recreancy" for having ever left it and its "ghosts." [20]

In the 1920s Garland kept up with literary fashion when it decreed disgust for all things midwestern. On one of his visits he discovered "ugliness, crudity and monotony" in the lives and houses of his native valley. "Physically lovely and richly productive, its coulees are empty of interest." When, in 1926, the University of Wisconsin gave him an honorary degree, his first, he thought to himself how much more nicely Harvard went about honoring the illustrious sons of Massachusetts. "Alas! . . . my native state is too far away from literary centers and too foreign to the literary traditions of my ancestors." [21] Old, famous, rich, Garland had restored for himself those once-crumbling idols of the past.

---

20. Hamlin Garland, *A Daughter of the Middle Border* (New York: The Macmillan Co., 1921), pp. 404–405, and *Afternoon Neighbors: Further Excerpts from a Literary Log* (New York: The Macmillan Co., 1934), p. 502.

21. Garland, *Afternoon Neighbors,* pp. 128–130, 333.

Garland owed his Wisconsin doctorate largely to his good friend Zona Gale. She was not only the state's outstanding woman writer; she was its outstanding woman, a feminist, pacifist, progressive, and active member of the university board of regents. The Garlands liked to call on her at her pleasant home—on the grassy Wisconsin River bank, with a vista of the Baraboo Hills—in Portage. "It is a drab little city—most unpromising material for the novelist, and yet Zona has found in it a mine of humorous and pathetic fiction," Garland noted in his diary after one of his visits. "She is the one Wisconsin author who remains in the place of her birth." [22]

"Portage, Wisconsin." Lovingly Zona Gale put down the words in a 1928 essay. "Here it is, with its memories, its traditions, and its settings, and not even the people who pass by on its seventeen through trains daily ever note its name." [23] The words "Portage, Wisconsin," stirred her in a way that such words as "Vienna," "Paris," "Pasadena," and "Calcutta" could never do. Yet even she had not always entertained feelings of that kind. She too had been a back-trailer—like so many other talented and successful Wisconsinites, including not only Garland but also Charles K. Harris, Bill Nye, Clare Briggs, and Ella Wheeler Wilcox. Zona Gale, however, had returned to Wisconsin to stay.

She was born in 1874, the only child of parents of old Yankee stock, her father a locomotive engineer. After graduating from the university in Madison, she thought that to achieve her ambition as a writer she must write of things "beautifully romantic—or romantically beautiful." [24] She could not conceive of anything worth writing about in Portage. She must escape. So she took off, first to Milwaukee and then to New York, to work as a newspaper reporter and a free lance. Yet Portage

22. Garland, *Afternoon Neighbors,* pp. 5–6.

23. Zona Gale, *Portage, Wisconsin, and Other Essays* (New York: Alfred A. Knopf, Inc., 1928), p. 5.

24. August Derleth, *Still Small Voice: The Biography of Zona Gale* (New York: D. Appleton-Century Co., 1940), pp. 40–41.

remained with her, and it was the scene of most of the stories and novels that she began to turn out in profusion. It was the Friendship Village of a very popular series of novels, which were serialized in women's magazines and then brought out in book form. The people of Friendship Village were sweet and kind and good.

Then came the First World War and with it a change in Zona Gale's outlook on small-town life. She conscientiously opposed American participation in the war. Even old neighbors began to wonder about her, and many of her fellow citizens had no doubt. Some could not entirely hide the fear and hatred they thought due her as a traitor. For her, much of the sweetness and kindness and goodness of the small town evaporated. In 1920 she published *Miss Lulu Bett,* a rather grim novelette about an old maid who is the victim of a selfish and narrow-minded community. This brought her critical acclaim and, as a play on the New York stage, a Pulitzer prize. She continued to write in the new vein, telling stories sympathetically but with more of a sardonic than a sentimental touch. She was now practicing the veritism that Garland once had preached.

One of her literary friends and fellow war objectors was William Ellery Leonard, a professor of English at the university, a truly accomplished scholar and linguist as well as poet and playwright. A New Jersey native, Leonard was thirty when, in 1906, he arrived in Madison after studying in Germany and earning graduate degrees at Harvard and Columbia. In Madison he was at first self-conscious as an outsider; he felt still less welcome after his wife, a Madisonian, committed suicide, and her relatives and friends—including prominent campus and community figures—blamed him for her death.

Leonard replied to his traducers through a medium that gave him distinctly the upper hand. That medium was poetry. He used more than three thousand lines of it, in perhaps the most unusual and self-revealing sonnet sequence ever to appear—*Two Lives,* which he composed in 1913 but did not publish until 1923. The poem begins with an invocation of Madison, ''The shining City of my manhood's grief,'' predicts for it a future comparable to the past of Florence or Geneva, and hopes that a ''solemn part'' of its fame will arise from ''The things whereof this story is to tell.'' [25] Clearly, the poet was not only defending himself but was also asserting a right to belong and, indeed, expressing a sense of belonging.

Leonard found time to dip into Wisconsin history as well as to delve into ancient and modern literature in several languages. In the drama *Red Bird* he presented a sensitive portrayal of the tragic Winnebago chief who had led a hopeless uprising a century before. Red Bird speaks: ''You say there is one law both for the White Man and for the Indian. But when the Long-Knives come and slay the Indians, they call it a victory; when the Indians come and slay the Long-Knives, they call it a massacre.'' [26]

Though he longed to revisit Europe, Leonard did not have the option of becoming a back-trailer, even temporarily. He was confined by a phobia, one traceable to a childhood trauma but triggered by the more recent emotional shock. He could not even get near a railroad track, to say nothing of getting on a railroad train. This phobia he transmuted into literature in *The Locomotive God* (1927), a unique autobiography of the psyche, comparable only to his own *Two Lives,* to which it was a prose sequel and supplement. For sheer mastery of words, as shown especially in this pair of books, he probably had few if any equals anywhere.

Edna Ferber, born in Michigan, also came to Wisconsin as a stranger, but she remained one for a much shorter time than Leonard. She was ten in 1897 when her parents, after unhappy, anti-Semitic experiences in Ottumwa, Iowa, re-established their variety store in Appleton, then a ''tree-shaded, prosperous, civi-

25. William Ellery Leonard, *Two Lives: A Poem* (1923; New York: The Viking Press, 1933), p. 1.

26. William Ellery Leonard, *Red Bird: A Drama of Wisconsin History in Four Acts* (New York: B. W. Huebsch, Inc., 1923), p. 121.

lized" place of about sixteen thousand. "If Ottumwa had seemed like some foreign provincial town in its narrowness and bigotry," she was much later to recall, "Appleton represented the American small town at its best." [27] Its mayor was a Jew, and it contained some forty Jewish families. Edna was quickly at home in Appleton among Jews and gentiles alike.

When, at seventeen, she graduated from Ryan High School in Appleton, she had to go to work to support her parents, her father having begun to lose his sight. She took a succession of newspaper jobs with the *Appleton Crescent,* the *Milwaukee Journal,* and the *Chicago Tribune.* She was beginning in much the same way as Zona Gale had done, and when she chanced to meet that already well established author, she noted her delicate, birdlike appearance and was a little envious of her fame. Eventually she was to outdo her by far in popular success. *Dawn O'Hara,* by Edna Ferber, was the beginning; published in 1911, it was a romance about a girl reporter in Milwaukee. Other novels followed in rapid succession, the first best-seller in 1925. Several formed the basis for moneymaking movies, and one also for a musical-comedy hit, *Show Boat.* The prospering author back-trailed from Chicago to New York and later to Connecticut. Only her *Come and Get It* again had a Wisconsin locale, the Fox River Valley in the roaring heyday of the lumbermen, but *Cimarron, So Big,* and others embodied bits of observation from a bright-eyed Wisconsin adolescence.

The greatest commercial success was Edna Ferber, but a greater critical success in the 1920s was the boy wonder of Wisconsin letters, Glenway Wescott. Literary critics compared him to F. Scott Fitzgerald and Ernest Hemingway and compared Thomas Wolfe to him. Each of these writers acted as if responding to an updated motto: Go east, young man. Each spent a period of self-imposed exile in Europe. In the case of Wescott and his contemporaries the back-trailer became the expatriate.

27. Edna Ferber, *A Peculiar Treasure* (New York: The Literary Guild, 1939), pp. 57–58.

"I was born in April 1901, on a farm in Wisconsin, near Milwaukee, of restless and long-lived pioneer stock," Wescott said in an autobiographical note, long after cutting off all connection with the state. He also said he was "slightly but inspiringly educated in Wisconsin public schools." [28] He might have added that he was strongly attached to his mother but could not get along with his father and, while in high school, left home to live with relatives. He was never to marry. After two years at the University of Chicago he moved to New York and then, in 1925, to Paris.

At twenty-four, Wescott published his first novel, *The Apple of the Eye;* in it a Wisconsin farm boy confronts a choice between the moral teachings of his parents and the hedonistic principles of his friends. His second, *The Grandmothers,* was the novel of the year in 1927. In it the author seemed to be seeking his own identity through an imaginative reconstruction of his family history. The story's narrator, Alwyn Tower (Wescott himself), admires his Wisconsin pioneer ancestors and is proud to be their heir, an American. Yet Tower also feels their many frustrations and failures. "Whenever he had come back from Chicago to the country he had looked about him with a half willing, almost bitter enthusiasm," he records near the end. "Neither Chicago nor Wisconsin had justified its existence." [29] Plainly, Wescott had not quite got away from Wisconsin; in imagination he was still there.

The next year, in a collection of short stories with an introductory essay, Wescott said *Good-Bye Wisconsin* (1928). In the essay he described his return from Europe for a Christmas visit in the state, the place with "the worst climate in the world." On the "milk-train" he gets attention with his exotic accoutrements, his cigarette lighter, gloves, and black Basque beret.

28. Glenway Wescott, *Images of Truth: Remembrances and Criticism* (New York and Evanston: Harper and Row, 1962), p. 311.

29. Glenway Wescott, *The Grandmothers: A Family Portrait* (New York and London: Harper & Brothers, 1927), pp. 372–373.

He seems to feel himself a prince among peasants. The preciosity of his manners was matched by the preciosity of his style. "How much sweeter to come and go than to stay; that by way of judgment upon Wisconsin." In the stories, Wisconsin was only a symbol for the Midwest, and the Midwest was only "an abstract nowhere." [30]

In his subsequent writings, Wescott looked elsewhere for his materials. But he continued to be haunted by the theme of Odysseus seeking the homeward way, the theme of the popular song "Show Me the Way to Go Home," the theme that formed "a principle question in the very nature of mankind: the way home." [31] Perhaps home for Wescott, as for Garland, was to be found only in a remembered or imagined past.

August Derleth knew where home was. For him it was without question Wisconsin and more particularly Sauk City and the surrounding area. His German ancestors were among the founders of Sauk City, and there he spent his entire life. He devoted much of it to his Sac Prairie Saga, an ambitious attempt to record and interpret, in fiction and poetry, the life of the community from the beginning. He set a high standard for himself: "The serious novelist has a duty to sift the facts of history; he may embroider them, but he may not alter them; he may imagine historical scenes and recreate them in his fiction, but he may not so distort them that they convey to the reader something other than the truth of history." [32] For the series he projected fifty volumes, the first of which appeared in 1937 under the title *Still Is the Summer Night*. He did not have time to complete the saga; he was busy with many other authorial and editorial projects, among them the writing of a biography of Zona Gale and the publication of the works of science-fiction writers. Derleth was prodigiously productive, an "American Balzac."

30. Glenway Wescott, *Good-Bye Wisconsin* (New York and London: Harper & Brothers, 1928), pp. 5, 32, 38–39.

31. Wescott, *Images of Truth,* pp. 8, 10.

32. August Derleth, "On the Use of Local History in Fiction," *Wisconsin Magazine of History,* 41 (Winter 1957–1958), p. 83.

5

Some say that Southerners have been the most history-conscious of Americans, but as good a case or an even better one could be made for Midwesterners, especially Wisconsinites. The argument could be launched with a mention of Wisconsin fictionists like Garland, Wescott, and Derleth. It could be advanced by reference to the public support and widespread influence of the State Historical Society of Wisconsin. And it could be capped with a listing of Wisconsin-bred or Wisconsin-trained historians, of whom the most notable by far was Frederick Jackson Turner.

Wisconsin had its historical society before it had its statehood. The society, in Madison, began as a private organization in 1846. Wisconsin as an American possession did not yet have much of a past, but it was bound to have a glorious future, or so the organizers of the society hoped. They aimed to speed the territory's and then the state's development by using history as advertising. For several years, however, no determined hand took hold, and the society languished.

Its reviver, its real founder, was Lyman Copeland Draper. Since his childhood in western New York he had been fascinated by the exploits of his country's heroes, particularly those heroes who had led the way for settlement beyond the Allegheny Mountains. As a young man he traveled from the Alleghenies to Alabama and Mississippi to call on old settlers, collect or copy any manuscripts they might have, and—as an early practitioner of oral history—question them and take down their reminiscences. He brought a mass of historical material with him when, in 1854, at the age of thirty-nine, he arrived in Madison to accept the new paid position of corresponding secretary, or executive officer, of the historical society.

The society now was beginning to receive a subvention from the legislature. Draper took the lead in reorganizing the institution, maintaining and increasing the state appropriation, obtaining gifts of money or materials from private donors, building up the documentary as well as the manuscript collections, and putting into effect a publishing program. In the size of its holdings the Wisconsin society overtook and passed the older historical societies of most of the eastern states. It provided a model for western states like Minnesota and Iowa. At Draper's retirement in 1886 the society's library contained more than 110,000 volumes, a very impressive number for the time. They dealt with the history of the region, the nation, and the world as well as the state.

Draper was not much of a writer, and he was still less of a theorist. Nevertheless, he helped to prepare the way for the development of a historical theory by making available the historical sources that he did. It was to be known as the "frontier theory," and the essence of it was that the West had somehow accounted for the Americanness of the American people. This was not a wholly new idea. George Catlin, for one, had adumbrated it when, after visiting Wisconsin Territory and neighboring states in the 1830s, he wrote of the Mississippi Valley: "It is here that the true character of the *American* is to be formed. . . ."[33] As late as the 1880s, however, it still remained for someone to bring the hints and suggestions together and make a definite theoretical formulation. That someone was Frederick Jackson Turner.

Turner was born in Portage in 1861, thirteen years before Zona Gale in the same village (and one year after Garland in West Salem, halfway across the state). The place was just emerging from its pioneer past, and reminders of that past were still around, such as the ruins of Fort Winnebago. Frontier ways had not yet disappeared entirely. When Turner was a boy of eight, he saw a desperado hanging by the neck from a tree—the second of two lynchings in town within a single week. As he grew up, he learned history from his father, locally prominent Republican politician, editor and publisher of the *Portage Register,* author of articles and pamphlets on the community's pioneers, and one of the founders of its Old Settlers' Club. Consciously or not, young Turner was finding patterns for American

33. Catlin, *North American Indians,* 2:180–181.

history in his own locality's development. In his conception the United States was to be essentially Columbia County, Wisconsin, writ large.

As an undergraduate at the state university in the 1880s, Turner came under the influence of Professor William F. Allen, a transplanted New Englander who taught his students to use maps, investigate original topics, and view the country's settlement as an extension of European civilization into an American environment. As a graduate, using manuscripts in the Draper collection, Turner wrote his master's thesis on the Wisconsin fur trade, in which he found much more than merely antiquarian interest. "The Indian village became the trading post, the trading post became the city. The trails became our early roads," he concluded. "In a word, the fur trade closed its mission by becoming the pathfinder for agriculture and manufacturing civilization." [34]

At the John Hopkins University, where he went for his doctorate after joining the Wisconsin faculty, Turner reacted both positively and negatively to a wide range of new influences. These came to him through both books and instructors, two of whom were Woodrow Wilson and Herbert Baxter Adams. He agreed with Wilson that the East had claimed too much importance in American history in comparison with the South and the West. But he could not accept Adams's view that American institutions, such as the New England town, were simply recent forms of medieval English and ancient German prototypes. He made it his mission to disprove and discredit this historiographical "germ theory," this notion that every seemingly new and different feature of American life was not distinctive at all, that it was nothing more than the outgrowth of some old, old Teutonic germ.

Turner gave the classic statement of his own interpretation when, a thirty-two-year-old assistant professor at the University of Wisconsin, he addressed the American Historical Association

34. Everett E. Edwards, ed., *The Early Writings of Frederick Jackson Turner* (Madison: University of Wisconsin Press, 1938), p. 15.

in 1893. The historians were meeting at the Chicago world's fair, the World's Columbian Exposition, which was timed (with a year's delay) to celebrate the quadricentennial of Christopher Columbus's discovery of America. Turner presented a paper on "The Significance of the Frontier in American History." By "frontier," he meant a line, a region, and a process—the imaginary line moving west with the movement of population and, at any given moment, dividing the settled from the unsettled portion of the country; the fringe region on both sides of that line; and the process by which society in that region was broken down and built up anew. "The existence of an area of free land, its continuous recession, and the advance of American settlement westward explain American development." At last, as the census of 1890 showed, the whole country had become more or less settled. "And now, four centuries from the discovery of America, at the end of a hundred years of life under the Constitution, the frontier has gone, and with its going has closed the first period of American history." [35]

On that hot July evening in 1893 nobody paid much attention to what Turner had to say. Ordinary fair-goers preoccupied themselves with the riding and shooting of Buffalo Bill and his Wild West performers, the belly dancing at Little Egypt, or the lakefront arrival of a Viking ship. Even the historians were not, for the moment, unduly impressed by their colleague's paper. Within a few years, however, his ideas begin to catch on, first inside the profession and then outside it as well.

The Turner theory met an emotional need of the American people as they confronted the disturbing trends of the time— business depression and unemployment, strikes and violence, monopolistic combination, war, imperialism, and war again. In a sense his conclusion might seem ominous. Surely the end of the frontier would mean the restriction of opportunity: People down on their luck could no longer go west and start over. And domestic conflict could be expected to worsen as the "safety valve" for social discontent ceased to operate. Yet in other

35. Edwards, *Writings of Turner*, pp. 186, 229.

ways the theory was encouraging, for it stressed the national character that the frontier experience presumably had engendered. The undying pioneer spirit, the ingrained traits of ingenuity and self-reliance, would enable Americans in the future to deal successfully with whatever difficulties they might have to face. On balance, Turner's was a message of hope and good cheer.

His optimism contrasted sharply with the cynicism of a contemporary social scientist, one who also was a native of Wisconsin. In *The Theory of the Leisure Class* (1899) and later books the highly original Thorstein Veblen sneered at the American society and economy as he effectively exposed its paradoxical wrongs. Veblen saw "conspicuous consumption" and "conspicuous waste" as characteristic of businessmen and their families. He himself favored the "instinct of workmanship," but he found it frustrated by the business principles of chicane and sabotage. He saw no future for either capitalism or democracy other than some kind of communistic or fascistic system.

Veblen's iconoclasm, like Turner's iconolatry, can be traced back to a Wisconsin boyhood. When *The Theory of the Leisure Class* came out, Veblen said he had got the general idea for the book when he was a boy, and he had got it largely from his father's remarks. His father, a Norwegian immigrant, had felt himself a victim of trickery when he lost out to a Yankee in a lawsuit over a pre-emption claim. The elder Veblen eventually acquired land in the wild forest of Manitowoc County, where in 1857 his fourth son, Thorstein, was born. The father never learned to trust Yankees or their business ways, and he never learned to speak English. Apparently Thorstein inherited the suspicion of Yankees, yet could not quite adjust to the Norwegian community with its puritanical rules and its theological disputes. He was a marginal man.

Thorstein was not yet nine when the Veblens moved away to Minnesota. At the age of twenty-three he returned to teach for a year at Monona Academy, a Norwegian Lutheran school in Madison. Later his unhappy professional career took him from one job and one state to another. During his last years, in the 1920s, he spent the summers in his native state, living and playing among the Icelanders on Washington Island. Only in these interludes did he manage to break out of an enveloping despondency. He was hoping to get back to Wisconsin when, in 1929, he died in California.

Turner meanwhile attained to heights of academic respectability that Veblen never approached. Turner's disciples at the University of Wisconsin, which was now becoming one of the largest producers of history Ph.D.'s in the country, went out as missionaries to take positions in other universities and colleges and make converts of their own students. Though Turner himself wrote comparatively little, the Turnerians published a great deal. As his fame and influence grew, he became a valuable academic property, and Johns Hopkins, Stanford, California, and other first-rate universities tried to lure him away. He refused to leave until Wisconsin regents, undergraduates, and citizens began to talk menacingly of overemphasis on research, especially in fields that were not practical. In 1910 he left for Harvard and, until retiring in 1924, made it the base of his national influence as a teacher.

Turner retired early because of his homesickness for Madison, but with the changes of fourteen years it no longer seemed like home. Besides, the frigid winters bothered him. After three years of discomfort he moved to Pasadena, to take a research position at the Huntington Library. There was a last trip home after his death in 1932. He was buried in Madison.

At that time his frontier interpretation was at its greatest sway. For popular writers and politicians as well as historians, it was the key to an understanding of the American experience. Someone has said that you could once have made a parrot into an economist by teaching him just two words: "demand" and "supply." You could have made the bird into an American historian, during the period in question, by teaching him only one word: "frontier." In 1932, Franklin D. Roosevelt proposed to deal with the Great Depression in the light of the Turner theory.

"Our last frontier has long since been reached," Roosevelt said in a campaign speech. "There is no safety valve in the form of a Western Prairie." [36]

Already a new generation of scholars was beginning to poke holes in the theory. Some of the criticisms were just; Turner at times had been imprecise in the use of terms, inconsistent, and inclined to exaggerate. The critics were unfair, however, when they called him an oversimplifier, a monocausationist. Actually he himself took a broad view, one that was informed by various social sciences, though some of his followers were narrow enough.

Despite the attacks, Turner's reputation remained high, at least among historians. When the American Historical Association's executive council undertook to list the six greatest American historical scholars of all time, every member of the council rated Turner first. As late as the 1960s and 1970s, he continued to be the subject of more articles than any other historian.

6

The Wyoming Valley, the future home and refuge of the most creative of American architects, was in the process of settlement when, in 1847, a Welsh immigrant family arrived with a five-year-old girl, Anna Lloyd Jones. When, at twenty-four, Anna was approaching spinsterhood, she married William Russell Cary Wright, a minister's son from Massachusetts, a widower seventeen years older than she. Wright accepted a call to serve as a Baptist preacher in Richland Center. There, on June 8, 1867, his new wife gave birth to a son. They named him Frank Lloyd Wright.

The boy's first eleven years were those of a wanderer as the father, in search of himself, moved the family from one place to another for a total of six stops in four different states. (The Wrights were living in McGregor, Iowa, while the Ringlings

---

36. Ray Allen Billington, *Frederick Jackson Turner: Historian, Scholar, Teacher* (New York: Oxford University Press, 1973), p. 447.

were there, and Frank Lloyd was three when Al Ringling put on his amateurish parade and circus in the town. Did Mrs. Wright take her son to see the parade?) Then the family returned to Wisconsin, to the Wyoming Valley, where the elder Wright became the pastor of a Unitarian church, after having tried his hand elsewhere not only as a Baptist minister but also as a lawyer and a school superintendent. Young Frank Lloyd went to work on the farm of his uncle James Lloyd Jones and continued to work on the farm during summers after his restless father, having stayed only two years, changed the family residence to Madison, where he opened a music studio. In his sixtieth year he sued for divorce on the ground that Mrs. Wright was denying him "intercourse as between man and wife." [37] Then he disappeared.

Frank Lloyd, always close to his mother, dropped out of Madison High School to prepare himself for supporting her and his two sisters. His mother, he was later to say, had marked him for a career as an architect, even while he was still in her womb. He now took a job with a Madison civil engineer and, as a special student without a high school diploma, enrolled half-heartedly in a few courses at the university. He got his first real experience with design and construction when, as an assistant to a Chicago architect, he helped with the building of his Unitarian minister uncle Jenkin Lloyd Jones's Unity Chapel in the Wyoming Valley.

At twenty he took the plunge into big-city architecture. Going to Chicago he managed (apparently through Lloyd Jones family connections) to get a position with the firm of one of the city's leading architects—and perhaps the nation's most innovative—Louis Sullivan. After remaining with Sullivan from 1887 to 1893, he went into business on his own. Soon he was designing variations of his novel Prairie House, with its long, low, horizontal lines, for wealthy clients who were setting up in the suburbs. By the time he was forty, he was himself well-to-do

37. Robert C. Twombly, *Frank Lloyd Wright: An Interpretive Biography* (New York: Harper & Row, 1973), p. 12.

and a member of Chicago's social elite, and he was beginning to achieve international fame.

Wright's developing architectural style owed much to Louis Sullivan, who had taught him that form follows function, and whom he ever afterward referred to as "Dear Master." It also owed at least a bit to Japanese art; he had visited Japan and made himself an authority on the philosophy and technique of Japanese prints. But it owed most to his communion, as a farm-laboring youth, with the Wisconsin countryside. "It had come to me by actual experience and meant something out of this ground we call America." [38]

Wisconsin already had a tradition of distinctive though untutored architecture. As early as the 1830s this part of the country had a fine amateur architect in the Italian-born Dominican missionary Samuel Mazzuchelli. In designing churches, Father Mazzuchelli created a style of his own by simplifying classical patterns and adapting them to the means and materials available. After him many another architect, amateur or professional, anonymous or known, used native materials in such a way as to produce local variations of prevailing national modes. The Greek Revival or the Italianate, for example, acquired a fresh look when done in cream-colored brick from a Milwaukee area clay (Milwaukee early acquired the nickname Cream City from the color of its brick buildings). The familiar fashions also looked different in Wisconsin stone. And the tan or gray stone houses blended well with their environment, matching as they did the nearby rock outcroppings, tan or gray.

To such surroundings, to the scenes of his youth, Wright eventually came back. After twenty years of marriage, in 1909 he left his wife and children in Oak Park and went off to Europe with a client's wife, Mamah Cheney. He planned a permanent home for her and for himself in Wisconsin. By 1911 he was reconnoitering the Wyoming Valley. "Now I wanted a *natural* house to live in myself. I scanned the hills of the region where

38. Frank Lloyd Wright, *An Autobiography* (New York: Duell, Sloan and Pearce, 1943), p. 168.

the rock came cropping out in strata to suggest buildings." The yellow-brown rock above the green slopes was "part of the countenance of southern Wisconsin. I wished to be part of my beloved southern Wisconsin, too." He rediscovered a favorite place of his boyhood where, "in the March sun while snow still streaked the hillsides," he used to look for purple anemones. "I turned to this hill in the Valley as my grandfather before me had turned to America—as a hope and haven." [39]

His Welsh relatives had Welsh names for their places, and he chose one for his new house of brownish yellow local stone— Taliesin. That was the name of a poet who had sung of the glories of fine art in ancient Wales. The word meant "shining brow," and it certainly fit the brow of Wright's chosen hillside. To Taliesin he brought Mamah Cheney. She had her divorce, but he did not yet have his. His conduct shocked the people of Spring Green, the village metropolis a few miles away on the other side of the Wisconsin River. The *Spring Green Weekly Home News* saw his behavior as an "insult to decency" and a "menace to the morals of a community." [40]

On August 14, 1914, almost exactly three years after bringing Mamah Cheney to Taliesin, Wright was in Chicago on business. At home Mamah Cheney was having lunch with her two visiting children, three Taliesin employees, and a local craftsman's son. In a fit of madness the recently hired Barbadian chef locked them in the dining room, set fire to the house, and waited with an ax for those who tried to get out. All six died, and the house was left a charred and blackened ruin.

In 1925, as he was approaching the age of fifty-eight, Wright brought a newfound love to a rebuilt and remodeled Taliesin. She was the dark and exotically beautiful Yugoslavian-born Olgivanna, more than thirty years younger than he. She had a divorce, but not the legal custody of her daughter, who was with her. Wright again was seeking a divorce, this time from his second wife, Miriam Noel Wright (he had not yet married

39. Wright, *Autobiography*, pp. 167–168.
40. Quoted in Twombly, *Wright*, p. 110.

Mamah Cheney when she died). He became a fugitive from arrest under the Mann Act when he hid out in Minnesota with Olgivanna and her daughter to keep Olgivanna's former husband from recovering the child. Eventually the mess was straightened out. Wright and Olgivanna were wed, and they lived happily ever after.

For Wright, these years of domestic trouble were years of professional slump. His reputation and genius were reconfirmed in 1923 when his Imperial Hotel withstood the shattering Tokyo earthquake. After his productive phase of the 1890s and early 1900s, however, he designed few other truly notable structures until the 1930s. Then, as he neared his seventies, his second great burst of creativity began. Among his later triumphs were the Johnson Wax Company administration building (1936) and research tower (1946) in Racine and the Herbert Jacobs residence (1937) in Madison.

During his long career Wright made many architectural contributions, especially to residential construction and design. He either originated or furthered such innovations as the following: concrete slab floors and roofs (with the elimination of basements and attics), cantilevering, radiant floor heating, corner windows, continuous fenestration, overhanging eaves to shade windows in summer and admit sunlight in winter, and carports. He introduced the open floor plan and the intimate indoor-outdoor relationship. He tried new techniques and new technology in, for example, the prefabrication of components and the use of steel I-beams. More broadly, he insisted that a house should "grow"—it should grow from the site, from the culture, from the needs of the prospective occupants, and from the imagination of the architect. Most significantly, he showed an aesthetic daring to match his engineering boldness.

Wright hoped to perpetuate his concepts through his own architectural school. In 1932 he had opened the school—the Taliesin Fellowship, he called it—in a remodeled schoolhouse near his home. He proceeded to construct a complex of buildings for the institution. A larger number of eager would-be disciples applied for admission than he could accommodate, though the tuition was very high. After an attack of pneumonia in 1937 he followed his doctor's advice and decided to stay away from Wisconsin during the cold months. He bought land in Arizona, and there he built a winter home, Taliesin West, and winter facilities for the Taliesin Fellowship.

He threatened to leave Wisconsin for good when Iowa County taxed his school property despite his insistence that, as an educational institution, it was tax exempt. He felt unappreciated in his native state. The state authorities rejected his offer to design "butterfly" bridges for river crossings at Spring Green and Wisconsin Dells. The authorities never consulted him professionally or honored him in any way. Indeed, they all along had ignored him except when quarreling with him over his taxes, his morals, or his political views, which some of them considered pro-Communist. But the people of his own community had long since made up with him. As part of its centennial, in 1957, the village of Spring Green held a Frank Lloyd Wright Day. Later the local paper said of his relationship with his neighbors: "It's a love affair." [41] He was then past ninety.

Wright died in Phoenix on April 9, 1959, two months before his ninety-second birthday. His body was flown home, home to the Wyoming Valley. Tributes to his greatness were coming in from all over the world as the coffin was lowered into the family burial ground near Unity Chapel, the very first piece of architecture in the shaping of which he had had a part.

41. Quoted in Twombly, *Wright,* p. 274.

6

The Wisconsin Idea

*C*AN politics ever be pure . . . ?'' a writer in the *National Observer* asked in 1975, in the wake of the Watergate scandal. ''Not really,'' he went on, replying to his own question, ''but in a handful of states it comes close. Wisconsin may be the cleanest political state in the Union, and you have to wonder why.'' [1]

Wisconsin had enjoyed a reputation not only for the purity but also for the progressiveness of its politics. It had set an example for other states in governmental and social reform. It had helped to prepare the way for the Square Deal and the New Deal, for the transformation of the federal government from a laissez-faire umpire into an active and beneficent regulator of the game of life.

You have to wonder why. Why Wisconsin? Many progressives found the answer in an idea and a man. Somehow there once had arisen in the state a special, activist philosophy of government—the Wisconsin Idea. And there had appeared a remarkable politician, a man of contagious energy and idealism—Robert M. La Follette. His two sons inherited his mission, and for nearly half a century, from 1901 to 1947, a La Follette was either the governor or a United States senator; during some of

---

1. The writer was James M. Perry, and his *National Observer* article was reprinted in the *Madison Capital Times,* August 6, 1975.

those years one was a senator and another was the governor at the same time. The La Follette family presumably made Wisconsin different.

The true story of Wisconsin's Progressive movement is not quite so simple as that. Nor has the state's political reputation been consistently one of either progressivism or purity. Senator Robert M. La Follette, Jr., was succeeded by Senator Joseph R. McCarthy, and the state began to attract national attention not for La Folletteism but for McCarthyism. Before the La Follette dynasty began—during the first half-century of statehood—Wisconsin had been more conspicuous for corruption and bossism than for political enlightenment and reform.

1

After only a decade of statehood, at least a few of the state's more thoughtful men had begun to question the soundness of the Wisconsin character. One of them was the German-born Carl Schurz, a lawyer-politician who was a liberal and a Republican. Another was the Irish-born Edward G. Ryan, also a lawyer-politician but a conservative and a Democrat. Speaking at the university as one of its regents in July 1859, Schurz praised the people of the state for their pioneering boldness and their skill and hard work. But, he said, there was a "dark side of the picture." The "spirit of materialism" and the "pursuit of gain" had gone too far; they had taken almost "exclusive possession" of the people's souls.[2] Addressing the State Historical Society in February 1860, Ryan said the early pioneers had been honest as well as industrious, but later Wisconsinites valued success above honor and money above integrity. Wisconsin, which he himself once had called the "paradise of western civilization," now seemed in danger of becoming a "paradise of folly and knavery."[3]

2. Quoted in Chester V. Easum, *The Americanization of Carl Schurz* (Chicago: University of Chicago Press, 1929), pp. 207–210.

3. Quoted in Alfons J. Beitzinger, *Edward G. Ryan, Lion of the Law* (Madison: University of Wisconsin Press, 1960), pp. 52–54.

Schurz and Ryan uttered their jeremiads in the midst of the business depression following the panic of 1857, at a time when the economic outlook in itself was enough to arouse feelings of gloom. But the speakers—and their hearers as well—had more than that in mind. All were familiar with public evils that recently had occurred around them: mob lawlessness, vote stealing, unblushing bribery, spectacular frauds, even a sex scandal involving a highly respected politician.

Lynch law had taken over soon after Wisconsin, the third of the states to do so, got rid of capital punishment in 1853. The next year there was a lynching in the state, and the year after that there were two more. Defenders of the mobs argued that, since the government refused to impose the death penalty, the people were bound to see justice done through their own efforts. "Wisconsin," the *New York Times* commented, "is rapidly gaining a reputation for disregard of law and contempt for legal tribunals." [4]

Some Wisconsinites, even those in high places, also had a disregard for democratic processes, as they showed by their attempt to steal the gubernatorial election of 1855. The election was very close, and for several weeks the outcome remained in doubt. Finally the state board of canvassers, all Democrats, certified the incumbent governor, William A. Barstow, also a Democrat, as the winner by a mere 157 votes. The Republicans raised the cry of fraud, and their candidate, Coles Bashford, decided to contest the election. On inauguration day, while Barstow was taking the oath of office in a public ceremony, Bashford met privately with the state's chief justice, a Republican, who swore him in as governor.

So for a few months in 1856 Wisconsin had two governors, or two men claiming the governor's office, at any rate. At first the Barstow men feared a Republican coup, and to head it off they prepared a cache of arms in Madison and brought in a few companies of Irish and German militiamen, all loyal Democrats. Bashford, however, looked not to armed retainers for redress

4. Quoted in the *Milwaukee Sentinel*, August 13, 1855.

but to the state supreme court, two of whose three members were Republicans.

Startling evidence came to light in the case of *Bashford* v. *Barstow,* in which Edward G. Ryan led the prosecution on behalf of the Republicans, though he was himself a Democrat. Several weeks after the election, "after all the official returns had been in some days," as Ryan summed it up, a "shower of supplements" came in and "changed the entire result." These supplementary returns were forgeries, the products of the Democratic board of canvassers. Ryan expostulated: "It is a grievous reproach upon the whole State—a bitter and terrible reproach—that any man can be found to claim the meanest and lowest office—even that of fence-viewer or dog-killer—on such frauds as these." [5]

The supreme court gave a unanimous judgment in favor of Bashford. Already Barstow had resigned, hoping thereby to save the governor's office for the Democrats. Now occupying the office was Arthur McArthur (grandfather of General Douglas MacArthur, whose father changed the "Mc" to "Mac"). McArthur had been elected lieutenant-governor, and since the validity of his election was not in question, the Democrats thought there was at least a chance that he could make good his succession to the governorship. But McArthur quietly got out of the governor's chair when Bashford along with a few dozen other determined men arrived to demand possession of it.

The final victory of Bashford over Barstow turned out to be no triumph of virtue over vice, as was shown when the state government proceeded to dispose of Wisconsin's first federal land grants for railroad construction. President Byron Kilbourn and other officials of the LaCrosse and Milwaukee Railroad spared no expense in their efforts to get the lion's share of the land. They succeeded. As an investigation revealed two years

5. *The Trial in the Supreme Court, of the Information in the Nature of a Quo Warranto Filed by the Attorney General, on the Relation of Coles Bashford vs. William A. Barstow, Contesting the Right to the Office of Governor of Wisconsin* (Madison: Calkins & Proudfoot and Atwood & Rublee, 1856), pp. 297, 300, 340.

later, in 1858, they had distributed more than $800,000 in cash and railroad bonds as "pecuniary compliments" to friendly newspaper editors, members of the legislature, and state office-holders. Governor Bashford received the largest bribe of any of the politicians—$50,000 in bonds.

When the panic of 1857 forced Kilbourn's and other rail-roads into bankruptcy, additional instances of business mis-management, corruption, and fraud came to light. Company officers were shown to have watered the stock, misused cor-porate funds for private ventures, contracted with construction firms in which they had secret interests, and defrauded stock-holders in other ways. The stockholders who suffered the most were those farmers who had exchanged mortgages for stock and who now stood in danger of foreclosure and the loss of their farms.

On top of these exposures came the revelation of sexual mis-conduct on the part of Sherman M. Booth, Wisconsin's an-tislavery leader, the great hero of Republican idealists and re-formers. On a February night in 1859 Booth, then forty-six, was at home in Milwaukee while his wife was away at a wedding in Waukesha. Also spending the night at the Booth house was a baby-sitter, a well-developed neighbor girl of fourteen. Af-terwards, on the complaint of the girl's father, Booth was brought to trial for seduction and "illicit connection." He de-clined to appear in court, and his attorney conceded that he had been in bed with the girl. Nevertheless, the lawyer insisted that his client was not guilty under the Wisconsin statute. Reflecting the extreme antifeminine bias of the time, the law required proof of both seduction and penetration and, besides, of the previous "chaste character" of the alleged victim. In a far-fetched effort to make a "lewd woman" of the fourteen-year-old, the defense introduced as witnesses prurient neighbors who testified that she had often "exposed her person." That is, they had managed to get glimpses of her legs or even her nipples while she was carelessly playing in the yard or street. The defense contended that the prosecution was simply a "Demo-cratic conspiracy" to bring down the "great champion of Republicanism.'' [6] The jury was hung, seven members voting for conviction, five against, and so Booth was acquitted. But the effort to blacken the girl's reputation had not whitewashed his own. Nor had it saved the fresh, young, moralistic Republican party from acute embarrassment.

2

The Republican party was fathered by idealism and, at least according to Wisconsinites, was born in their state. Here, as elsewhere in the Old Northwest, the party rose precociously to power. It was to dominate the politics of Wisconsin for a full century. At first, in the 1850s, it went to extremes in the defense of personal liberty. By the 1880s and 1890s it was to be preeminently the defender of corporate privilege.

Ripon, Wisconsin, boasts of being the birthplace of the Republican party, and the case for Ripon is at least as good as that for Jackson, Michigan, the other chief claimant of the honor. On February 28, 1854, a group of Whigs, Free-Soil Democrats, and Liberty party men gathered in Ripon at the call of Alvan E. Bovay, a local lawyer who had been born in New York state and college-educated in Vermont. The purpose of the meeting was to protest the Kansas-Nebraska bill then pending in Congress, a bill for opening to slavery a part of the Louisiana Purchase territory that previously had been closed to it. The Ripon gathering resolved that, if the bill should pass, the friends of freedom from all parties should unite to form a great new northern party. Bovay proposed for it the name "Republican." After the passage of the Kansas-Nebraska Act, a convention met in Jackson, Michigan, on July 6, 1854, to start a Republican organization for that state. One week later a convention met in Madison to do the same for Wisconsin.

The Republicans proceeded to revolutionize Wisconsin poli-

6. *The Trial of Sherman M. Booth for Seduction: Evidence and Summing up of Counsel in the Case of the State versus S. M. Booth, for Seducing Caroline N. Cook* (Milwaukee: Wm. E. Tunis & Co., 1859), pp. 140, 146–147.

tics. At the state's beginning in 1848 the Democrats had been in complete command. By 1857, less than three years after the birth of the new party, the Republicans had elected not only a governor, the corrupt Bashford, but also an overwhelming majority of the state legislators, all three of the congressmen, and both of the United States senators.

In their rise to power the Wisconsin Republicans made the most of the freedom issue. They could, and did, argue that freedom was at stake not only in the distant territories but also in Wisconsin itself. Near Racine, in 1854, was living Joshua Glover, a black man who had run away from slavery in Missouri. A deputy federal marshal, enforcing the federal fugitive-slave act of 1850, seized Glover and held him in the Milwaukee jail for his owner to reclaim him. An antislavery mob freed him and sent him on his way to Canada and safety.

Sherman M. Booth, a Liberty party editor from New York and Connecticut, one of the founders of the Republican party in Wisconsin, was arrested by the federal authorities on the charge of instigating the mob. A state judge ordered the release of Booth. After the federal district court had convicted him, the state supreme court took the case on appeal, dismissed the indictment, and declared the federal fugitive-slave act unconstitutional. In effect, the state was nullifying a federal law.

The federal marshal in Milwaukee, S. V. R. Ableman, a herculean figure of more than three hundred pounds, sued for the custody of Booth, and the case went to the Supreme Court of the United States. In *Ableman* v. *Booth,* 1859, Chief Justice Roger B. Taney and his colleagues reversed the decision of the highest Wisconsin judges. Marshal Ableman then proceeded against Booth, imprisoning him briefly in the Milwaukee customhouse and attaching his property in an effort to collect a thousand-dollar fine. This came on top of the disgrace that Booth suffered in the morals case despite his acquittal on the charge of seducing Caroline Cook.

While the Wisconsin court yielded to federal authority, the Wisconsin governor, Alexander Randall, took occasion to reassert in his own way the sovereignty of the state. His actions set going a chain of events that, as fate would have it, were to culminate in one of the most horrendous disasters in all the nautical history of the Great Lakes—the wreck of the *Lady Elgin.*

The fateful events began with Booth's rearrest. One of his admirers introduced in the legislature a resolution that, whereas the state was duty bound to protect the liberty of its citizens against foreign powers, therefore the governor should be directed to declare war against the United States. The speaker of the assembly ruled the resolution unconstitutional, and that was the end of it. But if a war declaration was fanciful, some kind of armed clash seemed a real possibility. Governor Randall worried about the dependability of some of the state's militia officers in case a showdown with the federal government should come. Would the officers remain loyal to him as commander-in-chief of the militia of Wisconsin—or would they side with President James Buchanan as commander-in-chief of the army and navy of the United States?

When questioned, Captain Garrett Barry of the Milwaukee Union Guards said he would not obey an order from the governor to resist federal forces; he would not commit the crime of treason. So Governor Randall ordered that Captain Barry be stripped of his commission, that his militia company be disbanded, and that its arms be returned to the state government. Now, Barry and his Union Guards were Irish, Catholic, and Democratic, and the Irish, the Catholics, and the Democrats throughout the state took Barry's side. With their encouragement, he determined to keep his company going as an independent unit. He gave back the guns that belonged to the state, but he took advantage of an opportunity to buy others, discards from the federal government, at a bargain price.

Cheap though the guns were, they would take money, and to raise the money the friends of the Union Guards arranged a grand benefit, an excursion to Chicago on a lake steamer. They chose the *Lady Elgin,* a fast and magnificent triple-decked side-wheeler, about three hundred feet from stem to stern, one of the favorites on the lakes in those days. Returning from Chicago on the night of September 7, 1860, with more than four hundred excursionists on board, the *Lady Elgin* in the midst of a sudden squall was rammed and sunk by a storm-driven lumber schooner. About three hundred of the passengers were drowned. For weeks, bodies kept appearing at widely scattered points, and there was a continual dirge in Milwaukee, especially on the Irish south side. Two months after the sinking the body of Captain Barry was washed ashore in Indiana.

In 1860–1861 the states of the South carried the doctrine of states' rights to the extreme of actually seceding from the Union. For several years before that, however, the most thoroughgoing champion of states' rights in defiance of federal authority had been none of the southern states. It had been Wisconsin. Of course, Wisconsin had invoked the doctrine in opposition to, not in support of, the institution of Negro slavery. And when Abraham Lincoln won the presidential election of 1860, thus precipitating the southern states into secession, the Wisconsin Republicans quickly forgot about their own recent heresy. They—especially Governor Randall himself—now tried to outdo all other northern patriots in support of national power and presidential authority.

The Civil War brought increased strength to the Republican party in Wisconsin. It divided the Democratic party. War Democrats supported and even joined the Republicans. Antiwar Democrats, or Copperheads, went to self-destructive extremes in opposition to President Lincoln and his war aim of emancipation. Edward G. Ryan, the leader of Wisconsin Copperheads, stated their position in a widely circulated 1862 "Address to the People." In it he said the "proper condition of the African was subjection in some form to the white." He blamed the Republicans for secession and the war—"the abolition party at the North produced the disunion party at the South"—and he blamed the Wisconsin Republicans in particular for setting a bad example with their assertion of the doctrine of states' rights.[7] When Lincoln was running for re-election in 1864, the *La-Crosse Democrat* denounced him as a traitor. "And if he is

7. Quoted in Beitzinger, *Ryan,* pp. 67–71.

elected to misgovern for another four years, we trust some bold hand will pierce his heart with dagger point for the public good.'' [8] Such rhetoric on the part of Democrats made it all the easier for Republicans to identify their own party with patriotism as well as humanitarianism.

After the Civil War the Republicans continued to enjoy the advantage of identification with noble causes, with the war aims of Union and freedom. To keep war memories alive and thus maintain this identification, they made an issue of the Union veterans, backing them in peace as in war, promising them generous pensions and preference in political jobs. One man among the Republican politicians early managed to rise above the others as pre-eminently the Soldiers' Friend. That was Lucius Fairchild, himself a veteran, one who had lost an arm at Gettysburg; always afterward he wore his empty sleeve conspicuously as a badge of patriotism. With the support of Wisconsin members of the Grand Army of the Republic, the national organization of Union veterans, Fairchild did what no politician had done before—he won three terms as governor (1866–1872).

As late as 1887, when he was national commander of the G. A. R., Fairchild was still busy blowing on the coals of wartime hatred. Like other Republicans he was sure the election of a Democratic president would mean a rebel sympathizer in the White House. He thought he saw proof when President Grover Cleveland issued an order for giving back to the South a number of Confederate battle flags that had been captured during the war. Addressing the veterans at their national encampment in Saratoga, New York, Fairchild called upon God to palsy the brain that had conceived, the hand that had written, and the tongue that had uttered the order to return the battle flags. Thereafter, among the irreverent, he was known as Fairchild of the Three Palsies.

The postwar Republican party had more to offer than patrio-

---

8. *La Crosse Weekly Democrat,* August 24, 1864, quoted in Frank Klement, ''Brick Pomeroy: Copperhead and Curmudgeon,'' *Wisconsin Magazine of History,* 25 (Winter 1951):106.

tism and pensions. The party also provided internal improvements—federal funds to improve practically every creek and inlet in Wisconsin, which regularly received more than its share of the annual pork barrel, the rivers-and-harbors appropriations act. So long as the party controlled both the state and the federal government, it could add the gift of both state and federal jobs.

By the 1880s the Republicans in Wisconsin were functioning like a well-oiled machine. A triumvirate of bosses governed, or misgoverned, the state. These three men were quite different from earlier leaders of the party, quite different from antislavery radicals such as Sherman Booth or professional superpatriots such as Lucius Fairchild. The new men were more practical than ideological; they had little or nothing to do with political rhetoric.

The three were Philetus Sawyer, Henry C. Payne, and John C. Spooner. Sawyer, the Oshkosh lumber baron, made no resounding speeches; in fact, he made no speeches at all. Nevertheless, as a congressman (1865–1875) and a United States senator (1881–1893), he introduced and got passed hundreds of bills, probably more of them than anybody before or since. Most were special, private pension bills, of the kind that Congress hurried through—and President Cleveland vetoed—in batches. But Sawyer also distinguished himself by his handling of river-and-harbor bills, so much that he was recognized as the foremost logroller of his time.

Payne, Massachusetts-born, twenty-seven years younger than Sawyer, started in business in Milwaukee as an insurance man. By the 1890s he was Wisconsin's biggest public-utilities magnate, an executive in railroad, telephone, electric light and power, and street railway and interurban companies. Meanwhile, as postmaster of Milwaukee (1876–1885), Republican national committeeman (1880–1904), and postmaster general (1902–1904), he served the Wisconsin organization well, especially in the distribution of federal patronage.

Spooner, a Hoosier by birth, about the same age as Payne, was the only one of the trio with a record of Civil War service. He was also the only one with a college education, holding both a bachelor's and a master's degree from the University of Wisconsin (Payne was a graduate of a Massachusetts academy, but Sawyer had only a few years of common schooling). A highly successful railroad lawyer residing in Hudson, Spooner went to the United States Senate in 1885. According to rumor, Sawyer bought the election for him from the state legislature, and no doubt Sawyer and others did spend money freely on the Spooner campaign. Spooner was not a vote-getting orator; he had little appeal and still less liking for the masses. But in the Senate, as in the courts, he was a sharp and effective debater, especially on fine points of constitutional law. He gave a touch of scholarly elegance to the Wisconsin organization.

The Republican machine gained and held popular support, then, not through the magnetism of personality but through the attractions of patriotism, pensions, patronage, and the pork barrel. The machine used its power for the particular benefit of railroad and lumber companies. These had their way with the state legislature as well as the national Congress, winning positive favors in grants of land and rights while checking attempts at effective regulation.

Only twice in the nineteenth century did the Republicans lose control of the state, and then only briefly—in 1873 and in 1890. On both occasions they lost because they made the mistake of provoking ethnic on top of economic discontent. The first time, the party alienated many of its German Protestant voters by sponsoring a temperance act; the second time, by espousing the Bennett Law, which required private as well as public schools to use English as the medium of instruction. In 1873, not only wheat growers but also wheat dealers demanded that the state step in to reduce railroad rates. Once in office, however, the Democrats and their new-found reformist allies succeeded in passing only the pretense of a regulatory measure. Even this was soon repealed.

Reformers could expect no more help from Democratic than from Republican leaders. Though Wisconsin Democrats still claimed to be Jacksonian representatives of the common man, their leadership included the greatest plutocrat of all, the banker and railroad magnate Alexander Mitchell, until his death in 1887. After him came the more illustrious but equally conservative if somewhat less wealthy William F. Vilas. A native of Vermont, Vilas had graduated from the University of Wisconsin, served in the Union army, and taught for seventeen years as a law professor in the university. He led the state's Bourbon Democracy as a member of Cleveland's cabinet (1885–1889) and as a United States senator (1891–1897).

By the 1890s the Democrats were beginning to threaten the rule of the Republican bosses, though not the existing system of institutionalized corruption. Not only did the Democrats get temporary control of the legislature, thus managing to replace Spooner with Vilas in 1891; they also carried the state for their presidential candidate in 1892—the first time they had done so since 1852. The real threat to both the bosses and the system, however, was not to come from the Democrats. It was to come from some of the Republicans themselves, from a faction of dissidents. Already, in 1892, one of them was making up his mind to challenge the intrenched leadership of his own party. His name was Robert Marion La Follette.

3

Robert M. La Follette was born in Primrose Township, Dane County, on June 14, 1855, five years after his parents had arrived to convert a piece of the wilderness into a farm. The La Follettes had come from Virginia by way of Kentucky and Indiana; earlier they had migrated to America as Huguenot exiles from France. As a youth of fifteen, La Follette undertook the operation of the farm to support his mother and his invalid stepfather. When nineteen he entered the University of Wisconsin, meeting his expenses at considerable sacrifice to himself and to his mother, now a widow. At the university, though only five feet, five inches tall, he stood out as an actor and still more as an orator, the best among midwestern college students, the winner of the Interstate Oratorical Contest his senior year. After graduation he took a few law courses, served briefly as a lawyer's apprentice, and was admitted to the bar. As soon as he was well enough established, he married a classmate, Belle Case of Baraboo. Mrs. La Follette went on to get a law degree from the university, the first woman ever to do so. She never practiced, but she became her husband's legal and political adviser as well as a woman's-rights advocate and the mother of two sons and two daughters.

As a practicing attorney, La Follette made good use of both his dramatic and his forensic art. A newsman once described him addressing a jury in a murder trial, "now shaking an index finger at a witness, now half sitting upon the reporters' table, now with a point[er] in hand by the map on the wall." He was "ever restless, ever eager—always in deadliest earnest" as he thus "set his stage scenery." Then the play itself: "Now his face was calm—now a thunder cloud—now full of sorrow. Here his voice arose almost to a shriek—there it sank to a whisper." [9] The show, as usual, deeply impressed the jurors.

In politics, winning election first as district attorney of Dane County and then as a congressman, La Follette demonstrated the same kind of histrionic talent. He was also persuasive when off the platform, exerting an almost hypnotic influence in conversation. He liked to mingle, and he carried his campaign in person to farmers throughout his constituency.

During three terms in Congress, 1885–1891, La Follette was unexceptionable as a party regular, an organization man. He was careful to keep on good terms with Senator Sawyer. Then, in 1891, something happened that caused a sudden and complete break between the two. Exactly what happened was the point of the dispute. Sawyer said he had offered La Follette some money as a retainer fee; La Follette said Sawyer had offered him a bribe. Sawyer had an interest in an upcoming law case in which La Follette's brother-in-law was to be the judge, but Sawyer denied previous knowledge of the relationship. Once Sawyer had begun to circulate his version of the incident,

9. *Wisconsin State Journal,* no date, quoted in David P. Thelen, *Robert M. La Follette and the Insurgent Spirit* (Boston: Little, Brown and Co., 1976), p. 17.

La Follette felt he had no choice but to tell the truth as he saw it.

La Follette was out of office, having been swept out in the Democratic surge of 1890. If he was to get back into office, if he was to have any future in Wisconsin's Republican party, he would now have to make his way against the bitter resistance of the party bosses. As a politician, he could retire or he could rebel. He was too young, only thirty-six, and too ambitious to retire. So he determined to get control of the party. The first step was to try and capture the governorship. In 1894 he persuaded a prominent Norwegian politician, Nils P. Haugen, to seek the Republican nomination—in vain. Then, in 1896, La Follette went after it himself.

In his revolt against the bosses, La Follette was encouraged by his success in gaining allies among various groups that held grievances of their own. Numbers of bright, young, ambitious men felt that their chances for political careers were hurt by the Sawyer-Payne-Spooner ring's monopolistic grip on public jobs. Norwegians believed that the machine discriminated against them, faithful Republicans though they were, in its distribution of political favors. The dairy leader and ex-governor, William D. Hoard, along with Hoard's faction of Republicans and the state's dairy farmers in general, resented the bosses' favoritism toward railroading and lumbering as against dairying, and they had a rankling memory of Payne's record as a lobbyist for the oleomargarine interests.

With the support of the disaffected Republicans, La Follette was confident, when the state convention met in 1896, that the nomination would be his. According to his count, a clear majority of the delegates were pledged to him. In the course of the balloting, however, so many of his delegates defected that he lost out. He was convinced that the machine had bought their votes. Hiding his bitterness for the time being, he campaigned that fall for the Republican state ticket and also for the national ticket, headed by William McKinley. La Follette was the conservative McKinley's friend and admirer. In no sense a Populist, he did all he could to save the country from McKinley's populistic opponent William Jennings Bryan.

To some Wisconsinites, however, La Follette was soon to sound, himself, like a Populist or worse. He was pondering the lesson to be learned from his recent defeat in the state convention—a lesson that finally taught him to become a reformer, even a seemingly radical one. "Under any system which would have ensured the expression of the views of the Republicans of Wisconsin I would have been nominated three to one," he wrote privately to an associate. "The result of this contest but makes it more certain that some radical change should be made in the laws relative to nominations in order that machine methods and money domination no longer control." [10] To win the game, he would have to change the rules.

La Follette now discovered the direct primary, which reformers in Wisconsin and other states had been advocating for some time. Presumably the voters, by choosing candidates in a primary election, would take the nominating power away from the machine. "Abolish the caucus and the convention," La Follette spoke out to demand early in 1897. "Go back to the first principles of democracy; go back to the people." [11] During the fall he toured the state to educate the public on the direct primary and to help elect assembly candidates who would legislate in favor of it. Again, in 1898, he underwent a personal defeat at the Republican convention, and again he blamed it on the bosses' last-minute use of bribes.

Through his conversion to political reform, however, La Follette was attracting more and more Wisconsinites to his support. These citizens were already converts to the reformist cause. Suffering through the depression of the 1890s, they blamed their troubles largely on the corporations and on the politicians who were subservient to them. Prominent among the popular leaders and educators was Assemblyman Albert R. Hall, a farmer-manufacturer from rural Dunn County. For years Hall had been

10. La Follette to George F. Cooper, September 7, 1896, quoted in Herbert F. Margulies, *The Decline of the Progressive Movement in Wisconsin, 1890–1920* (Madison: State Historical Society of Wisconsin, 1968), p. 35.

11. Robert M. La Follette, *La Follette's Autobiography: A Personal Narrative of Political Experiences* (Madison: Robert M. La Follette Co., 1911), p. 196.

crusading against the railroads, demanding higher taxes on their property, the regulation of their rates, and the prohibition of free passes, which they distributed as bribes to legislators and state officials. A group of young lawyers set up the Republican Club of Milwaukee to combat the corrupt coalition of Republicans and Democrats who ran the city for the benefit of the utilities. Whatever the evil that a particular set of reformers attacked, all could see some advantage in altering the nomination process so as to give them an increased part in it.

By 1900, La Follette had gained new allies among standpatters as well as reformers. Most valuable among the newcomers was the multimillionaire lumberman of Marinette, Isaac Stephenson, who, like Sawyer, had turned his money to good account in politics. Stephenson was bitter because of the bosses' refusal to give him, in 1899, the United States senatorship that he thought his just reward for years of service and subsidy. So he went over to La Follette and began to bankroll him. By the time the convention met, Sawyer was dead, Payne was ill, and Spooner was preoccupied with Washington affairs. Since the machine was falling apart, most of its subalterns decided to seek an accommodation with La Follette. He agreed to maintain party harmony at least for the duration of the campaign. So, at long last, the nomination was his, and his by the convention's unanimous vote.

The state Republican platform of 1900 lauded President McKinley and Senator Spooner and called for the direct primary, governmental economy, equal taxation, and antitrust measures of some kind. But La Follette gave leading businessmen confidential assurances that, as governor, he would be fair with them in such matters as railroad and other corporation taxes. In return, some of the corporations contributed to his campaign fund. He carried his message to the people as no candidate in Wisconsin had ever done before, traveling (according to somebody's count) 6,433 miles back and forth through the state and speaking 208 times to a total audience of nearly 200,000. His message now was mild: He refrained from denouncing corporations, and he stressed the reduction of state expenses more than the introduction of the direct primary or the increase of railroad taxation. But the message was effective. La Follette carried every one of the state's seventy counties except for six of the most overwhelmingly German and Democratic.

La Follette took office in 1901 as the first Wisconsin governor who was a Wisconsin native. Before long he was at outs with his recent conservative allies. He flayed them for betraying the platform, and they accused him of double-crossing them. But his progressive followers hailed him as the great practitioner of a new idea in government—the great practitioner of what was soon to be known as the Wisconsin Idea.

4

The origin of the term "Wisconsin Idea" is obscure, and its definition has been changeable. Essentially it means governmental reform and administration by, or at least on the advice of, academic experts. It assumes an educated electorate, one enlightened enough to recognize and appreciate the necessary expertise. Indispensable is the role of the state university, which trains or lends the needed specialists and which undertakes to instruct the entire people, the boundaries of the campus being the boundaries of the state. Implicit is a happy combination of research and reform.

The general concept—better government through better education—was already widespread when the University of Wisconsin was founded in 1848. This university was the first, however, to bring the notion into focus and give it practical meaning. Even the University of Wisconsin was slow to act. Not until the presidency of John Bascom (1874–1887) did it extend its influence through agricultural short courses and farmers' institutes. President Bascom was a universal scholar and also a firm believer in the Social Gospel, the doctrine that governments should put Christian ethics into practice. "It was his teaching, iterated and reiterated, of the obligation of both the university and the students to the mother state that may be said to have originated the Wisconsin Idea in education." [12] So believed La Follette, who had studied under Bascom.

Bascom thought highly of a book on the labor movement that the young Johns Hopkins economist Richard T. Ely published in 1886—though many critics considered the book much too sympathetic with labor. Ely agreed with Bascom that the state had a duty to encourage human progress. In 1892 Ely came to Madison to organize and head a graduate program in the social sciences. Two years later he was the center of a storm over academic freedom. One of the university regents accused him of radicalism, and the *Nation* magazine and the *New York Evening Post* took up the charge. Defending himself, as the affair gained more and more national publicity, Ely said he was only an advocate of Progressive Conservatism. After a thorough hearing, the board of regents vindicated both Ely and academic freedom. They resolved: "Whatever may be the limitations which trammel inquiry elsewhere we believe the great State University of Wisconsin should ever encourage that continual and fearless sifting and winnowing by which alone the truth can be found." [13] This became a corollary of the Wisconsin Idea.

When the vacant presidency was to be filled in 1903, Governor La Follette favored his old friend and classmate, now a geology professor at the university, Charles R. Van Hise. The regents appointed him. In his inaugural Van Hise proposed that faculty members serve as advisers to the state government. He backed Ely in bringing John R. Commons to the faculty in 1904 and Edward A. Ross in 1906. Commons, like Ely, was an authority on labor history and a meliorist who expected workers to improve their condition through collective bargaining, not through revolution. Together, the two men developed what came to be known as the Wisconsin school of institutional, or

12. La Follette, *Autobiography,* p. 27.

13. From the plaque at the main entrance to Bascom Hall on the Madison campus. President Charles K. Adams wrote the words. The class of 1910 had the plaque made after another threat to academic freedom, but the university authorities did not put it up until 1915.

welfare, economics. Ross, one of the most prestigious sociologists of his time, preached the Social Gospel in *Sin and Society* (1907), a book that both reflected and reinforced the progressive spirit of reform.

In formulating and applying the Wisconsin Idea nobody was to have a more important part than Charles McCarthy. A student of Frederick Jackson Turner, the Massachusetts-born McCarthy earned a doctorate in history in 1901, with a dissertation that won an American Historical Association prize. That same year he took a job as a librarian for the legislature. He proceeded to expand his functions, not only providing information for the lawmakers but also giving them assistance in the drafting of bills. Recognizing what he had done, the legislature in 1907 set up a legislative reference bureau with McCarthy at the head of it. Thus he played a key role in the enactment of laws that put Wisconsin in the forefront of the Progressive movement.

While governor from 1901 to 1906, La Follette struggled against conservative legislators and corrupting lobbyists to secure the passage of his reform program. This included the control of lobbying, the introduction of the direct primary, the increase of railroad taxation, the prohibition of free railroad passes, and the establishment of a commission to regulate railroad rates. For all the screams of the opposition, the La Follette program in action was comparatively mild. True, the direct primary was new, the first to be put into effect statewide. But several states had railroad commissions before Wisconsin had one, and some of the others were given greater powers. The Wisconsin commission, with political-economy professor Balthasar Meyer as its chairman, could not reduce intrastate charges; it could only equalize them. This—an end to discrimination—was what most businessmen, as shippers, desired. And the railroads were satisfied.

La Follette left Madison in 1906 to go to Washington as United States senator. From then on, he had nothing directly to do with Wisconsin lawmaking, though, of course, he could exert an indirect influence on it through his particular friends in the legislature. In his absence his successors in the gubernatorial office had a much greater impact on state legislation. They were James O. Davidson (1906–1911) and Francis E. McGovern (1911–1915). Both were progressives, but neither was a La Follette man. Davidson, Wisconsin's first Norwegian-born governor, had won his nomination against La Follette's hand-picked candidate in a primary race. McGovern broke with La Follette in 1912, refusing to assist him in his presidential hopes.

Under Davidson there was a lull in legislation, while the genial governor patched up relations with Republicans whom La Follette had antagonized, including Hoard and other progressives as well as the antiprogressives or stalwarts. But under McGovern there was a legislative explosion. In the one session of 1911 the legislature passed a larger number of important reform laws than in six sessions under La Follette. The McGovern legislation included measures of more far-reaching social and economic consequence than the La Follette ones, the aim of which had been restricted pretty much to making government more responsive to the people, less submissive to the "interests." The difference in programs reflected a difference in constituencies: La Follette's was essentially rural, McGovern's urban, centering on Milwaukee, his home city.

Among the laws of 1911 were some designed to benefit the farmer by encouraging co-operatives, loans for farm improvements, and school courses in agricultural and domestic science. More impressive was the legislation to protect the worker by limiting the hours of women and children, requiring factory safety, and providing compensation for injury or death. The workman's compensation act, the design of Professor Commons, was the first actually to go into effect in any state. Other measures were intended to regulate the insurance business through the competition of a state insurance fund and to increase the businessman's and the corporation's share of government costs by imposing an income tax, something no state had successfully tried before. Still other laws controlled industrial activity and encouraged conservation by creating forest reserves and a forest commission and by regulating the use of waterpower.

Of the many new agencies that the legislature set up, the most unusual was the board of public affairs, which had a mandate to look into any and all state or local governmental operations and to recommend means of increasing their efficiency. As members of the various boards and commissions, forty-six professors undertook to serve the government while also serving the university. Many of the professors, in addition to Commons, had helped McCarthy and his legislative reference bureau in the shaping of reform bills.

Wisconsin was attracting national and international attention with its wave of progressivism. Journalists and reformers from the outside flocked into the state to find out what was going on, and Wisconsin participants in the movement put into print their own versions of events. Articles, almost all of them highly favorable, appeared in the national magazines—nearly a hundred articles between 1910 and 1914. Whole books were devoted to the subject, three of them in 1911–1912.

"The story of the State of Wisconsin is the story of Governor La Follette," the widely read muckraker Lincoln Steffens reported in 1904, after interviewing the governor in Madison.[14] La Follette himself agreed with this in the autobiography he published as a campaign document in 1911, when he was seeking the Republican nomination for the presidency. The La Follette program will be a success, he posited, if it can be shown "that Wisconsin is a happier and better state to live in, that its institutions are more democratic, that the opportunities of all its people are more equal, that social justice more nearly prevails, that human life is safer and sweeter."[15] Here was a test of progressivism not only for Wisconsin but for other states.

Wisconsin, commentators said, was indeed a model for the rest. "Under the influence of university men," one writer declared in 1910, "Wisconsin has become the recognized leader

14. Lincoln Steffens, *The Struggle for Self-Government: Being an Attempt to Trace American Political Corruption to Its Sources in Six States of the United States* (New York: McClure, Phillips & Co., 1906), p. 79. This book incorporated Steffens's 1904 article on Wisconsin.

15. La Follette, *Autobiography*, p. 369.

in progressive and practical legislation, the New Zealand of the United States.'' [16] The most authoritative exponent of this theme was ex-President Theodore Roosevelt, who visited Madison and addressed the legislature in 1911, while getting ready for his own hoped-for return to the presidency. Writing an article for the magazine *Outlook,* Roosevelt said Americans needed no longer look abroad for examples in the "work of human betterment." Before going to Madison he had heard "well-meaning men" speak "with a certain horror of Wisconsin, as if it were a community engaged in reckless experiment." But he found no dangerous radicals in charge.

> After my visit I felt like congratulating Wisconsin upon what it had done and was doing; and I felt much more like congratulating the country as a whole because it has in the State of Wisconsin a pioneer blazing the way along which we Americans must make our civic and industrial advance during the next few decades. [17]

Enthusiastic writers made much of the metaphor of laboratory experimentation. For McCarthy's book *The Wisconsin Idea,* Roosevelt contributed an introduction in which he said Wisconsin had become "literally"—he doubtless meant "figuratively"—"a laboratory for wise experimental legislation aiming to secure the social and political betterment of the people as a whole." [18] In *Wisconsin: An Experiment in Democracy* (1912) the prominent journalist Frederic C. Howe described Wisconsin as an "experiment station in politics" and as a "state-wide laboratory" for the testing of popular government. [19]

Years later the New Deal theorist and propagandist Thurman

---

16. E. E. Slosson, *Great American Universities* (1910), pp. 210–244, quoted in Vernon Carstensen, "The Origin and Development of the Wisconsin Idea," *Wisconsin Magazine of History,* 39 (Spring 1956):187.

17. Theodore Roosevelt, "Wisconsin: An Object-Lesson for the Rest of the Union," *Outlook,* 98 (May 27, 1911):143–145.

18. Charles McCarthy, *The Wisconsin Idea* (New York: The Macmillan Co., 1912), p. vii.

19. Quoted by Carstensen in "Origin of the Wisconsin Idea," p. 181.

W. Arnold was to dismiss as the "sheerest fantasy" the belief "that state governments watch the legislation in other state governments as experiments are watched in the laboratory." [20] Arnold was merely trying to dispose of an argument some critics of the New Deal used against the continual increase of federal power. He was not referring to Wisconsin; apparently he was not even aware of its earlier role. The fact is that, in the heyday of progressivism, reformers in other states had watched the legislative experiments in Wisconsin and had used them as prototypes. Other states adopted or adapted the legislative reference bureau (twenty-seven of them by 1917), the direct primary (forty-four by 1940), the country schools of agriculture and domestic economy (Georgia, Alabama, North Carolina, Oklahoma, Arkansas, California, Michigan, and New York by 1913), and the income tax, among other innovations. By the 1920s the state of North Carolina had made the Wisconsin Idea its own, and the university at Chapel Hill was distinguishing itself as both a center for social research and a source of reforming energy.

Meanwhile the rage for reform was interrupted in Wisconsin itself. Stalwart Republicans made issues of rising taxes, government extravagance, and swelling bureaucracy. They complained of "reform run wild, humanitarianism without common sense, education to the verge of bankruptcy, and an insolent interference with the liberties of the people." In 1914 they secured the nomination and the election as governor of Emanuel L. Philipp, a successful Milwaukee businessman. Governor Philipp said his victory was a "complete repudiation of the much heralded Wisconsin Idea." [21] At first the new governor demanded the resignation of McCarthy, but the two soon made their peace, and McCarthy stayed on. During Philipp's three terms (1915–1921)

---

20. Thurman W. Arnold, *The Folklore of Capitalism* (New Haven: Yale University Press, 1937), p. 95.

21. Both quotations are from Writers' Project, Works Progress Administration, *Wisconsin: A Guide to the Badger State* (New York: Duell, Sloan and Pearce, 1941), p. 62.

none of the major progressive reforms was repealed. Though some of the boards and commissions were consolidated, their functions were expanded rather than curtailed.

The Wisconsin Progressive movement received a shattering blow, however, with the entrance of the United States into the First World War. La Follette himself survived and more than survived, and so did the spirit of reform, but only after a disintegration and a reintegration of the forces behind him and behind it.

5

La Follette's senatorial career (1906–1925) divided into two parts, or two distinct careers, with the First World War (1914–1918) as a transitional period. In the course of the changing times he went, in the minds of a great many Wisconsinites, from the heroic to the hateful—and back again to the heroic. He lost old friends and gained new ones, among the latter some strange bedfellows. Orginally he and other progressives had competed with Socialists, presenting their own brand of reformism as the preferable alternative to socialism. Before the war was over, he found himself and Socialists acting in parallel.

Senator La Follette came naturally by his opposition to American involvement in the European war. Involvement would put at least a temporary end to the ongoing federal reform program to which he was committed. Impressive indeed was the record of progressive legislation in which he had an initiating or contributory role: laws invigorating the Interstate Commerce Commission, evaluating railroad property for purposes of rate making, prohibiting certain corrupt practices on the part of lobbyists, shortening hours for workers on common carriers, improving working conditions for seamen, strengthening the banking and currency system, providing for the direct election of senators, and imposing a federal income tax. Yet there was more to be done.

From the outbreak of war in Europe, La Follette maintained a perfectly consistent position in regard to American policy. He stood all along for what President Woodrow Wilson stood for only at the beginning—strict neutrality. As late as 1916, this was still acceptable to enough Wisconsin Republicans that La Follette could, quite easily, obtain a third term in the Senate. By early 1917, however, because of his resistance to the administration's warlike measures, the previously friendly *Wisconsin State Journal* had begun to stigmatize him as un-American, and President Wilson had singled him out as one of a "little group of willful men" who had "rendered the great Government of the United States helpless and contemptible." [22]

When, in April 1917, Wilson asked Congress for a declaration of war, La Follette was one of six senators who voted resolutely against it. Afterwards he did not try to obstruct the war effort, but he continued to disagree with the decision to intervene, and he persistently criticized the administration policies that encouraged profiteering and discouraged the free expression of thought. As between Wilson's way and La Follette's view, the old progressives soon indicated their choice. Most of the politicians went for Wilson and for war without stint or limit, and so did most of the intellectuals, the Wisconsin Idea people, including President Van Hise and Professors Ely and Commons of the university and Dr. McCarthy of the legislative reference bureau.

In the eyes of superpatriots all over the state—all over the country—La Follette had marked himself quite clearly as a traitor. Referring to him, the ebullient Theodore Roosevelt told a Racine audience: "I abhor the Hun without our gates, but more I abhor the Hun within our gates." While a subcommittee in Washington deliberated over a resolution to expel him from the Senate, the legislature in Madison adopted the following resolution: "We condemn Senator Robert M. La Follette and all others who have failed to see the righteousness of our nation's cause . . . and we denounce any attitude or utterance of theirs which has tended to incite sedition among the people of

---

22. *New York Times,* March 5, 1917, quoted in Margulies, *Decline of the Progressive Movement,* p. 193.

our country and to injure Wisconsin's fair name before the free peoples of the world.'' [23] The unkindest cuts of all came when university students burned him in effigy after a loyalty rally, the Madison Club with its large membership of professors expelled him, and all but four members of the faculty signed a circular that censured him for giving aid and comfort to the enemy.

When in 1918 a La Follette man was running against a super-patriot in a Republican senatorial primary, the *New York Times* characterized the election as ''a battle between Germany and the United States for the possession of one of the United States.'' President Wilson was moved to write a public letter about the ''critical senatorial contest'' in Wisconsin. ''The attention of the country will naturally be centered on it,'' Wilson averred. ''And the question will be in every patriotic man's mind whether Wisconsin is really loyal to this country or not.'' [24] The La Follette man lost—which was temporarily reassuring to conservatives and chauvinists.

Not reassuring at all, however, was the fact that an antiwar Socialist ran third in the 1918 senatorial race with more than a quarter of the votes, enough to have given an easy victory to a combined progressive and Socialist pacifist-radical ticket. The Socialist candidate was Victor L. Berger. An Austrian-born Jew, Berger had received some university education in Vienna and Budapest before he arrived in Milwaukee at the age of about twenty-one. During the 1880s, after becoming a convert to the strictly Marxist and revolutionary Socialist Labor party, he left it to advocate a nonviolent, gradualist, parliamentary approach to socialism. Along with Eugene V. Debs, he helped to found the more moderate Socialist party of the United States. In Milwaukee he attracted a following not only among industrial workers of German origin but also, to a less extent, among workers and even middle-class reformers of Yankee and other non-German backgrounds.

23. *Wisconsin State Journal*, September 19, 1917, March, 6, 1918, quoted in Margulies, *Decline of Progressive Movement*, pp. 210, 212.
24. Margulies, *Decline of Progressive Movement*, pp. 220–221.

Another Milwaukee Socialist leader was Emil Seidel, who was born in Pennsylvania and brought to Wisconsin as a baby. Seidel spent several years in Germany studying the woodcarver's trade and also learning Marxist doctrine. In 1904 he and eight of his comrades were elected as Milwaukee aldermen in the Socialist party's first Wisconsin success. The party won a spectacular victory in 1910, when it made Berger the first Socialist ever to go to Congress, and Seidel the first ever to serve as mayor of a large American city. Both men were kept from reelection by a conservative coalition of Republicans and Democrats. But the Socialists put Daniel Hoan in the Milwaukee mayor's office in 1916, and they were to keep him in that office for a total of twenty-four years. Cleaning up the mess that Republican-Democratic corruptionists had made, the Socialists gave Milwaukee a new distinction for honest and efficient municipal government.

When the issues of neutrality and preparedness arose, the Wisconsin Socialists got an opportunity to attract votes from German Americans who had little love for radicalism but still less for Wilsonian diplomacy. As editor of both the German-language *Vorwaerts* and the English-language *Leader,* Berger wielded a powerful pen on behalf of peace. As a public speaker, though, he was ineffective. Still worse for his cause, he turned away some well-wishers by his domineering, grating personality, and he antagonized other potential adherents by his anti-Catholic disputatiousness. He did not even lead all the Socialists; they divided on the issues. Mayor Hoan was persuaded to march at the head of a preparedness parade.

The American declaration of war deepened the Socialist party split. Just two days after Congress passed the declaration, the party, convening in St. Louis, adopted a resolution denouncing it and urging resistance to the war effort. Berger voted for and defended the antiwar plank, but a minority of Wisconsin's Socialist leaders did not. Hoan was one of these; he confined himself to blaming the capitalists for American involvement and demanding, like La Follette, taxes that would take away the profits of the profiteers. The Milwaukee Socialist Algie Simons

went further; he repudiated the St. Louis platform as treason-
ous, and he became a propagandist for the superpatriotic Wisconsin Defense League. Simons thought Berger ought to be shut
up.

The Wilson administration thought so, too. Wilson's postmaster general struck at Berger by withdrawing second-class
mailing privileges from his *Milwaukee Leader* and then discon-
tinuing delivery even of first-class mail addressed to the newspaper. Undaunted, Berger ran for Congress in 1918. He won the
election, with almost three times as many votes as any Socialist
had ever received in Wisconsin. Before the new Congress met,
however, he was brought to trial in a federal court on a charge
of seditious utterances under the wartime Espionage Act. He
was convicted and sentenced to twenty years in prison. Out on
bail while appealing the verdict, he went to take his seat in
Congress, but the majority of his peers voted to exclude him.
His constituents sent him back in a special 1919 election, and
again Congress turned him away. In 1921 the United States
Supreme Court upset his conviction, and the next year he ran
for Congress once more.

La Follette came up for re-election to the Senate that same
year. A Red Scare still gripped the state and the country, the
hysteria of fear and hatred having been transferred at the war's
end from Huns to Reds. The national hysteria received much of
its stimulus from Wisconsin events, such as the defiance of
Congress by Berger's constituents. No less a national figure
than Vice-President Calvin Coolidge informed Americans that
the universities were hotbeds of radicalism and the University of
Wisconsin was the worst of all, having much the largest Socialist club. In fact, the university had fallen under timid and conservative leadership, and well-known radicals were being denied
the right to speak on the campus.

The state elections of 1922, with both La Follette and Berger
running for office, raised apprehensions to a new pitch in some
conservative quarters. "The fact has to be faced," a Wisconsin
correspondent warned in a national magazine, the *Outlook,*
"that in the Wisconsin primary election of September 5 Social-

ism gained the greatest victory that it has ever won in American politics.'' [25] The writer was referring to La Follette's renomination, which he said was the result of a tacit alliance between La Follette and Berger, between progressives and Socialists. It was, the writer went on, an endorsement of La Follette's and Berger's antiwar stand, an indication that a record of 1917–1918 war service was now a political liability in the state.

Certainly renomination and re-election, by overwhelming votes, gloriously vindicated the much abused La Follette. The votes came from a remade constituency. It was composed in part of old-time progressives who had remained loyal, prominent among them William T. Evjue, who in 1917 had founded the *Madison Capital Times* to counter the bellicose *Wisconsin State Journal*. The La Follette constituency also included a new element, a large body of German Americans who now saw him as a champion of civil rights and ethnic self-respect. Vindication likewise came to Victor Berger when, in November 1922, he was again elected to the House of Representatives, to be twice re-elected and to occupy his seat from 1923 to 1929.

Wisconsinites again showed their respect for La Follette when, in 1924, he ran as the Progressive party candidate for the presidency of the United States. He opposed Communism and favored disarmament, government ownership of railroads, farm relief, and labor legislation. He had the endorsement of black leaders, Socialists, woman's-rights advocates, and the heads of most of the labor unions. He carried his home state.

After his death—which followed his strenuous campaign by less than a year—still more honors came to "Fighting Bob." Wisconsin recognized him as its greatest statesman by placing his statue in the national Capitol's Statuary Hall. And the United States Senate, after polling American historians, hung his portrait along with four others in the Senate lounge to memorialize him as one of the five outstanding senators of all time.

25. John Ballard, "The Revolt Against the Yankee," *Outlook,* 132 (November 1, 1922):366.

6

"The Wisconsin Idea is dead—in Wisconsin," a writer in the magazine *World's Work* declared after La Follette's death.[26] But the announcement was premature. Old Bob's sons carried on his tradition, Robert, Jr., being elected to fill out his Senate term, and then re-elected in 1928, and Philip winning the governorship in 1930. The structure of progressive reforms still stood in the state, with little loss or alteration, and it was to receive significant additions with the coming of the Great Depression. Moreover, it was to provide models for federal reforms under the New Deal.

During the first several years under Old Bob's heirs and successors, the political reputation of Wisconsin continued to fluctuate. "Most Americans, asked to name the most radical American State, would undoubtedly nominate Wisconsin," a contributor to the *American Mercury* said in 1929. "Yet the plain fact is that Wisconsin is one of the most conservative States in the Union." The iconoclastic author went on to say: "The Wisconsin Legislature, I believe, is the cleanest and least venal in America. The State officials, in the main, are honest and capable. But Wisconsin is not, and never was, Progressive. Least of all is the La Follette machine." [27]

When hard times came and tempers tautened, some voices became shrill. One of the shrillest was that of John B. Chapple, a Wisconsin Republican of the stalwart faction, who published a screed he called *La Follette Socialism* (1931) and a sequel he titled *La Follette Road to Communism* (1936). "Why do we find LaFolletteism and Communism together?" Chapple asked rhetorically.[28] The two isms were essentially the same, he insinuated through frequent rhetorical questions and through quo-

26. French Strother, "The Death of the 'Wisconsin Idea,'" *World's Work,* 50 (October 1925):622.

27. Bennington Orth, "The Progressive Holy Land," *American Mercury,* 18 (November 1929):266, 270.

28. John B. Chapple, *La Follette Road to Communism—Must We Go Further Along That Road?* (n.p., published by the author, 1936), plate 20.

tations and photographic reproductions of "documents" consisting of other testimony just like his own. According to him, "LaFolletteism"–Communism centered on the university, and it was responsible for godlessness, immorality, unemployment, and even the perennially bad performance of the Badger football team. The *Chicago Tribune* took up Chapple's charges and gave them currency as acknowledged facts throughout "Chicagoland."

Visiting Wisconsin in the depth of the depression, the well-known journalist Elmer Davis discovered that, if he lived there, he would have to pay about five times as much in income taxes as he paid in his home state of New York. Still, Davis was well impressed. As he reported in *Harper's Magazine,* the feuding stalwarts and progressives keep pretending, both of them, to be "saving the commonwealth from a gang of scoundrels; yet Wisconsin goes on being governed pretty honestly whichever side wins." What Wisconsin papers occasionally exposed as a scandal would hardly be newsworthy if it happened in some other state. "Yes, in business and in politics the State of Wisconsin is, by contrast with the rest of the nation and most notably by contrast with Illinois and the city of Chicago, a happy land." Davis was reminded of Old Bob's remark that his Progressive movement would be a success if human life were made "safer and sweeter" in Wisconsin. Davis concluded: ". . . it certainly makes life safer and sweeter to have an honest and dependable government, even if it comes high." [29]

Wisconsin politics flip-flopped in response to the terrors of the depression and the charms of Franklin D. Roosevelt. In 1932 the state went Democratic, giving a majority to both the gubernatorial and the presidential candidate of the Democratic party, as it had done only once before, in 1892. The overturn left Phil La Follette out of a job, and it left Young Bob with a dubious prospect for retaining his. There seemed no immediate future for the progressives as a faction of the Republican party. Pre-

29. Elmer Davis, "Wisconsin Is Different," *Harper's Monthly Magazine,* 165 (October 1932):613–615, 620–621, 623–624.

viously the La Follettes, father and sons, had always run as Republicans except in the presidential race of 1924, when Old Bob carried a separate Progressive banner. Even on that occasion, however, the progressive candidates for all other offices had continued to bill themselves as Republicans. Now, converting their faction into an independent party and cultivating the support of Socialists, the La Follette brothers headed a complete Progressive slate in the elections of 1934. With the co-operation of President Roosevelt the new party put into office a governor, a senator, seven congressmen, and a majority of state legislators.

Roosevelt recognized the La Follettes as good New Dealers. Governor La Follette during his first term (1931–1933) set a precedent for the New Deal when he sponsored a public-works program that not only gave jobs to the unemployed but also made the state a still safer place by constructing highway overpasses and underpasses at dangerous railroad crossings. During his second and third terms (1935–1939) Governor La Follette brought into being Wisconsin's own "Little New Deal," with state agencies for developing electric power, giving marketing assistance to farmers, fixing standards of fair business competition, and settling labor disputes. Senator La Follette meanwhile helped to shape federal legislation for the relief of drought-stricken farmers and unemployed workers. He also led an investigation into employers' use of spies to discourage and disrupt labor unions.

Apart from the specific roles of the two La Follettes, Wisconsin made additional contributions to the development of the New Deal. The Wisconsin Idea bore yet more fruit in the form of the brain trust and the Social Security Act. In relying on academic experts of all kinds, President Roosevelt was doing on a national scale what the first Governor La Follette had begun to do in Madison more than three decades earlier. In designing the social security system, the administration made use of Wisconsin precedents as well as Wisconsin experts.

Wisconsin was the first of all the states to provide unemployment insurance. The Wisconsin act of 1932 was the culmination of a dozen years of striving on the part of Professor Commons and some of his students. Professor Edwin E. Witte of the university's economics department served as executive director of the technical board that advised on the drafting of federal social security legislation. Witte brought to the task the special skill he had acquired as Charles McCarthy's successor to the headship of the Wisconsin legislative reference bureau. The federal law of 1935 incorporated the principles of Wisconsin's act of 1932. Not till after the passage of the federal law—which provided federal assistance to state programs—did any other state insure its people against the loss of jobs.

Strains appeared in the working arrangement between the La Follette Progressives of Wisconsin and the New Deal Democrats of Washington as President Roosevelt began to place more and more emphasis on preparations for war. The La Follette brothers, like their father before them, believed that a foreign adventure would make a casualty of domestic reform. Young Bob La Follette had no ambition beyond continuing in the Senate; rather quiet and studious, he hardly had even the personality of a politician. But Phil, a fiery orator, was ambitious to rival and replace Roosevelt. In 1938 Phil launched what he called the National Progressive party and what he described as no third party but soon to be the one and only party. It was a fiasco.

By 1940, with war again in Europe, Wisconsin politics was in flux. The state went Democratic in the presidential election, Republican in the gubernatorial, and Progressive in the senatorial—sending Robert M. La Follette, Jr., back to Washington. After the Pearl Harbor attack, Senator La Follette supported the administration's conduct of the war but tried, again like his father, to devise taxes that would pay war costs out of war profits.

At the war's end, Wisconsin seemed as distinctive as ever in its political character. It was "probably the most isolationist of American states," John Gunther said in *Inside U.S.A.* It was also "one of the two or three best-run and best-governed" and, "on almost all domestic issues, one of the most liberal." The

"La Follette tradition," Gunther thought, was still very much alive.[30]

7

In 1944, when a book appeared with the title *McCarthy of Wisconsin,* everyone interested in the book knew perfectly well that it was about Dr. Charles McCarthy, the distinguished founder and former head of the state legislative reference bureau, the great expounder and practitioner of the Wisconsin Idea, who had died in 1921. Wisconsin was yet to make the transition from McCarthy to McCarthy, from the progressivism of Dr. Charles to the reactionism of Senator Joe.

During the 1950s Wisconsin figured more largely in the public eye than it had done for decades, but then it was identified with McCarthyism, not La Folletteism. "McCarthyism" became a dictionary word, with the following definitions:

> 1. public accusation of disloyalty, esp. of pro-Communist activity, in many instances unsupported by proof or based on slight, doubtful or irrelevant evidence. 2. unfairness in investigative technique. 3. persistent search for and exposure of disloyalty, esp. in government offices. [The etymology:] from Joseph R. *McCarthy,* 1909–1957, U.S. Senator, + -ISM.[31]

Joseph Raymond McCarthy, Wisconsin-born of Irish Catholic parents, was in the Senate for the last ten years of his rather short life. The first three of the ten were years of obscurity; the next four, of international notoriety; and the last three, of subsidence.

Though unknown in 1944 to the world at large—even to the state .at large—Joe already enjoyed a considerable local fame. This was not confined to his hometown, Appleton, or even to Outagamie County, but extended throughout an eight-county

---

30. John Gunther, *Inside U. S. A.* (New York: Harper and Brothers, 1947), pp. 318–321.

31. C. L. Barnhart, ed., *The American College Dictionary* (New York: Random House, 1963), p. 754.

judicial circuit. McCarthy was the circuit judge and had been for five years, ever since switching from the Democratic to the Republican party and getting himself elected at the tender age of thirty.

How he had won election to the judgeship, he was afterwards quite willing to explain. Campaigning, he had visited as many farms as he could in each of the circuit's eight counties. "Now, farmers aren't interested in politicians, you know. They're interested in cows. So I'd ask a farmer how his cows were. He might answer: 'They're all right, except Old Bess there. She's got sore teats.' Of course, I didn't know anything about cows, but the next farmer I saw, I'd ask him about it, and he'd say: 'I've always found a mixture of kerosene and lard is good in cases like that.' As soon as I'd get back to my car, I'd dictate a letter on the dictating machine to the first farmer, telling him what to do for Old Bess."

McCarthy and his campaign workers had also compiled a list of members of all the farm families in the circuit. On the Saturday before the election the workers mailed, from their headquarters in Madison, a postcard to each of the families. A typical card read something like this:

Dear Herman,

 I hope you will go out and vote tomorrow, and I hope your wife, Beulah, will vote, and also your son Willie and your daughter Myrtle. I'm sorry your son Jimmie and your daughter Susie aren't old enough. I don't care who you vote for, but do exercise your democratic right to vote. Sincerely yours,

Joe McCarthy.

The card would be delivered on Monday while the farmer was at work in the fields. "When he came in, his wife would ask him: 'Say, who's this Joe McCarthy?' and he would say: 'I don't know. Never heard of him.' 'Well, he knows us—look!' And she would show him the card. The next day they would all go out and vote, and they would vote for me."

To his fellow Appletonians, Judge McCarthy in the 1940s seemed neither the patriotic angel nor the fascistic ogre that

Senator McCarthy was to seem to many Americans later on.
The judge was friendly, unpretentious, quick to greet, easy to
approach. "You'd better come on down to the courthouse," he
once told a person he had just met. "I've got a couple of good
adultery cases coming up." Seated on the bench, he asked the
clerk to remind him of the facts of the first case. Then he rested
his chin on his fist after the manner of Auguste Rodin's "The
Thinker."

When, in 1946, McCarthy sought the senatorship, he did so
not because of any disagreement with or grievance against Senator La Follette. This he made plain when he spoke that spring to
a political science class at Lawrence College. As casually but as
emphatically as he could, he kept calling attention to his military record, which presumably distinguished him from the incumbent. Every once in a while he uttered a "hell" or a
"damn," and each time he quickly apologized: "You coeds
must excuse me. I was a tail-gunner in the Marines, you
know." When asked point-blank just how he differed with La
Follette on any issue foreign or domestic, he replied: "I don't
differ with him. For that very reason, it's going to be a dirty
campaign." [32]

In 1946 and afterwards, outsiders wondered how Wisconsin,
after keeping a La Follette in the Senate for forty years, could
possibly have turned to McCarthy. There was really nothing
mysterious about it. La Follette, we must remember, had been
for more than a decade a Progressive, not a Republican, and
was now trying to make his way back into the Republican party.
This had been left to the domination of the conservatives. Some
of the recent Progressives, instead of returning with La Follette
to the Republican fold, preferred the Democratic as potentially
the more liberal. So La Follette was at a serious disadvantage to
begin with, though he did not seem to be aware of it at the time.
He did practically no campaigning, whether because he was
overconfident, indifferent, or preoccupied with legislative mat-

32. This and the preceding quotations of McCarthy reproduce, according to my recol-
lection, his remarks as made to me or in my presence in Appleton in the spring of 1946.

ters—he was busily at work on a plan for the reorganization of Congress. He suffered from another handicap: he had incurred the hatred of Communists and fellow travelers in the Milwaukee CIO because of his strictures on Josef Stalin's postwar expansionism. McCarthy, then, enjoyed the backing of both conservatives and Communists. Moreover, he received the votes of many Democrats in the primary (the primary was always "open" in Wisconsin; anyone could "cross over"), since they thought he would be easier to beat than La Follette in the general election. Having got the Republican nomination, McCarthy rode into office along with the rest of the Republican ticket.

McCarthy began to attract publicity when, early in 1950, he announced that there was in the State Department a large number of Communists who had been and still were making American foreign policy. He was speaking at a very sensitive moment, soon after the fall of mainland China to Communism and the exposure of Communist espionage in the United States. Recent events gave the appearance of credibility to his charges, even when he extended them to include "the whole group of twisted-thinking New Dealers" who had "led America near to ruin at home and abroad." [33] But he went too far when he accused the army of coddling Communists. The televised Army-McCarthy hearings in 1954 exposed him—to millions who had never had a chance to see him in action before—as a bullyragger who could not tell the difference between innuendo and evidence. His fellow senators then made bold to censure him. After losing his grip on the public imagination, he turned more and more to drink.

McCarthy, dead, continued to hold the admiration of right-wingers throughout the country. He remained a prophet not without honor at home in Appleton. His friends placed a bust of him in the Outagamie County courthouse, and they kept fresh flowers constantly in front of the bust. Every year they held memorial services at his grave. But left-wingers everywhere re-

33. Quoted in Richard N. Current, T. Harry Williams, and Frank Freidel, *American History :A Survey* (New York: Alfred A. Knopf, 1961), p. 838.

membered McCarthy as a horrible example, the prototype of an American Hitler. In death, as in life, he had a seldom-equaled power to evoke love and devotion on the one hand and fear and loathing on the other.

In retrospect, some presumed experts concluded that the change from La Follette to McCarthy had signified no sharp break in the Wisconsin political tradition. Certain eastern historians and social scientists, not well informed about Wisconsin's past, intimated that McCarthyism and La Folletteism were essentially the same thing. These writers left the impression that, even in the heyday of reform, the state had seethed with dark, fascistic impulses, that Old Bob La Follette as well as Joe McCarthy had exploited such tendencies, and that, in short, Joe was Old Bob's legitimate heir. Now, the question of La Follette's constituency in comparison with McCarthy's is somewhat complicated, since La Follette's underwent a transformation in consequence of the First World War. Still, we must agree with the Wisconsin historian who wrote:

> The historical evidence indicates that La Follette and McCarthy did not take similar political positions and that they had different political styles. Their political support came from different individual political leaders, different interest groups, and different parts of the state. Indeed, to a considerable extent, La Follette's supporters were McCarthy's enemies, and vice versa. The hypothesis of a connection . . . does not stand up under scrutiny.[34]

All along, anti-McCarthy Wisconsinites protested not only that McCarthyism had little or nothing to do with progressivism but also that it was less a state phenomenon than a national one. They pointed to some cogent facts. For the most part, McCarthy directed his witch hunts away from his home state, sparing both Lawrence College and the University of Wisconsin. He impressed his philosophy upon neither the cultural nor the political life of the state. Actually, he was never a great power in its politics. Unlike the La Follettes, he headed no organization that

---

34. David A. Shannon, "Was McCarthy a Political Heir of La Follette?" *Wisconsin Magazine of History,* 45 (Autumn 1961):8.

controlled or swayed the state government. He did not even have a strong political base in Wisconsin. His first election to the Senate, as has been seen, was more or less fortuitous. When he came up for re-election in 1952, after McCarthyism had become a national issue, he ran far behind the rest of the Republican ticket in the state.

Indeed, in the view of many Wisconsinites, the state distinguished itself more for anti-McCarthyism than for McCarthyism. It did so especially in the recall effort of 1954. Among the twelve states that had adopted constitutional amendments for the recall of elected officeholders, Wisconsin was the last (in 1926), but it was the first to make a really spectacular attempt to put such a procedure into effect. According to the amendment, there would be a new election if 25 percent of the voters in the previous gubernatorial election signed a petition for it. The "Joe Must Go" movement therefore needed 404,000 signatures. It obtained only about 400,000, and so it failed, but it nevertheless made its point. "More people had signed the protest than had ever signed any notarized petition in the nation's history, and they had dealt a massive blow to the myth of McCarthy's invincibility." [35] This rebuke, coming on top of his poor showing in the 1952 election, undoubtedly helped to overcome the terror in which his fellow senators seemingly had held him. Wisconsin, that is to say, encouraged the rest of the country to take a stand against McCarthy—such a stand as the Senate finally took in its 1954 resolution condemning him.

Unwittingly McCarthy contributed to the resurgence of the Democrats in Wisconsin. The Republican stalwarts held him in fond embrace, but progressives left him and the Republican party in disgust. They joined and reorganized the Democratic party, giving it a more and more liberal orientation and greater and greater electoral attractiveness. In the 1957 election to fill McCarthy's unexpired term, the winner was a Democrat, only the second one to go from Wisconsin to the Senate in the twen-

35. David P. Thelen and Esther S. Thelen, "Joe Must Go: The Movement to Recall Senator Joseph R. McCarthy," *Wisconsin Magazine of History,* 49 (Spring 1966):200.

tieth century. In the 1958 gubernatorial election the winner again was a Democrat, the sixth member of his party to serve as governor in the entire hundred-and-ten-year history of the state (there had been twenty-six Republicans, one Progressive, and one Whig). Wisconsin was entering upon a period of genuine two-party politics.

8

Among the states, Wisconsin was a maverick as well as a model. Here the passion for reform had not extended to rewriting the constitution itself, which, except for amendments, none of them very drastic, retained the form in which it had been drawn up in 1847. It came to be the oldest of the state constitutions still in effect. Written at a time when strong government was a thing to be shunned, it provided for no great consolidation of power in Madison. Eventually other states began to centralize governmental functions, but Wisconsin held back. Its counties and municipalities retained or recovered authority despite the growth of progressive bureaucracy.

"Wisconsin is the only state in the Union where responsibility for the maintenance and improvement of all state trunk highways is lodged with county government," the magazine *Better Roads* reported in 1942.[36] Except for a shift from township to county administration in 1907, the state had resisted the centralizing trend with regard to highways. In response to a federal requirement, a Wisconsin law of 1931 made the state government nominally responsible for maintaining federally financed roads. Even so, the actual administration remained with the counties, and county highway departments continued to keep up federal as well as state highways. Moreover, county policemen went on patrolling state and federal highways in Wisconsin long after state police systems had gone into operation elsewhere.

In the 1960s and 1970s the legislature kept tinkering with

36. Quoted in the *National Municipal Review*, 31 (December 1942):638.

both state and local administrative machinery in an effort to modernize it and make it more efficient. The legislature had considerable leeway even without constitutional amendments, for the constitution was unusually brief and general. Yet Wisconsin was not being transformed into some kind of superstate. As a rule, the state agencies still had to operate through the counties and municipalities, which carried out an exceptionally large number of governmental functions. The state bureaucrats could set standards for, give advice to, and use persuasion on the local governments, but could seldom dictate to them. Wisconsin was distinctive for (among other things) the persistence among its people of strong feelings of local independence.

Suggestions for Further Reading

Wisconsin has been a history-conscious state from the beginning, and countless books and articles have been written about its past. Only a selected few of the many titles will be mentioned here. The purpose of this listing is only to give a start to the reader interested in further exploration of the subject. The purpose is not to indicate the sources for the present book. Some of the sources—but only those from which quotations have been taken—are indicated in the footnotes. These notes also serve as suggestions for further reading.

The State Historical Society of Wisconsin is in the process of publishing *The History of Wisconsin* in six volumes, which, when completed, will constitute a standard reference work. So far, the first two volumes have appeared: *From Exploration to Statehood* (1973) by Alice E. Smith, and *The Civil War Era, 1848–1873* (1976) by Richard N. Current. The most up-to-date, scholarly, and sophisticated one-volume account is Robert C. Nesbit, *Wisconsin: A History* (Madison: University of Wisconsin Press, 1973). Expertly condensed is Larry Gara, *A Short History of Wisconsin* (Madison: State Historical Society of Wisconsin, 1962). An indispensable reference is the *Dictionary of Wisconsin Biography* (Madison: State Historical Society of Wisconsin, 1960). The fullest treatments of many aspects of the subject are to be found in the *Wisconsin Magazine of History,* which the State Historical Society puts out four times a year. Articles on historical topics also

217

appear in *Wisconsin Trails,* a handsomely illustrated quarterly that Howard Mead publishes in Madison.

The geographical setting is authoritatively discussed in Lawrence Martin, *The Physical Geography of Wisconsin* (Madison: Wisconsin Geological and Natural History Survey, 1916), which is available in a more recent edition from the University of Wisconsin Press. Important period studies include the following: George I. Quimby, *Indian Life in the Upper Great Lakes, 11,000 B. C. to A. D. 1800* (Chicago: University of Chicago Press, 1960); Robert E. Ritzenthaler, *Prehistoric Indians of Wisconsin* (Milwaukee: Milwaukee Public Museum, 1953); Louise Phelps Kellogg, *The French Regime in Wisconsin and the Northwest* and *The British Regime in Wisconsin and the Northwest* (Madison: State Historical Society of Wisconsin, 1925, 1935); Frederick Merk, *Economic History of Wisconsin During the Civil War Decade* (Madison: State Historical Society of Wisconsin, 1916), a classic of its kind, available in a recent reissue; Herbert F. Margulies, *The Decline of the Progressive Movement in Wisconsin, 1890–1920* (Madison: State Historical Society of Wisconsin, 1968); and Leon D. Epstein, *Politics in Wisconsin* (Madison: University of Wisconsin Press, 1958).

In local and area studies Joseph Schafer sets a high standard in his Wisconsin Domesday series, two volumes of which are *A History of Agriculture in Wisconsin,* a prefatory volume dealing mainly with the pioneer period, and *The Winnebago-Horicon Basin: A Type Study in Western History* (Madison: State Historical Society of Wisconsin, 1922, 1937). Bayrd Still does an exemplary job with *Milwaukee: The History of a City* (Madison: State Historical Society of Wisconsin, 1948). Merle Curti and his associates analyze Trempealeau County with new quantitative historical techniques in *The Making of an American Community: A Case Study of Democracy in a Frontier County* (Stanford, Calif.: Stanford University Press, 1959). Merle Curti and Vernon Carstensen provide an excellent institutional study in *The University of Wisconsin: A History, 1848–1925* 2 vols. (Madison: University of Wisconsin Press, 1949).

Recent, readable, reliable biographies of outstanding Wisconsin figures are David P. Thelen, *Robert M. La Follette and the Insurgent Spirit* (Boston: Little, Brown and Co., 1976); Ray Allen Billington,

Frederick Jackson Turner: Historian, Scholar, Teacher (New York: Oxford University Press, 1973); and Robert C. Twombly, *Frank Lloyd Wright: An Interpretive Biography* (New York: Harper & Row, 1973).

Practically all the items mentioned here contain notes or bibliographies which will guide the curious reader to more detailed studies.

Index

Ableman, S. V. R., 180
Adams, Herbert Baxter, 164
Agriculture: pioneer farming, 21, 67, 75; soil erosion, 22–23, 25–26; diversification, 67, 69, 71–73, 89; effect of Hoard on, 74, 75, 81; farm machinery, 68, 123–126; use of ensilage, 75–76, 88; cattle testing, 80–81. *See also* Canning; Dairying; Meat packing
—crops: wheat, 67, 68–71; corn, 68, 72, 85, 88; hops, 71–72; ginseng, 72; alfalfa, 75; clover, 75; peas, 67, 85; other, 67, 89
—livestock: cattle, 74–75, 80–81, 83, 84; sheep, 72; hogs, 78, 85–86
Allen, William F., 164
Allis-Chalmers Company, 127–128
Aluminum, 119–122. *See also* Manufacturing
Aluminum Company of America (Alcoa), 121
Aluminum Manfacturing Company, 120
American Historical Association, 164–165, 168, 193
American Motors Company, 131
American Protective Assn., 53
Anderson, Rasmus D., 58, 61
A. O. Smith Corporation, 129–130
Appleby, John F., 123, 124
Appleton: hydroelectric plant, 105; streetcar, 105; papermaking, 117; and Edna Ferber, 158–159; and Joseph McCarthy, 208, 211. *See also* Lawrence College
Armour, Philip D., 86–87
Arnold, Thurman W., 196–197
Automobiles: frames, 123, 129–130; steam-powered buggy, 128; first race, 128–129; four-wheel drive, 129; speedometer, 129; tire-patching kit, 129; automatic assembly line, 129–130;

Rambler, 130; Kissel Kar, 130; Nash, 131
Aztalan, 15, 16, 17

Babcock, Stephen Moulton, 83–84
Babe, the blue ox, 116
Badger Ordnance Works, 23
Badgers, 9
Baraboo, 134–139 *passim,* 187
Barnum, Phineas T., 133–134, 137
Barnum & Bailey, 134, 135, 137
Barry, Garrett (captain), 181–182
Barstow, William A. (governor), 176–177
Bascom, John, 191–192
Bashford, Coles (governor), 176–178, 180
Beaumont, Dr. William, 81–82
Beef Slough war, 112–115
Beer, 66, 67, 89–94
Belgians, 37, 40, 43, 49, 59
Beloit, 124, 126, 129
Bennett, Henry H., 28
Bennett Law, 52–53, 185
Berger, Victor L., 200–203 *passim*
Best, Jacob, 90
Black Hawk (Chief), 18–19
Blacks, 37, 39, 46, 50, 55, 203
Blatz, Valentin, 51, 90, 92, 94
Bond, Carrie Jacobs, 146
Booth, Sherman M., 178–181, 184
Borden, Gail, 80
Bovay, Alvan E., 179
Brain trust, 206
Braun, John, 90
Brewing (industry), 89–94. *See also* Beer
Briggs, Clare, 149, 156
British, early settlements, 37, 38; and politics, 48, 52; Americanization of, 56, 63; as brewers, 89
Bryan, William Jennings, 188

220